THE VIEW FROM THE FENCE

THE VIEW FROM THE FENCE

The Arab–Israeli Conflict
from the Present to its Roots

NEILL LOCHERY

continuum

'For my wife and children'

The Continuum International Publishing Group

The Tower Building
11 York Road
London SE1 7NX

15 East 26th Street
New York
NY 10010

www.continuumbooks.com

First published 2005

British Library Cataloguing-in-Publication Data
A catalogue record for this book is available from the British Library.

ISBN: 0–8264–8679–7

Typeset by Free Range Book Design & Production
Printed and bound in Great Britain by Cromwell Press, Trowbridge, Wiltshire

Contents

Acknowledgements

I would like to thank my colleagues at University College London for their help in the writing of this book especially John Klier, Ada Rapoport-Albert, Mark Geller, Michael Berkowitz, Tsila Ratner, Helen Beer and the Vice-Provost for Arts, Michael Worton. As ever, my agent, Louise Greenberg was full of enthusiasm for the project and constantly reminded me about the importance of clear and precise prose. Many administrators at the various archives I visited helped me with my research and without their assistance I would have struggled to locate the evidence I was looking for. The staff at the Public Records Office at Kew in London were particularly kind. At Continuum, Robin Baird-Smith was simply wonderful to work with as were Ben Hayes and Anya Wilson. Finally, I would to say a big thank you to my wife and children who put up with me closing the door to my office at home for long periods of time during the winter and spring of 2004–5.

University College London
July 2005.

Introduction

I was born on a chilly winter's day in late January 1965.
Sir Winston Churchill had just died and his body lay in
state at Westminster awaiting the funeral that was to
bring much of the country to a standstill. The death of
Churchill was an important symbolic event in post-war
Britain. After a long, and sometimes chequered, political
career, Churchill was remembered as the leader most
associated with the struggle of Britain to survive against
Nazi aggression during the Second World War. Later in
1965, the political career of David Ben-Gurion, Israel's
first prime minister, and viewed by many Jews as the
Israeli equivalent of Churchill, came to a sudden halt.
Defeated and humiliated in elections, Ben-Gurion was
effectively forced to permanently retire from political life.
Though he did not die until 1973 it was a sad end for the
leader who most symbolised Israel's struggle and fight for
survival during its formative years. As two symbolic
leaders departed, the career of another was just beginning.
On 1 January 1965 a new Palestinian group was created,
known in English as the Movement for the National
Liberation of Palestine. The group, however, soon came

to be known by its Arabic acronym, Fatah (victory). Its leader was identified within Palestinian circles by his *nom de guerre*, Abu Ammar, but his real name was Yasser Arafat. For nearly 40 years until his death in November 2004, Arafat would be the symbol and leader of the Palestinian national struggle in its confrontation with Israel, and at various times also with the Arab world.

Being born in 1965 means that my first recollection of the Arab–Israeli conflict is the October 1973 War, which Israelis term the Yom Kippur War and Arabs call the Ramadan War. I mention this early memory because of its importance in shaping my mindset towards the conflict. When I hear people talk of Israel as a regional superpower my mind is cast back to the grainy black and white television images of Israel being driven back during the initial stages of the War, and the reporters talking of the possible destruction of Israel. As an eight year old boy I understood little of the detail but was deeply struck by the vulnerability of Israel. Had I been able to remember the 1967 Arab–Israeli War when the Israelis captured East Jerusalem, the West Bank, the Gaza Strip, the Sinai and the Golan Heights, I might have been more easily seduced by the simplistic vision of Israelis and Arabs using the David and Goliath context (weak Arabs – strong Israelis). Since 1973, I have retained a strong interest in the affairs of the Middle East, and the Arab–Israeli conflict in particular. Over the years my interest has developed from keen amateur observer to professional academic. I remain, however, an outsider to the region, despite having lived there and undertaken numerous trips for research purposes. In short, I inhabit twin worlds with different perspectives: as an outsider looking in, but also at times, by virtue of my work, an insider looking out.

It appears that I was not alone in following events in the Middle East. Everyone you meet seems to have a point of view about Israel and the Arab–Israeli conflict. Often, it is said that if only the Israelis would give back the land they stole from the Palestinians in 1967, all would be resolved; or, that if only the Palestinians would really accept Israel's right to exist, all would be resolved. Mention the conflict between Pakistan and India, however, and the responses are likely to be more muted, if not blank, with people quite happy to admit their unfamiliarity with the disagreements in that part of the world.

In truth, the outpouring of popular debate about the Arab–Israeli situation has not led to enlightenment, or even a partial understanding of the problems, on the part of most people. The recent attempts by the left in Europe to view Israel as the new Apartheid state, and the clear linkage in some people's minds between Israel and South Africa, have lowered the intellectual bar even further. The major error that most people make is to look at the intractable dilemma from either a solely Jewish/Israeli or a purely Arab perspective. Anyone informed who picks up copies of a selection of Middle Eastern papers in London will soon see the limitations of such approaches. Both, in reality, are frequently propaganda for those committed to a certain dogmatic political line, be it pro- or anti-Israel. Fuller accounts of recent history in the region have leaned heavily on diplomatic history, when it would be more productive to probe the convictions and attitudes that make both parties continue the fight. Many of these accounts are politically coloured and add little to the debate. Some have been clear attempts to present a particular narrative of history that suits the interests of the authors. Others have been written in response to previous narratives that the author disagrees with.

This book provides an analysis of the issues which drive the conflict: the development of the State of Israel, the transformation of the Arab world, including both Palestinian and Arab states, and the role of the external powers in the area. It is important to develop an understanding of just how related these three areas were to each other using this comprehensive or inclusive approach and to see how changes in one area impacted upon the other. It is the old case of the swinging balls – move one ball and they will all shift. There is, in short, a need to understand all the factors that lay behind the causes of the conflict and its continuation.

Central to the last decade of the conflict have been the attempts by the United States to broker a settlement. The so-called 'New World Order', outlined by President Bush Sr, meant that the USA, freed from the shackles of the Cold War, took a more proactive role in trying to achieve a resolution. These attempts, however, were doomed to failure from the outset, as recently published accounts by political leaders, advisors and mandarins in the United States reveal. The conclusions that these writers arrive at for the failure of the diplomatic processes range from citing the significance of a particular tragic event to apportioning blame to a specific individual. In most US accounts, two main reasons are put forward for the failure to end the conflict: the assassination of Yitzhak Rabin by a Jewish extremist opposed to the handover of land to the Palestinians, or the personality and political judgement of Yasser Arafat. This is superficial reasoning and this book attempts, in part, to expose the myth of both explanations.

As we shall see, the death of Rabin – or 'the sacrifice' as the Israeli left labels it – made little difference to the outcome of the negotiations with the Palestinians. While it is understandable that both Israelis and the outside world should immortalise Rabin, that is an emotional response and does not reflect the political realities of the era. This book also probes the belief that Rabin was the only Israeli leader capable of making peace with the Palestinians and the wider Arab world. Prior to his death, Rabin had started planning what we now know as separation from the Palestinians and the creation of a security fence, which today dominates the agenda of the conflict, and is linked in most minds with the current Israeli Prime Minister, Ariel Sharon. Back in 1995 Rabin understood two things better than most: the peace process with the Palestinians was in terminal decline, and his re-election chances for 1996 looked very shaky indeed. Had he lived, the evidence suggests that, faced with Arafat's failure to deal with Hamas and Islamic Jihad, Rabin would have sent the army in to do Arafat's work for him – just as we saw happen under his successors Benjamin Netanyahu, Ehud Barak and Ariel Sharon. This book, as a result, starts with a history of the Security Fence from Rabin through to Sharon and the development of the wider thinking behind it – at the heart of which is the admission that the Oslo Accords failed to end the conflict between Israelis and Palestinians.

For his part, Yasser Arafat was no political novice. He saw six US Presidents come and go. Arafat, as one leading member of the Israeli peace camp claims, was not a committed terrorist, but neither was he a committed statesman. The central Israeli narrative of events is that Arafat never really wanted peace with Israel and that he was eventually unmasked when an Israeli PM, Ehud Barak, made him generous offers that no peace-loving leader could have refused, at Camp David and Taba in 2000. Having destroyed the chances for peace, and blamed by the Clinton administration and wider world for the failure, Arafat returned to what he knew best, violence. This version of how the current Palestinian unrest started is only partially correct, and this book looks at the economic reasons for the Palestinian unrest as well as the wider political explanations.

Traditional diplomatic history lends itself to naming and shaming those that the writer believes to be responsible for the failure to end the Arab–Israeli conflict.[1] True, Arafat's role in the failure to secure peace cannot be ignored, but it was not the explanation in itself, as many Israelis appear to believe. This book, as a result, will try to steer clear of criticism of individuals and look at the deeper lying causes of the conflict. Certainly, political leaders on both sides have made mistakes, as have the mediators charged with trying to bridge the gaps between the parties. From Ben-Gurion and Nasser through to Barak and Arafat, all Middle Eastern leaders have taken incorrect roads and as a result inflamed the conflict – sometimes for reasons of political self-preservation, while on other occasions simply due to bad judgement. These mistakes, however, have normally been made when a leader is under pressure, usually from their domestic constituencies. Here, it is difficult to think of two broader churches of people than Israelis and Arabs with both communities ranging from far left to far right and from secular to highly religious – a fact that makes successful national leadership all the more difficult.

Finally, if the reader takes only one thing from this book, I hope it is that conflict in the Middle East is not simply about Israel versus the Arabs. Splits between the various Arab states, and between these states and the Palestinians have played just as an important a role in the region as the battle between Israel and the Arab world has done. Additional factors that have come to play a role in the conflict include the relative failure of modernisation in the Arab world, difficulties over the allocation of resources, and the diminishing amount of the region's natural resources. Of course, the Arab–Israeli conflict is partly to blame for many of these problems. Any look at the percentage of GDP that Middle Eastern states devote to military expenditure provides some explanation for the economic difficulties that large parts of the region have faced in the last century. Countries of the Middle East still spend easily more money on arms than any other part of the world.[2] Much of this military spending, however, has less to do with the Arab–Israeli conflict and more to do with maintaining certain Arab dictators in power, and acts as a deterrent – or offensive strategy – for dealing with other Arab states. To this extent, the Arab–Israeli conflict has served as a reliable excuse for the lack of change and reform in the region. Given all this, the historical high profile of the conflict, and its ability to polarise opinion across the globe, it is important to present a three-dimensional account of the conflict amidst the wider development of the Middle East.

Notes:

[1]   For an example of this see reviews of two books by A. Shlaim (2004), 'The Nation: the Lost Steps', *Political Studies Journal*, Volume 47(4).

[2]   A. Cordesman (2004), *The Military Balance in the Middle East*, Westport and London: Praeger, p. 29.

1

❧❧❧

Understanding the Present: Good Fences make Good Neighbours

Some images appear to tell a story so directly and starkly that words can add little to the raw power of the photograph or video footage. In recent history, the fall of the Berlin Wall would be one such example, as would the sight of the planes flying into the World Trade Centre on 11 September 2001. In the Middle East, the Rabin–Arafat handshake in September 1993, the funeral of the assassinated Yitzhak Rabin in Jerusalem in 1995 and the sight of the helicopter carrying the body of Yasser Arafat landing in Ramallah in November 2004 would all fit into a similar category. Perhaps the most striking images from recent Middle Eastern history, however, are those that focus on Israel's Security Fence, which, when finished, will run for approximately 622 km, nearly the entire length of the disputed West Bank.[3] Anybody who has seen the 8–9 metre high concrete sections of the fence, either from close up or from a distance, as it snakes its way across the West Bank skyline, cannot fail to be either suitably impressed or appalled – depending on one's political colour. In reality, the fence, which the Palestinian Authority routinely refers to as the Apartheid Wall or Israel's Racist Separation Fence, is a mixture of concrete sections, ditches, razor wires, electronic monitoring systems and patrol roads, the materials used depending on the area and its proximity to Palestinian villages and towns.[4] The Great Wall of China it is not, but it is already much more imposing than its modern day equivalent, the Berlin Wall and the fence that divided the rest of Germany. That fence formed the East–West front line during the Cold War, part of the Iron Curtain, as Churchill referred to it.

The Israeli fence differs from the German one in that its role is to prevent people (specifically Palestinian suicide bombers) from getting into Israel, rather than stopping people leaving the country, as was the case with the East German/Soviet-constructed fence. This main aim of stopping potential suicide bombers was confirmed by the Israeli Attorney General, who, in a recent Cabinet meeting, argued that the route of the fence must be governed by this aim, and not any wider security issues such as trying to stop any missiles and rockets being launched from the West Bank. Where the aims of the Israeli and German fences merge, however, is in the strategic thinking behind their respective constructions. Both fences form part of a wider political goal of separating peoples. Though this comparison might appear a little crude on the surface, it remains the case that, within Israeli thinking, the construction of the fence is really political code for shutting up shop, locking the door – and an acceptance of the fact that, in the short-to medium-term, Jew and Arab simply cannot live together.

Different visions: integration versus separation

There is a major misconception held by many people that the plan for Israel's Security Fence was originally formulated by the Israeli right wing. This argument, which is often aired in both the Western and Arab medias, charges that the creation of the fence represents a blatant attempt by the Israeli right to grab lands in the West Bank from the Palestinians. This, the critics argue, would help ensure that there could be no Palestinian control of lands close to the Green Line border that marks Israel's internationally recognised border with the West Bank. The truth is of course much more complex.

The original idea of a fence came from the late Israeli Prime Minister and leader of the centre-left Israeli Labour Party, Yitzhak Rabin, who first proposed the idea in late 1994, and started detailed discussions on its viability in early 1995. It is possible to trace the rationale behind Rabin's thinking even further back in time, to the 1992 elections that brought him to power.[5] Rabin's response to the murder of a 16 year old schoolgirl, Helena Rapp, in Bat Yam (south of Tel Aviv) on 24 May 1992, by a Palestinian from Gaza during the campaign became an important factor in his subsequent election victory. Rabin argued that the Likud was bringing Gaza to Tel Aviv, and it was time to, in effect, take Gaza out of Tel Aviv by creating two distinct entities so the populations could avoid points of friction.[6] Central to Rabin's thinking in 1994–5 were two factors: the need to maximise the personal security of Israelis in the wake of the campaign of suicide bombings by Hamas and Islamic Jihad, and to create a physical barrier that would encourage the separation of Israelis and Palestinians.

Back in 1994–5, such thinking by Rabin and his advisors was nothing short of revolutionary. For the Palestinians, one of the major fillets for signing the Oslo Accords had been the hope that Israel would remain economically closely linked to any future Palestinian state. Some Palestinians went much further and talked of an economic confederation between Israel, Palestine and even Jordan. If a Palestinian state was to prove economically viable, then, at the very least the 128,000 legal Palestinian workers who crossed into Israel each day – earning salaries on average 61 per cent more than in the West Bank and 85 per cent more than in the Gaza Strip – had to retain their jobs.[7] When Israel imposed closures on the Occupied Territories following attacks by Hamas and Islamic Jihad on Israeli cities, the impact was felt almost immediately by Palestinians. In 1995 and 1996, for example, when the closures imposed by Israel on the West Bank and Gaza Strip were extremely severe, Palestinian unemployment was as high as 25 per cent.[8] Not only were the workers not able to get to their jobs, but also Palestinian agricultural produce destined for export was not able to leave the West Bank and often simply left to rot, further adding to the economic difficulties of the Palestinians. Rabin's decision sent a clear message to the Palestinian leadership that his view of peace was one in which the two peoples were in effect separated by a fence, and that the Palestinians would have to look to the east (Jordan) to deal with their structural economic problems.

This crude form of Israeli separation brought to an end a quarter of a century of the Israeli policy of economic functionalism towards the West Bank. The architect of this policy was none other than another Israeli army general turned politician, Moshe Dayan, who argued that if Israel could convince those living in the West Bank that their economic futures were better served by remaining linked to the Israeli economy, then it followed that their nationalist aspirations to be part of a Palestinian state would, given time, recede. Consequently, political autonomy for Palestinians living in the West Bank and Gaza might have been enough to satisfy them, and this would have effectively allowed Israel to continue to control these disputed areas.

Much of the leadership of the Palestinian Authority, the quasi-state body set up following the signing of the first of the Oslo Accords in 1993, was caught unawares by Rabin's ideas. Though the extent of Rabin's thinking was not public knowledge at the time, the little that was in the public arena was met with harsh criticism by the Palestinian Authority leadership. Rabin, they charged, was attempting to pre-empt any final agreement between Israelis and Palestinians; in other words, putting facts on the ground. There was also, however, a sense among many of the young Palestinian leadership that it would never come to that: that, in effect, Rabin's actions were mere pressure tactics aimed at trying to motivate the security forces of the Palestinian Authority to do more to dismantle the infrastructure of groups like Hamas and Islamic Jihad. I myself recall addressing a group of Palestinian leaders who argued that the threat of a fence was being used solely to placate Israeli domestic public opinion, which was becoming less enthusiastic about the Oslo Accords with the Palestinians. The major criticism that most Israelis had at the time, in simple terms, was that the peace accords had actually led to an increase in violence and a decrease in their own feelings of personal security. Academic polling conducted by Tel Aviv University in 1994 found that some 57 per cent of Israelis were either worried or very worried about their personal safety – a significant increase on previous years. This figure was to steadily rise in subsequent years, peaking in 1999 when some 79 per cent of Israelis were worried about their safety.[9] With cities in Israel's wealthy coastal plain such as Tel Aviv and Netanya becoming prime targets for the first time by bombers, the power of such feelings of insecurity among the Israeli public should not be under-estimated.

Rabin was not to be put off by the essentially negative response to his proposals. Prior to his assassination, he had been busy starting to prepare strategies for the forth-coming elections in Israel that were due to be held by the summer of 1996. For many Israelis one of the major weaknesses in his record was the fact that he continued with the political negotiations with Arafat while there was still violence on the ground. The catch phrase that seemed to stick was 'negotiating under fire', something that all previous Israeli leaders had refused to publicly countenance. Tired of trying to get Arafat to act against the radical Islamic groups, and unable to send the Israeli army into areas controlled by the Palestinian Authority, Rabin saw the fence as the only way to present a case to the Israeli electorate that he was dealing with the terrorist threat on its eastern border.

Though the cost of the fence had not been fully calcu-lated, Rabin's military advisors were already working on its route and approximate costing. Initially, it was hoped that the United States could be persuaded to pay for part or all of the cost for the fence's construction, and that the CIA would play a role in the planning and selling of the idea to the sceptical Palestinians. The Clinton Administration, in short, did not disagree with Israel's desire to build the fence, but at the time it was not clear that the fence would not simply run along the existing Green Line that divides the West Bank and Israel. Though today the eventual route of the fence is highly fluid and subject to change by international pressure and the Israeli judiciary, the United Nations reported in 2004 that only 15 per cent of the intended route of the fence would actually run along the exact route of the Green Line that divides Israel from the West Bank. At its greatest point of intrusion into the West Bank, at the Ariel enclave, the fence is to be located some 22 km inside the West Bank. The UN claimed that the proposed route of the fence in 2004 would lead to some 140,200 Israeli settlers living between the fence and the Green Line, and some 93,000 Palestinians in effect being left on the wrong side of the fence.[10]

Though the notion of a Security Fence was by no means a secret, it did not top the political agenda during times in which the headlines continued to be dominated by the possibilities and opportunities that peace appeared to be bringing to Israelis, Palestinians and the wider Arab world. It did not seem odd to Israeli leaders that, at the same time as Rabin was preparing for separation with the Palestinians, his Foreign Minister, Shimon Peres, was attending regional economic conferences talking about the potential for joint Israeli-Palestinian economic projects and, in effect, trying to tie the economy of a future

THE VIEW FROM THE FENCE

Palestinian state to that of the Israeli economy as much as possible[11], for Peres saw the future peace in a very different light to that of his boss. For Peres, a Palestinian state would require a viable and stable economy if the state was to have any chance of long-term success, and Israel had a major role to play in helping to nurture the infant Palestinian Authority economy. Peres, quite simply, viewed a successful Palestinian economy as the best counter-balance to the actions of Hamas in the West Bank and Gaza Strip.

In the shadow of Hamas

The rise of Hamas in the West Bank and Gaza Strip marks one of the most interesting developments in Palestinian society. Founded in 1987–8 (its Covenant was not published until August 1988) it was initially seen by Yitzhak Rabin – then serving as Minister of Defence in a National Unity Government – as a counterbalance to the influence of the Palestinian Liberation Organisation (PLO).[12] Israel went as far as indirectly helping to fund the organisation. This usually took the form of ignoring the payments coming in to the Occupied Territories that were destined for Hamas, while at the same time continuing to intercept any payments that were going to the PLO in the same areas. In retrospect, the Israeli decision to help Hamas appears curious given the recent levels of conflict between the organisation and Israel, but at the time it appeared to make perfect political sense, given the Israeli government's hatred of the PLO. Unsurprisingly, Israel's flirtation with Hamas turned out to be short-lived: following Hamas involvement in the kidnapping and murder of two Israeli soldiers in mid-1989, contacts were broken off and Israel imprisoned several leading members of Hamas.

The Saudis primarily bankrolled the organisation – mainly wealthy Saudi individuals who viewed Hamas as a charitable organisation, and some whose motives were a little more sinister. At this time, Hamas concentrated its effort on winning support from Palestinians through the building of hospitals and schools that were of a high standard. The aim of such programmes was to develop strong ties between the organisation and the local population. In short, in exchange for free hospital treatment and schooling, Palestinians would give their support to Hamas. Put simply, Hamas succeeded in developing strong ties of dependency between itself and large segments of the Palestinian population living in the West Bank and Gaza Strip. Quite ironically, the model employed by Hamas for the development of a strong powerbase was none other than the labour Zionist movement. The political leadership of Hamas were known to have studied in detail how the labour Zionist movement was able to develop strong ties with the newly arriving Jewish immigrants in Palestine during the 1920s and 1930s. Back then the new immigrants soon came to rely on the movement for healthcare, education and other social services. The Zionist model had been proven to be very successful, and Hamas hoped to copy it with the Saudis acting as the provider of aid in the same way that Jewish donors such as the Rothschilds had done for the labour Zionist movement.

Back in 1994–5, the success of Hamas's strategy was clear for all to see, including Peres and his advisors. The Palestinian Authority was struggling to deal with the

Palestinian areas that were coming under its control. To a certain degree this was understandable, given the relatively small amount of land they controlled and the difficult economic situation they inherited in many of these areas. Donor aid promised when the Oslo Accords were signed did not materialise in full. Many countries grew increasingly sceptical about Palestinian Authority accounting practices. Although stories of German bankers being asked to leave brown sacks of cash at the bottom of staircases proved to be an exaggeration, there was a culture of suspicion and corruption. As a result, it was clear that, during the early years of a potential Palestinian Authority-led Palestinian state, Israel would have to be fully engaged in helping to support it. Many commentators, both Arab and Israeli, went further, arguing that the Israeli government had a moral obligation to help support a Palestinian state. The central theme of Shimon Peres's economic vision, which he outlined in his optimistically entitled book *The New Middle East* was, however, not moral, but pure, simple, economic logic.

For Rabin, known affectionately by Israelis as Mr Security, economics came a poor second to immediate Israeli security concerns, and the Security Fence was a very direct product of this line of thinking. His death in November 1995, however, effectively put any plans for a Security Fence on hold, as the period up to 1999 was characterised by deep fault lines in the Oslo peace process in Israel. Rabin's successor as Prime Minister, Shimon Peres, did not last in the job. Some seven months later, Benjamin Netanyahu secured a narrow, but decisive, victory in Israel's general elections. Thereafter, Netanyahu kept the question of building a Security

Fence firmly off the agenda for a number of political and ideological reasons.

In Israel, the Likud are the modern day descendents of the Revisionist Zionist movement. Central to the ideological belief of the Likud (and what largely separated them from the Israeli Labour Party) was the question of land. For the Israeli Labour Party, the Zionist priority was immigrants – land came second.[13] For the Likud it was the reverse. Likudniks believed in 'Greater Israel' – the right, as promised in the Bible, to a Jewish state in lands including the West Bank of the River Jordan (Israel and the West Bank). In other words, the West Bank was part of Israel itself, and so fences should not be built between Israel and the West Bank, as it gave the impression of reducing the Israeli claim on the land in the West Bank. For the same reason, Israeli Prime Ministers such as Menachem Begin, Yitzhak Shamir and Benjamin Netanyahu were much more reluctant than their Labour Party counterparts to impose security closures on the West Bank, hand over land, or, indeed, build physical barriers that would divide lands that they considered to be an integral part of Israel.

Palestinian and Arab responses to the construction of the fence and separation

The question of an Israeli Security Fence has brought interesting responses and rationales from the Palestinian leadership. It is worth pointing out that the Palestinian Authority, in a non-paper (not adopted as official policy) on the Palestinian vision for the outcome of permanent status negotiations, stated that the notion of minor changes to the Green Line were acceptable, providing they were reciprocal, equal and did not affect Palestinian territorial continuity.[14] In terms of the fence, this means that the Palestinian Authority is not adverse to some of it crossing into the West Bank, provided the Palestinians receive an equal amount of land in return somewhere else in the West Bank. This seemingly pragmatic response was never officially adopted, and in the arena of international diplomacy the Palestinians formally reject the construction of the fence over the Green Line.

Of far greater importance is the fact that the Palestinian leadership views the Security Fence as a public relations disaster for Israel, and consequently a golden opportunity for them to damage Israel's international standing, particularly among the member states of the European Union. In order to maximise the publicity, the Palestinian leadership adopted two strategies, both of which challenged the legality of Israel's decision. The first is going through international organisations such as the International Court of Justice and the UN, and concerns the overall validity of the fence. The second is a challenge to the specific route of the fence. To some degree both strategies proved fruitful. Israel did not attend the hearing at the International Court of Justice, arguing that the Court had no jurisdiction to hear the case. The ruling made headlines all over the world, with the Court declaring on 9 July 2004 – albeit predictably – that the fence was illegal, by a vote of fourteen to one, stating:

'The construction of the wall being built by Israel, the occupying Power, in the Occupied Palestinian Territory, including in and around East Jerusalem, and its associated regime, are contrary to international law.

12

Israel is under an obligation to terminate its breaches of international law; it is under an obligation to cease forthwith the works of construction of the wall being built in the Occupied Palestinian Territory, including in and around East Jerusalem, to dismantle forthwith the structure therein situated, and to repeal or render ineffective forthwith all legislative and regulatory acts relating thereto, in accordance with paragraph 151 of this Opinion.'[15]

Despite Israel's attempts to play down this ruling, it was difficult to disguise the fact that it presented the Palestinians with a major political, if not legal, victory in their battle to maximise the damage to Israel of its construction of the fence.

At the UN, the Palestinian delegation increased the rhetoric, claiming, among other charges, that the 'Israeli fascist colonial occupier' was imprisoning the whole Palestinian people and that the wall was the shame of the twenty-first century.[16] In 2004, the Secretary-General made it clear that he regards any deviation of the fence from the 1949 Armistice Line as illegal, and demanded that Israel stop and reverse the construction of the wall in the Occupied Palestinian Territory, including in and around East Jerusalem, arguing that it is in contradiction to relevant provisions of international law.[17] A motion had been submitted before the Security Council the previous year, which among the usual calls on Israel to halt all settlement activity, demanded the cessation of the construction of the fence in lands over the 1949 line.[18] On the specific route of the fence, the Palestinians have been joined by Israeli individuals and groups opposed to the fence. The Israeli court system has, in general, ruled in favour of those petitioning for a re-routing of the fence, and against the Israeli army who were responsible for devising its original route.

On a deeper level, the question of a Security Fence left Arafat and his Palestinian Authority leadership with some difficult decisions to make. In private, many members of the Palestinian Authority leadership were acutely aware of the need for strong economic ties with Israel. The fence was clearly going to make economic linkage much harder, if not impossible altogether. In public, no Palestinian leader could admit just how dependent they were on the Israeli economy for the foreseeable future. Some Palestinian intellectuals charged that the Oslo Accords were in fact an agreement between the large business classes in both Israeli and Palestinian society to help maximise their respective profits. In effect, the Oslo Accords were mutually beneficial to the Israeli and Palestinian business elites.

The threat of the fence and the resulting separation of the two communities led to a series of internal debates within the Palestinian Authority leadership and the wider Arab world. In Palestinian circles, the key question was if they could not rely on access to the Israeli markets for their goods and labour force as previously planned, where else could they look? In the wider Arab world, both President Mubarak of Egypt and King Abdullah II of Jordan expressed their concern, and argued that any solution to the Israeli–Palestinian conflict would have to be agreed upon at multi-party level and not at bi-lateral level, as attempted by the Oslo Accords. Not for the first time, both Egypt and Jordan expressed their concerns about the creation of a Palestinian state – one which they would be expected to help to bail out economically and whose workers would have to be allowed to enter their respective countries in order to earn money to send to their families back in the potential Palestinian state.

The Hashemite Kingdom of Jordan is especially nervous about the fence, and has quietly been leading the international opposition to its construction. Jordan's fears centre on what they cite as the potential for a Palestinian exodus eastward from Israel and the West Bank and into Jordan. With Palestinian workers unable to enter Israel for the foreseeable future, Jordan's fear is that they will try to enter the Jordanian jobs market. Around one-third of the Jordanian population is of Palestinian origin, with many families split between those members who live in the West Bank and those on the East Bank. The last thing Jordan needs at present is to have scores of both sets of Palestinians trying to enter Jordan to get work. A lack of economic viability is only one of many reasons why Jordanian leaders, in private, do not fully support the creation of a Palestinian state. In the sometimes surreal world of Middle Eastern politics, however, Jordan is aware that a Palestinian state will one day be created, but it wants such a state to be tied economically to both Israel and itself. In short, it hopes that both Jordanian and Israeli capital will be able to control a Palestinian state through making use of a good old-fashioned tactic: economic colonialism.

To be honest, Jordanian fears about the creation of a Palestinian state are not purely based on its lack of confidence in the economic viability of such a state. The origins of the ill will between the PLO and Jordan can be traced much further back to September 1970, when King Hussein moved against the PLO fighters in Jordan who had effectively created a state within a state (they were later to do the same in Lebanon). Earlier that summer, the King had survived an assassination attempt, and he blamed Yasser Arafat's fighters for the attempt on his life. The King's decision led to an attempted invasion of Jordan by another Arab state acting on the surface in the name of the Palestinian people, Syria. Only the threat of direct Israeli and US intervention to protect the King caused Syria to pull its troops out of Jordan. Meanwhile, after fierce gun battles, the Jordanian army succeeded in either killing the Palestinian fighters, or forcing them to flee. Yasser Arafat used up one of his many cat's lives, escaping Jordan dressed as a woman. The issue of Jerusalem since 1967 has also proved to be a point of confrontation between the PLO and Jordan. Following Israel's conquest of East Jerusalem and the Old City during the 1967 Arab–Israeli War, Jordan was given a special role in the running and maintenance of the Islamic holy sites in the City. The PLO always resented this fact, and when it became clear that the Israeli government during the late 1990s was considering allowing a PLO presence in the City, Jordan became even more concerned.

So the construction of the Security Fence has proved to be the catalyst in bringing a series of inter-Arab disputes to the surface, which might otherwise have remained relatively hidden from the West. The response of the Arab world in general has mirrored its somewhat confused reaction to the outbreak of the second Palestinian *Intifada* – and the resulting violence that persuaded the Israeli government to press ahead with the fence in the first place.

Why build the fence and why now?

If Rabin was the Israeli architect of the fence – and the thinking behind its construction – then Ariel Sharon was its builder. Sharon cited the wave of Palestinian violence known by Palestinians as the Second *Intifada* as his rationale for pressing ahead with the fence, which he hoped would make it harder for Palestinians to launch suicide attacks against Israeli targets. The Israeli government pointed to the fact that some 47 per cent of Israelis who have been killed in attacks by Palestinians since 2000 have been the victims of suicide bombers, with over two-thirds of deaths civilians.[19] During Sharon's first year in power in 2001, some 85 Israelis were killed in suicide attacks, and in 2002 this number peaked at 220. An additional problem for Israeli authorities was the increase in the number of organisations taking part in such attacks. During the 1990s, the attacks were almost exclusively the work of Hamas and Islamic Jihad. A look at the organisations who carried out successful suicide attacks in 2004 illustrates the growing number of groups carrying out attacks. The Israeli Defence Forces (IDF) reported that in this year, 55 Israelis were killed in total as a result of such attacks. Of the 55 killed, some 26.48% died as the result of multi-organisational attacks, 10.18% were killed by groups linked to Fatah, 3.5% to the Popular Front for the Liberation of Palestine and 16.29% deaths were attributed to Hamas.[20]

There was an Israeli precedent for the belief that a fence or barrier would help prevent attacks. A Security Fence had existed for many years, cutting off the Gaza Strip from the rest of Israel. Palestinians intent on entering Israel for work were forced to enter through a number of Israeli security checkpoints. In times of high tension Israel would simply close the checkpoints, thus making it very difficult for Palestinians to enter Israel. During the initial months of the second Palestinian *Intifada*, there were complaints from the leaderships of Hamas and Islamic Jihad in the West Bank that their respective 'brothers in Gaza' were not mounting enough attacks against the 'Zionist enemy'. On the other side of the fence in Gaza, Israeli military leaders were complimenting themselves on how successful the Gaza fence was in preventing attacks on Israeli cities from cells based in the Gaza Strip. Operations mounted by such cells usually took the form of suicide bomb attacks on crossing points and risked killing as many Palestinians as Israelis.

Israeli military planners argued that the success of the fence in Gaza could be transferred to the West Bank – an area where the majority of attacks against both Jewish settlers on the West Bank and Israeli cities within the Green Line were originating from. Much of the Israeli political leadership was convinced about the security value of such a barrier running the length of the West Bank, but deep divisions that cut across traditional party lines in Israel developed over the political pros and cons of the fence. The parameters of this debate went to the very essence of how Israeli lawmakers viewed the conflict with the Palestinians, and produced some interesting alliances.

The origins of the wave of Palestinian violence and Israel's military response, starting in October 2000, that led to the Israeli decision to turn Rabin's blueprint into physical reality are not difficult to trace. The political environment during the summer of 2000 was dominated by the failure of the Camp David summit, where it had been hoped that Israel and the Palestinians would be able to reach an agreement that would be the culmination of the Oslo peace process that had started some eight years previously. The failure at Camp David – as we will discuss later – did not mark the complete end of the Oslo process, but, at the very least it created a dangerous political vacuum in both Israel and the Palestinian Authority-controlled territories in the West Bank and Gaza Strip.

The political needs of Yasser Arafat cast a giant shadow over the Palestinian aims of its self-termed uprising. Widely blamed for the failure at Camp David by the Americans, the Israelis and even the generally pro-Arafat European Union, the Palestinian leader needed to do something to rekindle his declining popularity among Palestinians. True to his dramatic nature, Arafat saw the need to create a crisis in order to entice the Americans and Europeans back into the process, in the knowledge that any armed conflict with Israel would no doubt lead to images of Israeli tanks firing at Palestinians. In respect of the latter, Arafat must have noted the tragic television pictures of a terrified young Palestinian child being shielded by his father before being shot by the IDF. Arafat and the Palestinian Authority were, in short, looking for a reason to provoke the IDF into the situation whereby the world would witness an Israeli atrocity committed on Palestinians. This methodology of provocation was the last instrument left for Arafat to re-establish his international and domestic legitimacy to lead the Palestinians.

On a more philosophical level, Arafat had clearly decided that there was a need for a Palestinian state to be born out of blood. This message was not lost on Ariel

Sharon, who had defeated Ehud Barak by a landslide in Israeli elections in early January 2001. Sharon soon made it quite clear that, from an Israeli perspective, Arafat was no longer a partner for peace. He started, as a result, preparing for what became known as disengagement from the Palestinians, at the centre of which was the decision to build a Security Fence along the West Bank. Amidst the death and destruction of both human life and economies, the fence therefore remains the most physical result of the violence.

There is, of course, an additional reason why Israel needed to construct the fence. Since its creation in 1948, Israeli leaders have always worried about maintaining the Jewish nature of the State of Israel. They argue that Israel is a state for the Jews, and if it is to survive and remain a part of the group of democratic states, then the majority of its inhabitants must be Jewish. Today, the population of Israel is just over six million, of whom five million are considered to be Jewish. So on the surface the demographic question would appear not to be a major issue. A deeper analysis, however, reveals very real problems in the coming years for Israeli leaders in this area. If we take the area of land from the River Jordan to the Mediterranean (Israel and the West Bank), then research conducted by Israeli scholars predicts that Jews will be in the minority in the area by 2020. To a large extent, this change is a result of much higher birth rates among Israeli Arabs and their Palestinian brothers living in the West Bank than Jews living in the same areas – this despite the large size of many Orthodox and Ultra-Orthodox Jewish families. Though birth rates among the Palestinian Arabs are lower than in the wider Arab world, the gap between the two groups in Israel shows little sign of change.

The demographic time bomb, as some Israelis refer to it, is by no means a certain fact. Other Israelis charge that it is too simplistic to suggest that current rates of birth will be maintained. To add further confusion to the picture, some non-academic reports charge that the Palestinians have been exaggerating the levels of their birth rates in order to trick Israel into making territorial concessions. Key elements in the Israeli political leadership, however, appear to be taking the threat very seriously. What it in effect means is that Israel can not indefinitely postpone defining what its Zionist priority really is. To put it starkly, Israeli leaders know that if they attempt to annexe large chunks of the West Bank and Gaza Strip, there is a fair to better chance that the Jewish nature of the State of Israel will be lost.

Originally, back in the 1990s, it was hoped that the influx of millions of new Jewish immigrants from the ex-Soviet Union would avoid such a situation. Then it was hoped that this Soviet Aliyah (wave of Jewish immigrants) would settle in the West Bank where, given time, a Jewish majority – or at the very least a sizeable Jewish minority – would emerge. Somebody, however, had forgotten to ask the Soviet immigrants what their intentions were. In the period between 1991 and 2000, only 750,000 Soviet Jews made Aliyah to Israel. The number may sound high, but the truth remains that Israel had hoped for a lot more. Many Jews chose to remain in the successor states of the Soviet Union, where they were granted more religious freedoms than they had previously enjoyed under the old Soviet regime.

Even more worrying for those who foresaw a massive expansion of Jewish settlement in the West Bank, those immigrants who did arrive in Israel indicated a strong preference for living within the Green Line and in or near established large urban areas. The Aliyah, in short, were not pioneers willing to go out into the West Bank and develop new communities. Instead, their major concern appeared to lie in economic advancement; put simply, a concentration on the self rather than any so-called collective ideological fervour to secure the West Bank for Israeli goals.

The consequence of the failure to flood the West Bank with Jewish immigrants is that if Israel wishes to continue to rule the area, it will have to do so against the wishes of the vast majority of its inhabitants. Given that Israel can not simply annex these lands either, as this would threaten the Jewish nature of Israel, many Palestinian leaders fear that, in the light of all this, Israel will attempt to transfer the Palestinians out of the West Bank by force. Support for such a move, however, though growing within Israeli society, only enjoys support in parliamentary terms from the far right in Israel. So Israeli leaders are caught between trying to maintain the status quo of controlling the West Bank – without annexing the land and having to give Israeli citizenship to over 2.2 million reluctant Palestinians – or working towards trying to reduce the dangers to Israel of the creation of a Palestinian state in these areas. Recent Israeli governments from both sides of the political spectrum in Israel have chosen the latter option, and the creation of the Security Fence has been put forward as the best way of trying to reduce the threat to Israel of a Palestinian state.

The proposed withdrawal by Israel from the Gaza Strip as part of the Disengagement Plan presented by Ariel Sharon on 28 May 2004 needs to be viewed within this context. On the surface, the plan represented growing Israeli frustration at the lack of a Palestinian partner for negotiations with Yasser Arafat, who was under Israeli-imposed virtual house arrest in Ramallah. On a deeper level, however, the plan was a reflection of the Sharon government's aim to reduce points of friction between Israelis and Palestinians.[21] The plan was also a reflection of the demographic realities of Gaza, where Israel has only around 18,000 settlers. This was not the first time that the Likud had discussed such a withdrawal from Gaza. During the 1992 election that the party lost to the Labour Party under Rabin, senior Likud leaders had discussed supporting something approaching a full withdrawal from the Gaza Strip, but the then party leader, Yitzhak Shamir, finally rejected the proposal.[22] In 2004, Israeli and Palestinian cynics initially suggested that Sharon's plans were put forward to distract attention away from several investigations being conducted at the time by the Israeli police into the business affairs of Sharon and his family. The reality is that the Disengagement Plan reflects an attempt to define and formalise the concept of separation, with the withdrawal to behind the already constructed fence in Gaza marking the first step in the process of completing the fence in the West Bank, and subsequently pulling back behind this fence.[23]

While the short-term rationale for the fence, from an Israeli perspective, was merely to check the violence stemming from the second Palestinian *Intifada*, its continued longer-term need for Israel says much about how Israel envisages the conflict developing. In recent years, Israeli planning divisions in both the military and civilian sectors have concluded that the creation of a Palestinian state will not by itself end the Israeli–Palestinian conflict. Indeed, on the contrary, the creation of a Palestinian state might actually fuel – not fulfil – Palestinian nationalist aspirations. Proponents of this argument look at what they term likely scenarios for such a state. What happens if, once established, its economy stagnates and goes into deep recession, leading populist Palestinian leaders to blame Israel for the economic ills? This would likely lead to calls for a Palestinian state to expand and reduce support for the two-state solution to the conflict. Violent clashes could erupt as Palestinians eager for work try to enter Israel. Israeli planners believe that violence will continue after the creation of a Palestinian state, and that the fence is the best method for controlling and managing any social unrest in the Palestinian areas. Put simply, keeping the violence out of Israel.

In terms of economic issues, the Israeli government has already illustrated how committed it is to separation, but this has come at a heavy price. In effect, Israel has already replaced the Palestinian workers who used to cross into Israel with what it terms 'foreign workers', drawn largely from Asia and Eastern Europe. The Bank of Israel stated that in 2002, some 250,000 foreign workers were legally employed in Israel – a figure that was around ten per cent of the total Israeli workforce.[24] Israeli companies still prefer to employ foreign labour because it costs less than employing local labour. The Bank of Israel points out that to employ a foreign blue collar worker costs around

65 per cent less than employing an Israeli in the same position. Despite government attempts to reduce the number of foreign workers in Israel in 2004–5 by introducing new taxes and reducing the number of work permits for foreign workers, the issue remains problematic, as rates of unemployment among Israelis remain very high, particularly in the construction industry. In effect, the foreign workers are pricing the local workforce out of jobs in certain key sectors in the blue-collar part of the labour market. Though some of these problems existed before the process of economic separation began, they have been magnified by the influx of a far higher number of foreign workers into Israel than the number of jobs that had been previously undertaken by Palestinians. By 2004, however, it was clear that the effort to limit the numbers of foreign workers had failed, as the number started to increase once more. Moreover, in 2003 some 43,000 Palestinian workers were able to cross into Israel as the political climate marginally improved.[25] This placed further strains on the Israeli blue-collar market. Many Israeli companies appeared to be more dependent than ever on the use of foreign labour. Though exact figures are not readily available, it is clear that some of the 43,000 Palestinian labour force has been used in the largest on-going construction project in Israel – the 622 km long Security Fence. As we shall see in Chapter 2, the employment of Arab, or indeed foreign, labour went against the Zionist ideology of the Second Aliyah, the founding fathers of the State of Israel, who argued that the Jewish State should be built using Hebrew labour, whatever the economic implications of doing this.

On a deeper level it is not difficult to view the creation of the fence as a permanent border between two states: one Israeli and the other Palestinian. This means that the exact route of the fence is extremely important for both sides. Here Israel is open to criticism of, in effect, trying to pre-judge any future negotiations on borders between the two parties. In public, the official line of the Israeli government remains that the route of the Security Fence in no way reflects the final borders between Israel and a Palestinian state. In private, and given the cost of constructing the fence, this is clearly not an accurate reflection of the situation.

The reaction of the Palestinian leadership in both the Arafat and post-Arafat eras illustrates just how permanent they believe the fence will become: that it is effectively marking out the Israeli–Palestinian border. As we have mentioned before, the Palestinians, as well as maximising the public relations damage to Israel over the fence, have been involved in making several legal challenges to its route, particularly in the Jerusalem area. In private, far away from the media and their own constituents, Palestinian leaders resigned to the construction of the fence have been negotiating with Israel over its proposed route. To many Palestinians and their supporters, such actions probably represent capitulation and defeat. In reality, however, they reflect a growing political maturity among many younger Palestinian leaders, who argue that they need to be on the political inside shouting out, as opposed to the previous typical Palestinian situation of being on the outside shouting in.

The creation of a Security Fence in many ways turns the clock back to 1947 and the findings of the United Nations

Special Commission on Palestine (UNSCOP), whose report formed the basis for the creation of Israel on 14 May 1948. In its report, UNSCOP called for a partition of Palestine into two states: one Jewish, the other Palestinian.[26] Today, with certain deviations mainly caused by the expansion of Jerusalem and large scale Israeli settlement blocks in the West Bank, the borders between Israel and a Palestinian state will, to some degree, resemble those that UNSCOP recommended over 57 years ago. Back in 1947, the partition plan was rejected by both the local Palestinians and the wider Arab world, in the belief that a Zionist state was little more than a colonial settler state, and, perhaps as importantly, because they believed that their joint military forces could defeat the infant State of Israel.

It was not until the PLO statement of 15 November 1988, following a meeting of the Palestinian National Council, that the Palestinian leadership accepted the partition plan and called for the two states to live side by side in peace.[27] Yasser Arafat's subsequent speech to a special session of the United Nations General Assembly on 13 December 1988 appeared to confirm this change of policy.[28] Today, however, there are suspicions that many Palestinian leaders still do not accept a two-state solution, and view the establishment of a Palestinian state in the West Bank and the Gaza Strip as only the first stage in creating a greater Palestinian state that includes all the lands that are today called Israel. For many Israeli leaders, as a result, the building of the fence is an insurance policy which, after decades of conflict, they feel Israel needs in order to secure its future. Finally, in understanding the present day difficulties between Arabs and Israelis, it is important to go back and remind ourselves about the causes of the conflict, and look at the role which the international powers of the day played in shaping the scope of the conflict.

Notes:

3   Estimated figure from United Nations (2004), 'The Humanitarian Impact of the West Bank Barrier on Palestinian Communities', *United Nations Humanitarian Policy Group Report*, (1 September 2004), p. 8.
4   See the Palestinian Authority–Ministry of Foreign Affairs website (www.mofa.gov.ps) for its terminology of fence.
5   D. Makovsky (2004), 'How to Build a Fence', *Foreign Affairs*, Mar–Apr, p. 52.
6   N. Lochery (1997), *The Israeli Labour Party: in the Shadow of the Likud*, Reading: Ithaca Press, pp. 212–13.
7   Figures from World Bank (2002), 'Long Term Policy Options for the Palestinian Economy', *World Bank Report*, p. 4.
8   'Long Term Policy Options for the Palestinian Economy', *World Bank Report*, p. 3.
9   A. Arian (2003), 'Israeli Public Opinion on National Security 2003', *Memorandum No. 67*, Tel Aviv: JCSS (October 2003), p. 19.
10   Estimated figure from 'The Humanitarian Impact'. When East Jerusalem is included these figures increase to 318, 654 Israelis living in areas between the fence and the Green Line, and some 325,660 Palestinians living on the wrong side of the fence.
11   For details of the Palestinian economy's dependence on Israel see IMF (2003), 'West Bank and Gaza Economic Performance and Reform under Conflict Conditions', *Report of International Monetary Fund*, (September 2003), pp. 14–20.
12   B. Milton-Edwards (1996), *Islamic Politics in Palestine*, London: Tauris Academic Studies, p. 151.
13   N. Lochery (1997), *The Israeli Labour Party*, pp. 182–3.

[14]   Palestinian Authority (2002), 'Non-Paper: Palestinian Vision for the Outcome of Permanent Status Negotiations', 15 June 2002.

[15]   International Court of Justice (2004), 'Legal Consequences of a Wall in the Palestinian Occupied Territory', *Advisory Opinion of the International Court of Justice*, (9 July 2004), p. 1.

[16]   UN General Assembly, Comments by Nasser Al-Kidwa, Emergency Special Session of the UN General Assembly, (8 December 2003) A/ES-10/PV.23, p. 4.

[17]   UN Secretary-General, 'Israeli Settlements in the Occupied Palestinian Territory, including East Jerusalem, and the Occupied Syrian Golan', Report of the Secretary-General, (9 September 2004) A/59/343.

[18]   UN Security Council, Draft Resolution of the Security Council, Guinea, Malaysia, Pakistan and Syrian Arab Republic, (14 October 2003) S/2003/980.

[19]   Figures from IDF (2005), 'Ebb and Flow: a Summary of 2004, Strategic Trends', *Israeli Defence Forces Report*, p. 8.

[20]   'Ebb and Flow: a Summary of 2004, Strategic Trends', *Israeli Defence Forces Report*, p. 12.

[21]   Prime Minister's Office, Jerusalem (PMO), 'Disengagement Plan of Prime Minister Ariel Sharon – Revised', (28 May 2004), point 5, p. 1.

[22]   The proposals were made by Likud Campaign manager, Ronni Milo, see N. Lochery (1997), *The Israeli Labour Party*, p. 211.

[23]   Prime Minister's Office, Jerusalem (PMO), 'Address by Ariel Sharon to the Fourth Herzilya Conference', (18 December 2003); also, (PMO), 'Address by Ariel Sharon to the Fifth Herzilya Conference', (16 December 2004).

[24]   Bank of Israel (2004), 'Recent Economic Developments 103, April–September 2003', *Bank of Israel Report*, p. 15.

[25]   Bank of Israel (2005), 'Recent Economic Developments 108, July–December 2004, *Bank of Israel Report*, p. 7.

[26]   UN General Assembly, Recommendations to the General Assembly, United Nations Special Committee to Palestine, (3 September 1947) A/364/3.

27 Ministry of Foreign Affairs, Jerusalem, PLO Statement, (7 December 1988) MFA/9-10/408/1984–1988.
28 Ministry of Foreign Affairs, Jerusalem, Statement by Arafat to UN General Assembly, (13 December 1988) MFA/9-10/414/ 1984–1988.

2

Where to Start?
The Origins of the Conflict

In truth, finding a starting point for the conflict is no easy matter, and is not free from having to make difficult and admittedly contentious judgements. While some prefer to go back to ancient times, they are usually trying to use ancient history as a method for justifying their claim on the land known today as Israel. Such claims are more often than not accompanied by a heavy dose of religious history as justification for claiming a right to the land – such as the traditional use of the argument that the land was promised to a particular group in the Bible. In the modern world of history and political science, such claims mean very little to the non-committed. Admittedly, it would be foolhardy to ignore the role of religion in the conflict, but it would prove even more imprudent to be held prisoner by notions of religious legitimacy and ancient rights to the land. It is important to remember that the Arab–Israeli conflict has been fought by leaders who are either secular in nature or are only moderately religious. Leaders from both sides have conjured up religious symbols and tales from ancient times to attempt to justify and find a context for their actions. It should, however, be remembered, amidst all the current headlines about religious extremism in Israel and the Arab world, that Israel was built and created by immigrants and pioneers who, by and large, were not considered religious in nature; and that the majority of Arabs do not subscribe to fundamentalist forms of Islam.

For the non-committed 'modernists' there is at least a relatively clear starting point to the Arab–Israeli conflict. The arrival of the first Aliyah, starting around 1880, marked the arrival of the first group of Zionist immigrants. Between 1880 and the birth of the State in 1948, some six Aliyahs arrived in Palestine, literally transforming the physical and political landscape of the country. It was not simply a 'numbers game', in terms of getting Jewish immigrants into Palestine. It is equally important to look at what these immigrants achieved (and failed to do), and how their actions shaped the growing conflict with the local Palestinian Arab population and, subsequently, the wider Arab world. In looking at the various waves of Jewish immigration to Palestine, it is important to remember the reasons why they came, why they stayed, and, indeed, why some moved on and left. One of the most interesting features of the immigrants who came to Palestine is that a large number did not come in order to fulfil any Zionist ideological aspirations. Many, in short, came because of a lack of choice – political and economic persecution in their respective countries of origin, and, particularly after the United States closed its doors to Jewish immigration, a lack of an alternative country willing to take them.

The modern-day story of Israel begins at the end of the nineteenth century, when the first Aliyah began arriving in Palestine. Prior to their arrival, there were under 25,000 Jews living in Palestine, mainly in the four holy cities of Jerusalem, Hebron, Tiberias and Safed. These religious Jews spent most of their time in prayer and study, praying for the arrival of the Messiah and the redemption of the land, and were financially supported by funds collected by Jewish communities from outside Palestine. They greeted the arrival of the new, decidedly non-religious, Jewish immigrants, who had come to Palestine without divine help, somewhat coolly.

The period from 1882 to 1930 saw the arrival of the first four Aliyahs in Palestine, and the development of the Zionist political, economic and social structures that were to eventually form the basis of the State of Israel. During this time, it was the arrival of the Second Aliyah, and its subsequent battle for power with the First Aliyah, that proved to be the most politically significant event. To a large degree, the political leadership that was to dominate both the pre-State Jewish institutions in Palestine (Yishuv), and the early years of Israel, was determined by the outcome of this conflict. Of great importance to under-standing the various Aliyahs is the notion of the push and pull factors that led individual immigrants to come to Palestine. Push factors are determined by what made them leave their countries of origin, and pull factors represent the attractions in Palestine that persuaded them to come. The push factors ranged from persecution in the immigrants' country of origin to economic hardship. The pull factors were mainly Zionism and the hope for a better life in Palestine. In many cases, however, there were a number of push and pull factors that led an immigrant to Palestine. Again, it should be remembered that not all those immigrants that came to Palestine did so for Zionist reasons – many would have chosen another, less arduous, location if given a choice, or remained in their country of origin had they not been subject to persecution.

The First Aliyah (1882–1903) numbered between 20,000 and 30,000, and came to Palestine mainly as a result of the growing wave of anti-Semitism in Russia. Although the majority of the 2.5 million Jews who left eastern Europe at the time went to the United States, the minority that went to Palestine were ideologically committed to the Zionist movement, and had received formal training in Zionism from eastern European-based Zionist groups. The majority of the new immigrants came from relatively well-educated urban backgrounds. They had, however, little or no preparation or training in the agricultural skills that were required to develop the lands from barren wastelands into fertile ones. Despite this, they managed to set up agricultural colonies (moshavim) where the land was privately owned. Due to their lack of agricultural skills, the work itself was mainly carried out by hired Arab labour. In modern-day terms, the First Aliyah would have been extremely concerned about the construction of a Security Fence that would lead to Arab labour effectively being barred from Israel. Even today, Arab labour remains cheaper, better equipped and available in greater numbers than Hebrew (Jewish) labour, and in pure economic terms it still makes greater sense for Israel to employ it.

The First Aliyah's welcome from the religious Jewish colonies in Palestine was far from warm. The religious

Jews saw the immigrants not only as religiously incorrect, but also as competitors in the race to win the very limited charity funds from Jewish communities abroad. This first attempt at settling the land would have been doomed to failure but for two reasons. In financial terms, the First Aliyah was largely saved by 'import capital,' and, in particular, by funds from Baron Edmond de Rothschild. The intervention of Rothschild was, however, not without strings. Rothschild installed his agents as overseers, and the immigrants grew used to turning to his organisation for funds, and some, for sending their children to Paris for schooling. Unfortunately for the prospects of this Aliyah, many of the children sent overseas for schooling did not return, preferring the relative luxury of Europe to the physical and economic hardships of Palestine. In practical terms, the efforts of the First Aliyah were saved by the arrival of the Second Aliyah that brought new agricultural and organisational skills.

This Second Aliyah (1904–1914) mainly came out of the failed Russian revolution of 1905, and numbered around 35,000, the vast majority of whom were Russian (a few thousand were Romanian, and 2,000 came from Yemen). Of the 35,000, around 10,000 were pioneers in the true sense of the word, abandoning comfortable lifestyles back home for the difficulties of transforming the land in Palestine. However, many did not last the course, and left Palestine to return to their country of origin, or emigrated to a third country. Of those that stayed, the majority were single, young, highly-motivated socialists who were more innovative than their predecessors. Building on the basic foundations laid by the First Aliyah, they quickly developed new kinds of agricultural collectively owned settlements (kibbutzim), as well as other industries. Although not the largest numerically, the Second Aliyah proved to be the most important grouping for two reasons. First, the major leaders of Israel's formative years came from this group, for example, David Ben-Gurion (Israel's first Prime Minister), Yitzhak Ben-Zvi (Israel's second President) and Yosef Sprinzak (Israel's first Chairman of the Knesset). Second, the political parties and economic and social institutions that they founded came to dominate not only the pre-State Yishuv, but the early history of Israel as well.

It came as little surprise when conflict broke out between members of the First and Second Aliyahs. Members of the latter wanted to undertake physical work, but found themselves excluded by their natural employers, the First Aliyah – who continued to prefer to use Arab labour, which was cheaper, more experienced and available in greater numbers. The landowners of the First Aliyah argued that they were serving the Zionist interest by developing a viable economy. The Jewish labourers of the Second Aliyah, however, argued that Jewish (Hebrew) labour was an essential part of a viable economy, and, more specifically, that it would be difficult to attract large numbers of new immigrants if such work was not available. Eventually, the labourers won the support of the World Zionist Organisation for their stand, and thus won the battle for influence between the first two Aliyahs. However, the bitterness continued between these two groups and, to some degree, has been passed on from generation to generation. Today, it still resonates under the surface of Israel's complex social structures. To summarise the success of the leadership of the Second Aliyah: they did not make substantial gains in practical issues such as increases in the number of immigrants or political mobilisation of the labour force. However, they defined the course (aims) and developed a strong sense of internal cohesion (unity). Both of these factors were to prove important to the long-term aim of creating a homeland for the Jews.

Jewish immigration to Palestine was given further impetus by the publication of the Balfour Declaration on 2 November 1917, in which the British appeared to support a Jewish homeland in Palestine.[29] The declaration, however, in typical British understated prose, also stated that any potential Jewish homeland should not prejudice the rights of the existing (Palestinian Arab) population. Consequently, the document not only encouraged the building of a Jewish state, but also, in many people's eyes, made the land twice promised. From here on in, conflict appeared inevitable, as two sets of people competed for one piece of land. From the end of the First World War in 1918, and the start of the British Mandate which the League of Nations officially awarded to Britain in 1922, until May 1948, Britain was responsible for trying to control Palestine for its own strategic interests, and for keeping order between two national movements who both believed they had a right to the land.

The arrival of the 35,000 members of the Third Aliyah (1919–1923) brought the total number of Jews living in Palestine to 85,000, which was a similar figure to 1914, but compensated for those that had emigrated from Israel during the same period. The members of the Third Aliyah were mainly young, single males who originated from

Eastern Europe (Russia and Poland). Unlike many of their predecessors, they had been carefully prepared for their immigration, studying in education programmes – specialising in agriculture and political organisation – run by the Zionist movement in their respective countries of origin. In general, they brought with them a strong ideological fervour, choosing Palestine over any other destination, and a keen sense of the importance of political mobilisation and control. Put simply, they had come to Palestine to build a Jewish state, and had received detailed training in order to maximise their contribution to achieving this goal. They accepted the leadership of the Second Aliyah even though there was not much age difference between the two groups. Thus collectively, the Second and Third Aliyahs became known as the generation of the founding fathers (and mothers) of the State of Israel.

After the relative success stories of the Second and Third Aliyahs came more self-inflicted difficulties for the Jews in Palestine that centred upon the business practices of the Fourth Aliyah. Two major factors had led to the arrival of the Fourth Aliyah (1924–1930): the introduction of quotas by the United States in the 1920s aimed at limiting the number of immigrants, and second, a worsening political and economic situation for Jews living in Poland. This Aliyah numbered around 82,000 Jews, with some 25,000 arriving in 1925 alone. They were predominantly middle-class Poles, many bringing capital and a bourgeois orientation with them, in direct contrast to the pioneering Zionist socialism of the members of the Second and Third Aliyahs. In 1927, the problems started. There was a severe economic crisis that made it difficult for the Yishuv, which concentrated its economic efforts in the agricultural sector, to absorb these urban-orientated immigrants. The result was that out of the original 82,000 immigrants, some 23,000 left Palestine. In 1927, emigration was higher than immigration. Many argue that this Aliyah's bad capital management caused the economic crisis itself, in that they used their capital for property speculation as opposed to the development of industry or agriculture. This led to some 8,000 workers out of the total workforce being unemployed. This Aliyah was often rather cruelly referred to as that of 'capitalists without capital' or simply 'bad capitalists'.

The rise to power of Hitler and the growing anti-Semitism in Europe led to the arrival of immigrants of the Fifth Aliyah (1932–38). This Aliyah was massive in contrast to the previous ones, numbering some 200,000, with a record 66,000 Jews arriving in 1935 alone. Historians often refer to it as the German Aliyah, although in reality only around a quarter were German or Austrian Jews. The largest numerical group in this Aliyah was Polish, while there were fewer Jews from the Soviet Union, which had imposed restrictions on emigration. In numerical terms, the arrival of this Aliyah doubled the Jewish population in Palestine within a five year period. These European immigrants, in general, brought with them capital for investment. Like the Fourth Aliyah, they mainly came from urban, middle class backgrounds. Lessons had been learnt from the failed use of capital by the previous Aliyah, and this group was encouraged to invest in a much more constructive and successful way.

Although the Fourth and Fifth Aliyahs were the largest statistically, and made contributions to the economic development of the Yishuv, their influence on the socio-political system was less pronounced than that of the Second and Third Aliyahs. There are a number of reasons for this, but in simple terms the Second Aliyahs in founding the basic political, social and economic structures of the Yishuv (political parties, trade unions, welfare system, control of immigrant absorption) ensured that its leadership controlled these vital organisations. The newly arriving immigrants were initially highly dependent on these very institutions to help them be successfully absorbed into their new country. Consequently, despite their numerical superiority, the latter Aliyahs did not challenge the legitimacy of the Second and Third Aliyahs' leadership of the Jews in Palestine.

Jewish immigrants did not only have to do battle with the climate, the land, the various ruling powers (the Turks and the British), and, to a degree with themselves; they also faced a local Palestinian Arab population. This group grew increasingly hostile to the immigrants as their numbers increased, and as the objective of creating a Jewish state became a more realistic prospect. The starting point of the concept of Palestinian nationalism is harder to trace. The methods that the Palestinian Arabs employed to resist Jewish immigration, however, were much clearer, taking the form of protests and non-co-operation with the British Mandate Authorities, and, between 1936 and 1939, staging a major uprising. Raymond Hinnebusch, a leading Arabist scholar, argues that the rebellion failed due to internal division among the Palestinians, and British military might.[30] As a result of the Arab revolt or uprising, and the decision of British rulers that the Arabs were more important to furthering British interests in the region

40

than the Zionists, the British restricted the levels of Jewish immigration. This action was undertaken primarily in an attempt to appease Arab opinion.

The onset of the Second World War made the Middle East even more strategically important to Britain and the Allies. There were fears in London that if the British did not do enough to appease the Arabs, some or all of them would throw in their lot with the Nazis. There was little prospect of the Jews in Palestine doing the same. Indeed, mainstream Jewish defence forces fought on the Allied side. British–Zionist relations, however, never easy, worsened at the end of the Second World War in 1945, when Britain refused to allow the survivors of the Holocaust to enter Palestine. The Zionists responded by running illegal immigrant ships from Europe to Palestine, with mixed success. Some boats, such as the Exodus – whose story was told in a Hollywood movie starring Paul Newman – at least succeeded in drawing world attention to the desperate plight of the refugees and helped turn the opinion of many non-aligned countries against the British policy of barring Jewish immigration. It was also clear that the Zionists were receiving at least partial help from some European countries, notably France, in their efforts to get as many Holocaust survivors to Palestine as possible.

In Palestine, British forces were coming under increased armed attack from Zionist forces – both from armed militias of the labour Zionist movement and the Revisionists. Attempts at quelling what the British termed a Jewish rebellion were increasing the cost to Britain of maintaining a presence in Palestine, both in human and economic terms. Eventually, the set of scales that largely dictated British foreign policy during this era tipped in favour of handing over the task of finding a solution to the future of Palestine to the United Nations. In other words, the other side of the scales – the strategic value of holding on to Palestine – no longer out-weighed the costs of maintaining such a policy.

Passing the buck was perhaps the only viable move left to the British in 1947. Not only had they failed to quell Jewish unrest against the British presence in Palestine, but the growing opposition to British policies on Palestine from the United States and among many non-aligned states, particularly the prevention of the immigration to Palestine of the survivors of the Holocaust in Europe, threatened to make Britain the international pariah of the day. To be fair to the British, there was a certain truth in the point that Palestine was treated no better or no worse than any other part of the British Empire as the process of decolonisation of the Empire, including areas administered under by Mandatory Orders, started to gather momentum. The difficulties for the British were the obvious sensitivities caused by the Holocaust, and the international feeling that something had to be done about the plight of the survivors who were living in transit camps in Europe.

It is also fair to say that the Zionists, under the leadership of David Ben-Gurion, to some extent exploited the Holocaust issue for political gain. The survivors were clearly needed in Palestine to help in the coming battles against the Arabs, and great efforts were made to get as many as possible to Palestine in the illegal immigration ships. The majority of survivors, however, would not get to Palestine until after the State of Israel was declared on 14 May 1948. From that point, on many of the survivors flooding into Palestine were given a baptism of fire by being sent straight to the front lines in the 1948 War of Independence. In the pre-State period, however, the survivors effectively served a useful public relations purpose for the Zionists. Their presence in the transit camps helped to de-legitimise British rule over Palestine, and consequently strengthened the support for a Jewish state to be declared in the areas earmarked by the United Nations Special Committee on Palestine (UNSCOP).

The vote by the General Assembly of the United Nations by the necessary two-thirds majority to ratify the UNSCOP proposal to partition Palestine into two states on 29 November 1947 provided the international legitimacy required for the Zionists to declare a state when the British Mandate ran out in May 1948.[31] The extent to which guilt over the Holocaust had impacted upon the voting intentions of the member states of the UN remains hard to gauge. The Arab member states, for their part, steadfastly refused to accept partition, voted against it, and threatened war if a Jewish state was declared.[32] Clearly, however, the impact of the Holocaust was strongly felt among the non-aligned nations who in general voted in favour of partition – effectively accepting the notion of a Jewish state.

In the United States, President Truman was deeply affected by the Holocaust and subsequently the plight of the survivors and their attempts to get to Palestine. Zionist leaders such as Chaim Weizmann regularly lobbied the President in an attempt to win American support for the declaration of a Jewish state when the British Mandate on Palestine ran out. In order for a Jewish state to have any chance of success, it was imperative that it be recognised by as many countries as possible. It would have been almost unimaginable to press ahead with the declaration of a state that the United States would not give diplomatic recognition to. The political situation in the USA, however, meant that gaining such a commitment proved to be extremely difficult for the Zionist leadership. While President Truman was generally supportive of the creation of a Jewish state in May 1948, his Secretary of State, George Marshall, most certainly was not. Marshall took the view that the creation of a state for the Jews would lead to a further escalation of an already deteriorating situation on the ground in Palestine. Marshall's policy was governed by two logical fears: that if a Jewish state were to be declared, the violence in Palestine would spill over and become a regional war; and that the USA would be drawn into the conflict and might have to send troops to restore calm and police the peace.

In a stormy meeting between the two heavyweights of US foreign policy, Marshall argued that he simply could not endorse Truman's support for a Jewish state. Afterwards, and for much of the first part of 1948, Truman shifted between supporting the creation of a Jewish state, and backing Marshall's plan for an International Protectorate to govern Palestine when the British left in May, until the violence could be brought under control. The United States went as far as presenting its plans for what it termed a temporary UN trusteeship in Palestine to the UN Security Council on 19 March 1948.[33] Ben-Gurion led the Zionist opposition to the proposal, arguing in dramatic terms that the US decision was a surrender to the terrorism of the Arab gangs, armed by the British Foreign Office and brought to Palestine by its sufferance.[34] Eventually, however, Truman got his way and the USA announced that it would support the creation of a Jewish state; but tellingly, the President also stated that if a Jewish state were to be declared by the Zionist leadership in May 1948, it would stand alone. Under no circumstances would the USA come to its aid. The Zionists, in short, would have to face the Arabs alone, and effectively emerge victorious in the coming war, if the proposed Jewish state was to survive.

Declaration of statehood and war
The response of the Arab states to the declaration of the State of Israel by the Zionist leadership on 14 May 1948 appears, on the surface, to have been united hostility to Israel, and a seemingly selfless willingness to come to the aid of their Palestinian brothers with the instigation of military hostilities against the infant State.[35] A deeper analysis, however, reveals the shortcomings of such a simplistic take on the events of May 1948. To put it mildly, the Arab leaders were deeply divided over the Palestine question, and, as we shall see, there is at least some evidence to suggest a degree of collusion between the leader of the military attack on Israel, King Abdullah, and the Zionist leadership. Before looking at this and other charges, it is worth briefly recounting the major developments of Israel's War of Independence.

The military aspect of the conflict is generally divided by historians into three distinct time periods: the first from 14 May 1948 until the United Nations ceasefire based on UN Security Council Resolution S/801 of 29 May 1948 came into effect on 11 June.[36] The second phase took place from the resumption of hostilities at the end of the four week ceasefire on 9 July 1948 until 18 July, when a second UN truce came into effect based on UN Security Council Resolution S/902[37], and the third from October to the end of the war in the Negev Desert in early 1949.[38] During the first phase, the Arab armies went on the offensive, quickly gaining ground on all fronts and threatening to overrun the newly created Israeli Defence Forces (IDF). It came as little surprise that David Ben-Gurion and the Israeli leadership were keener on a ceasefire than their Arab counterparts, who sensed that victory was at hand, although in reporting to the Provisional Government on 3 June Ben-Gurion indicated that, while the threat to Israel was by no means over, a corner had been turned. Israel had survived the first wave of the Arab attack.[39]

During the subsequent ceasefire, Israeli officials, led by a young advisor to Ben-Gurion, Shimon Peres, used the break in hostilities to search the world, procuring vast quantities of arms. The work of Peres and others in changing the military balance of the conflict has become part of Israeli folk-lore. In reality, however, it revealed the extent of the willingness of several countries to sell arms privately to Israel, in violation of the arms embargo imposed on the region by a list of countries that included the United States. The end product of this covert arms trade was that, when hostilities recommenced, the balance of arms or firepower had been significantly altered in Israel's favour.

The second and third phases of the War are widely viewed as the Israeli offensive. As well as being better armed, the IDF made several changes to its strategy for fighting the War. Greater use was made of night-fighting, the element of surprise and launching smaller, almost guerrilla-style, attacks against the enemy. The tide of the War had clearly turned, and the IDF started to take over areas of land in the old Palestine that were not designated by the UN to form part of the State of Israel.[40] Indeed, by the end of the War, Israeli forces in the south were threatening deep into the Sinai – a move that made the British, in particular, very nervous, and came close to leading to a major confrontation between Israeli and British forces. There were two key events related to the War that came to have a significant impact on the conflict: the assassination of the UN-appointed Special Mediator to Palestine, Count Bernadotte, in Jerusalem, and the flight of a large segment of the Palestinian Arab population from Israel.

The assassination of the Special Mediator was important for a number of reasons – not least because of his efforts to secure a ceasefire and political solution to the conflict. His assassins were presumed to be Jewish, members of a hard-line Jewish militia linked to the Revisionist movement and were not at the time incorporated in the IDF. David Ben-Gurion used the assassination to bring all forces under the High Command of the IDF, and achieved an important pre-requisite for a government – a monopoly over the means of violence and coercion. Despite the actions of David Ben-Gurion on the diplomatic front, Israel's position was very badly damaged by the assassination. Much of the goodwill directed towards Israel from the non-aligned states as a result of the Holocaust was severely dented, and Bernadotte's peace plans, which called, amongst other things, for Israeli withdrawal, were viewed as his legacy and awarded a greater degree of international legitimacy than prior to his death.

THE VIEW FROM THE FENCE

The flight of the Palestinian refugees from Israel during the War, and the creation of the refugee crisis, remains one of the most emotive issues of the War, and its repercussions are still felt in contemporary political negotiations between the two sides. Central to the Arab viewpoint of events has been the charge that Israel, in effect, expelled thousands of Palestinian Arabs during the War, in order to ensure the Jewish nature of the State of Israel. Arab historiography also charges that some refugees were driven out by Israeli forces in order to gain control of specific areas that were deemed by the Israeli leadership to be of great strategic importance to Israel. Some Arab scholars claim that the expulsion of the Palestinian Arabs was a premeditated action, planned and executed by David Ben-Gurion, Israel's first Prime Minister, who also simultaneously served as Minister of Defence. In modern terms, the term used would be 'ethnic cleansing', and no doubt some Arab leaders would be calling for Ben-Gurion's arrest, trial and conviction on charges resulting from these actions. The reality is, of course, much more complex, and the question of the cause of the refugee issue has been clouded further by the selective release of a number of documents in Israel that cover the issue.

An Israeli scholar, Benny Morris, has devoted much time and attention to the matter, and concluded that the evidence that is currently available points to the fact that there was no premeditated order to expel the Arabs from Israel, and that there are a range of reasons for their departure in the period up to June 1948. In his memoirs, Yitzhak Rabin caused something of a political storm in Israel by alleging that Ben-Gurion had ordered him to expel a number of Arabs from villages that lay close to the

Tel Aviv–Jerusalem road. Rabin was himself the commander responsible for what he termed 'driving the Arabs out' of these areas. Such were the political sensitivities back in 1979 that the offending passages covering these events were removed by the Israeli military censor (it is routine for all ex-prime ministers in Israel to submit their memoirs to the censor). Another leading Israeli military officer who was also present at the same meeting, Yigal Allon, denied that Ben-Gurion had given any such order to drive the Arabs out, and argued that Rabin must have misunderstood Ben-Gurion's words or gestures.

History does matter, and the importance of it in shaping the present day has never been clearer than in the case of the refugees. Who caused the refugee crisis will greatly impact upon the outcome of contemporary negotiations over the future of the refugees, who continue to live in camps situated mainly near Israel's borders. In retrospect, it appears that the refugees fled Israel for a number of reasons – some caused by Israel, others by Arab leaders who told them to leave and return when the War was won, and the normal set of fear, rumour and gossip that takes hold during the fighting of a particularly bitter war.

Just how divided were the Arabs before and after the 1948 War?
The extent to which the Arabs were divided over the Palestine question is open to debate. Avi Shlaim, one of the leaders of Israel's new historians, who set out to challenge what they argue are the myths that surround Israeli history, argues that there was collusion between King Abdullah and the Zionists.[41] The central charge which Shlaim makes is that, in secret meetings between the King

and Zionist leaders, which took place before the war, an agreement was reached whereby Israel and Trans-Jordan would carve up the area the UN had designated for a Palestinian state between themselves. In short, there would be no independent Palestinian state, leaving Israel with more sustainable secure borders, and Trans-Jordan in control of the West Bank. On reflection, given the nature and the intensity of the conflict between Israeli and Jordanian military forces during Israel's War of Independence, Shlaim's views appear a little far-fetched, despite his spirited attempt to defend them using what documents are available on this question. During the War, some of the fiercest fighting took place in Jerusalem, where Israeli and Jordanian forces faced each other. At the conclusion of the War, only West Jerusalem remained under Israeli control, with both East Jerusalem and the Old City under the control of King Abdullah and Jordan. The fact that Israel and Jordan absorbed the lands designated by the UN for a Palestinian state appears to fuel the collusion theories. Again, with the lack of compelling documentary evidence, the most likely explanation remains the simple fact that Israel and Jordan tried to grab as much land as possible in the vacuum caused by the Palestinian rejection of the partition plan – a decision that, in legal terms, allowed Israel and Jordan to effectively carve up the lands between themselves.

Accepting for a moment that Abdullah did not have a formal agreement with Israel about the War, there remain question marks about his personal motives for taking Jordan to war. As commander of the Arab forces, Abdullah was responsible for co-ordinating the Arab attacks – a role that had been given to him by other Arab leaders whose attitude appears to have been governed by the old adage 'put those you do not trust up front and out in the open where you can see them'. During the War there is little evidence to suggest that he dedicated much time to this task. Instead, Abdullah concentrated his efforts on securing as much land as possible for Jordan, without mounting major attacks in lands which the UN partition plan declared to be in the Jewish State.

If Abdullah's motives for the War did not really have the best interests of the Palestinians at heart, the same can be said for the Egyptians. Up until the last minute, it was not even clear if Egyptian forces would intervene in the War at all. Eventually, the King decided to commit his largely untested army to battle. The motives for the King's decision were, to a large degree, to be found in appeasing Egyptian public opinion, which was actively calling for an intervention to help their Palestinian brothers in their hour of need. The court of Egyptian popular opinion was something the King and even his Free Officers' successors ignored at their peril. On the battlefield, the performance of the Egyptian Army did not match that of the British-trained Arab Legion of Jordan. Few of the Egyptian officer class had any experience of war, and, despite initial gains against Israel, the Egyptians were largely routed by the IDF. It says much that at the end of the War, battles were being fought on Egyptian soil rather than within the old borders of Palestine.

Given the nature of the War – a battle for survival for the Israelis, and a half-hearted intervention on behalf of the Palestinians that masked attempts to grab lands by Arab states – the outcome was not particularly surprising. Mixed Arab motives, divisions among their leadership, and, in places, questionable motivation to fight did not alone hand victory to Israel during the War. The Israeli war dead, accounting for some one per cent of the total population, provides evidence to the contrary. The Israeli narrative, however – that the War was won against all odds – reeks of a little bit of myth-making for the national historical narrative. For Israel, the real fear has always been a well-planned and highly co-ordinated attack on it by two or more Arab states. This clearly did not happen in 1948, and arguably the Arabs were only really able to launch such a well co-ordinated attack against Israel during the first phase of the October 1973 War.

The War concluded with a series of curious negotiations that took place on the Greek island of Rhodes. The arduous talks produced a series of Armistice Agreements between Israel and Egypt (24 February 1949), Israel and Lebanon (23 March 1949), Israel and Jordan (3 April 1949) and, finally, Israel and Syria (20 July 1949).[42] Even here, Arab disunity was apparent. The Syrian delegation was furious at the Lebanese for agreeing to sign an Armistice Agreement with Israel before Syria did – the Syrians believed that this move damaged the Syrian negotiating hand. As Syria's role in Lebanese affairs deepened over the years, so the Syrian leadership has always attempted to prevent Lebanon from dealing with Israel before Syria was ready to. At the present time in the Middle East, all parties are aware of the simple fact that when and if Israel and Syria sign a formal peace agreement, Lebanon will soon follow and do the same. Any attempts by Israel and Lebanon to move before such realities are in place will always be blocked by Damascus. The recent wave of anti-Syrian sentiment which swept

Lebanon in early 2005 is very much a product of the growing resentment of the Lebanese to decades of Syrian political and military domination. Though it remains early days, this new wave of support for democratic reform in Lebanon might lead to history repeating itself, with Lebanon signing an agreement with Israel before Syria does.

Back in 1949, the Armistice Agreements were meant to lead to the signing of full peace agreements between all parties within six months. Not only was this hope unfulfilled, but no meaningful peace negotiations ever took place. Instead, there was much criticism about the content of the Armistice Agreements. A young Yitzhak Rabin, who was a member of the Israeli delegation in Rhodes, went so far as to suggest that the agreements would lead to a second Arab–Israeli war. Central to Rabin's argument was his belief that Israel's borders, as agreed in Rhodes, remained indefensible.

In respect of borders, Israel's War of Independence changed much in the Middle East, with Israel gaining more land than had originally been given to it in the UNSCOP Partition Plan. From a military perspective, Israel showed the world that the State could survive a major military confrontation with the Arabs. For the Palestinians, the war proved to be a complete disaster. Following the Armistice negotiations – at which they were not represented – the Palestinian population was left either in Israel, or those who had fled during the War were housed in what were meant to be temporary refugee camps. The conditions in many of these camps were appalling, and, with the notable exception of Jordan, the refugees have always been denied any form of citizenship in their host countries. They were to all intents and purposes stateless, homeless and, for many, penniless. The story could have been very different, however, had the political leadership of the Palestinians accepted the UNSCOP's proposed two-state solution. In these circumstances, the Palestinians would have received a geographically viable state, which would resemble the state that they are still trying to create today. The failure to agree to this allowed Israel and the Arab states to essentially remove the Palestinians from the political map of the lands that had been known as Palestine during the period of the British Mandate.

Notes:

29 British Public Records Office, Kew, The Balfour Declaration (1917) CO 733/443/6.
30 R. Hinnebusch (2003), *The International Politics of the Middle East*, Manchester: Manchester University Press, p. 156.
31 Ministry of Foreign Affairs, Jerusalem (MFA), 'Future Government of Palestine, General Assembly Resolution 181 (II)', (29 November 1947) MFA/1-2/8/1947–1974.
32 (MFA), 'Arab Reaction to UN General Assembly Resolution 181–II', (29 November 1947) MFA/1-2/9/1947–1974.
33 (MFA), 'The US Proposes Temporary Trusteeship', (19 March 1948) MFA/1-2/10/1947–1974.
34 (MFA), 'Statement by David Ben-Gurion to Press Club in Tel Aviv', (20 March 1948) MFA/1-2/11/1947–1974.
35 (MFA), 'Arab League Declaration on the Invasion of Palestine', (15 May 1948) MFA/1-2/5/1947–1974.
36 (MFA), 'Establishment of a Truce, UN Security Resolution S/801', (29 May 1948) MFA/1-2/9/1947–1974.
37 (MFA), UN Security Resolution S/902, (15 July 1948) MFA/1-2/15/1947–1974.

[38] For a lucid account of the military campaign see E. Karsh (2002), *Essential Histories Number 28, The Arab–Israeli Conflict: the Palestine War 1948*, Oxford: Osprey.

[39] Ministry of Foreign Affairs, Jerusalem (MFA), 'Report to the Provisional Government of Israel by the Prime Minister and Minister of Defence Ben-Gurion', (3 June 1948) MFA/1-2/10/1947–1974.

[40] (MFA), 'Report to the State Council by Prime Minister Ben-Gurion', (27 September 1948) MFA/1-2/17/1947–1974.

[41] A. Shlaim (1988), *Collusion Across the Jordan: King Abdullah, the Zionist Movement and the Partition of Palestine*, Oxford: Clarendon Press.

[42] Ministry of Foreign Affairs, Jerusalem,' The Armistice Agreements', (1949) MFA/1-2/4-7/ III/.

3

Paths not Taken:
Searching for the Peacemakers
and Peacekeepers

Why was there no peace following the end of the 1948 War?

The domestic political background in both the Arab world and Israel remains an extremely important factor in understanding why there was no peace in the period following the ending of the 1948 War, and indeed why preparation for a second round of hostilities came to take precedence over everything else. At the end of the 1948 War there were many internal debates in the Arab world that centred on coming to terms with the outcome of the War. Rightly or wrongly, much of the Arab world blamed King Abdullah for the failure of the military campaign, arguing that his forces had essentially fought to secure Jordanian interests, and not Arab ones. The wider Arab public, in general, took the view that the military defeat was down to poor leadership and tactical mistakes, which would be rectified by the time there was a second major Arab–Israeli war. There was little in the way of closure for the Arab masses in relation to the Israeli question. Their hope was that next time, God willing – and with better luck – the Zionist entity would be removed from the map of the Middle East.

In truth, the Arab states and their leaders had much to worry about themselves. The state system, largely created by the imperial powers, was highly flawed. The need for modernisation in the Arab world was clear for all to see, and attempts to transform economies from being largely agriculture-based to more industrialised brought a set of social and economic problems that Arab rulers found hard to resolve. The role of the military added an extra dimension to the problems of the Arab world. The threat of coup and counter coup was never far away, with the boundaries of civil-military relations severely blurred.[43] A summary of the deposed and the fallen brings home the extent of the instability. In Egypt, the Prime Minister, Nokrashi Pasha, was murdered in the aftermath of the 1948 War, and in Syria the government was overthrown in 1949 by General Husni el-Zaim, who was subsequently overthrown in 1951. In July 1951, King Abdullah of Jordan was assassinated by agents of the Mufti of Jerusalem (the King was purported to have already secretly signed an agreement with Israel). In short, it is impossible to separate the Arab–Israeli conflict from the growing political and economic difficulties of several key front-line Arab states. Indeed, the conflict often provided a suitable smokescreen for the growing pains of these still relatively infant states. The old Arab adage, 'when in doubt blame the Israelis for all the ills of the world', was frequently employed by leaders who were experiencing some domestic turbulence.

THE VIEW FROM THE FENCE

In Israel, the 1948 War had illustrated to some leaders the need for a strong defence force and, in terms of secure borders, a need to hold on to lands, captured by Israel during the War, that were not designated for the Jewish State by the UNSCOP Partition Plan. Others placed more emphasis on trying to secure formal peace agreements with the Arab states as the best method for securing the long future of the State. And it was this debate which dominated the Israeli political agenda during the early years of the State. The ruling political leadership divided into two camps on this issue. On one side were the Prime Minister, David Ben-Gurion and his supporters, and on the other the Minister of Foreign Affairs, Moshe Sharett and his followers.

Much has been made of the different personal histories of Ben-Gurion and Sharett by way of explanation of their differing perceptions of the Arabs. The sum of Ben-Gurion's viewpoint was that Israeli security came first, second and third in order of priorities and that Israel's existence would be secured through a combination of military might and diplomatic skill, with a strong emphasis placed on the former. Ben-Gurion argued that Israel had no negotiating cards with which to trade with the Arabs. The two central demands of the Arabs were known, at the very least, to include Israel handing over lands that it had captured during the 1948 War that were originally intended by the UN to be part of a Palestinian state and a return of the Palestinian refugees to Israel. These latter were extremely problematic for Ben-Gurion on two grounds: they endangered the Jewish nature of the State of Israel; and many of the vacated homes and land had already been taken over by Israelis. At a more philosophical level, Ben-Gurion believed that the instability of Arab regimes meant that there was little chance of finding viable partners for peace among the Arabs. Taken together, Ben-Gurion and his supporters took the view that achieving peace with the Arabs on Israel's terms (for those were the only terms that interested them) was near-impossible for the foreseeable future. It comes as little surprise, therefore, to learn that Ben-Gurion thought that the best way of securing Israel's existence lay in establishing IDF military superiority over the corresponding Arab forces.[44]

Moshe Sharett took a counter-view to Ben-Gurion's. Though it is misleading to exaggerate the differences between the two men over relations with the Arabs, Sharett was certainly more hopeful that formal peace agreements with the Arabs could, and should, be reached. The dispute between the two political heavyweights of the early years of Israel did not only centre on policy differences, but was to a large extent driven by a personal dislike of each other, which was compounded by competition for power and influence between the two (particularly within the internal power organs of the ruling party, Mapai). Their rivalry, however, dominated Israeli political life, with Ben-Gurion always seeming to hold the upper hand over his rival until at least the mid-1950s.

In accepting the argument that there was little will for peacemaking in the Arab world and in Israel, it is important to summarise the political climate in conflict between 1949 and 1956. Just because there was no major Arab–Israeli war during this period does not mean that it was a time of calm. Indeed, quite the opposite was true. Frequent raids by Palestinian *fedayeen* groups into Israel were met with heavy retaliation raids by the IDF. For example, in 1955 alone, some 260 Israelis were either killed or wounded by *fedayeen* raids.[45] The Palestinian guerrillas enjoyed at the very least the tacit support of their host countries. These cycles of violence produced the admittedly embryonic system of deterrents that Israel developed over the years for dealing with the Arab threat. Israeli forces had two major aims in their raids: to illustrate that Israel could destroy the infrastructure of these groups, and to act as a warning to the Arab states where the raids originated that their communities and infrastructure would be targeted. Such tactics have been developed over the years, but the overall parameters of Israeli systems of deterrence have remained largely the same to the present day.

What the attacks by the *fedayeen* illustrated to Israel was the relative vulnerability of its borders and the need to strengthen its defences in these areas. Zionism called for the land to be widely settled, and Israel had built many communities near or along the border in order to reinforce this point. With border settlements came a strong IDF presence, usually situated in bases in or near the settlements. Though the Revisionist Zionist thinker and leader, Vladimir Ze'ev Jabotinsky, had first suggested the idea of an Iron Wall to protect the Zionists in what was then Palestine from the Arabs, the notion of a barrier or wall was used more in a philosophical sense. To have physically constructed a fence in the period between 1948 and 1956 would have been near impossible. The cost involved for a state that was struggling to survive economically would have been prohibitive. Also, the diplomatic damage caused by its construction would have been great at a time when

Israel was trying to win new friends and influence in the wider world. The labour Zionist leadership who dominated the national leadership during the first years of the State would have viewed the construction of a physical barrier between themselves and the Arabs as tantamount to admitting that there would never be peace between Israel and the Arabs. In short, at this early stage of the conflict, they were not able to foresee its longevity, or the fact that conflict would deepen in its intensity, rather than start to tail off.

It is worth remembering that at this time there were no peace agreements in place with either Egypt or Jordan, and that any fence would have had to run all the way from the border with the Gaza Strip, through the Negev, and along the entire border between Israel and the West Bank. Instead, Israel came to rely more and more on its ability to prevent attacks by *fedayeen* crossing into Israel with the use of patrols, intelligence gathering and the system of deterrents previously mentioned. This, of course, was not perfect, and many attackers did get through. What was noticeable, however, was that, as a result of such attacks, Israel was not tempted to evacuate these outlying settlements, but rather chose to strengthen them and its commitment to the border areas as a whole. Israel, in short, would not leave such areas just because the attacks were making life difficult for its citizens and soldiers in these areas.

What impact did Nasser have on the development of the Arab state and the Arab–Israeli conflict?
Of all the modern Middle Eastern leaders, President Abdul Gamal Nasser remains perhaps the most interesting. Few

leaders, with the possible exception of Ben-Gurion, have played such a large role in shaping events in the region, including the Arab–Israeli conflict, in which he presided over two major wars with the Israelis, both of which ended in heavy military defeats for the Egyptian army. 'Nasser the man' remains something of an enigma. Accounts of his life, and his army and political careers, remain highly politically coloured.[46] In Israel, his name is still demonised, with many Israelis simply regarding him as having been anti-Semitic and the senior cheerleader of the 'Israel haters club'. Such views are, of course, highly simplistic, and reflect the impact the mention of his name still has in Israel, rather than accurately reflecting his beliefs, character and career.

The Free Officers' coup that dispossessed King Farouk in Egypt was a largely bloodless affair. The King and his family were allowed to leave the country on his royal yacht to go into exile. At first, Israel and its Prime Minister cautiously welcomed the arrival of the Free Officers on the scene.[47] Nasser was not the head of the plotters, but he soon emerged as their leader, following an internal power struggle with Mohammed Naguib. Israeli leaders hoped that a strong Arab leader would bring a degree of stability to Egypt and perhaps even the wider Arab world. Israeli hopes were further raised when Nasser did not even refer to the Arab–Israeli conflict during his first major policy speeches. Nasser chose instead to focus on the need for internal reforms within Egypt.

At the centre of Nasser's attention appeared to be his belief that Egypt and the wider Arab world needed to rid itself once and for all of the continued influence of the old British and French colonial powers. Though Egypt had enjoyed political independence for decades, the economic story was very different. In Egypt, Britain enjoyed a great deal of economic influence that led many to suggest that the era of colonial rule had merely been replaced by a more subtle form of economic colonialism. The sum of this was that Egypt was not actually a fully independent nation in charge of its own economic or political destiny. For Nasser, this was unacceptable, as was the carving up of the Middle East by the British and French and the creation of the modern Arab state system. In rejecting this division of the region, Nasser embraced a rather peculiar form of Pan-Arabist thought, namely that there would be a unitary Arab state as all Arabs were brothers. Nasser, however, envisaged that such a state would be controlled and ruled by himself and his Egyptian cronies. In other words, Pan-Arabism served as a smokescreen for Egyptian attempts to achieve domination of the whole Arab Middle East.

Accepting the argument for a moment that Nasser did not view the Arab–Israeli conflict as an initial priority, it is important to outline why it did become so important to him personally and, in time, to the survival of his regime. Here the real weakness of Nasser's political strategy is revealed. In short, Nasser provided dispirited countries with differing national aims a common enemy to rally against. In the period prior to his use of the anti-Israel card, there had even been signs of his willingness to negotiate with Moshe Sharett, who had become Israel's second Prime Minister following Ben-Gurion's decision to retire (though in retrospect the term sabbatical might have been a more accurate reflection of his absence). Secret contacts took place in Paris between officials from

Israel and Egypt with the blessing of Nasser. The absence of available documentation in the Egyptian archives, which remain closed to researchers, means that we can only speculate as to Nasser's aims here. The two possibilities remain that either he was taking these talks seriously (negotiations would be too advanced a phrase for them), or that he was only using these talks to pacify Israel until he was able to transform the Egyptian military into a powerful modern fighting force, armed with the level of equipment that could defeat Israel on the battlefield.

Whatever Nasser's motives for engaging in the secret talks, they became redundant when a rogue Israeli spy ring was captured after a series of attacks in Egypt, in which they planted bombs in Cairo cinemas, a post office and the US Information Centres in Cairo and Alexandria. The aim of the operation appeared to be an effort to sabotage relations between the West and Egypt, at the time of negotiations over the British withdrawal from Suez. The capture of the spy ring in 1954 proved to be extremely damaging not only for Israeli–Egyptian relations, but also internally in Israel where it became known as the Lavon Affair – after the Minister of Defence Pinhas Lavon who was accused of having authorised the operation. From Nasser's perspective, the message that Israel was sending him could not have been clearer – the hardliners were in charge. Nasser thought, probably correctly, that either the more moderate Sharett, who was sending him signals stating that he had not authorised the attacks, was lying, or that the hardliners had, in effect, taken over from him. Whatever the motive, or whoever was really behind them, the attacks convinced Nasser to move forward with a strategy of confrontation with Israel. The secret channel in Paris was closed down and there were no more direct contacts between Egypt and Israel until long after Nasser's death. Of course, the significance of the impact of the captured Israel spy ring could only have been fully understood if we had a clearer picture of Nasser's true motives for allowing the channel to proceed in the first place. Rather unsurprisingly, the Arab historiography that covers the life and times of Nasser takes the view that this was a golden opportunity missed, in that Nasser was genuine in his efforts to resolve the 'Zionist question', as do some of Israel's new (revisionist) historians. For their part, many of the more traditional Israeli scholars view the issue of Nasser's motives with a great deal more scepticism.

It is worth remembering that, even if Nasser's intention was to try to end the conflict, it is not clear what chance he would have had in surviving either politically and physically had he signed a formal peace agreement with the Zionist enemy. The Nasser of 1954 was not the same man in terms of personal prestige and leadership as the Nasser of the post-Suez War period. It remains highly questionable, therefore, whether, even if Nasser had wanted peace, he would have been able to implement any potential peace deal that would have been highly unpopular among the Egyptian masses, intellectuals and much of the Egyptian military leadership. The signing of an agreement with Israel would in all likelihood have stopped any chance of Nasser achieving his major personal political goal to be the undisputed leader of the Arab world. Nasser's actions from here onwards need to be seen within the framework of this goal.

Israel was not the only country to worry about Nasser's intentions. The British and the French who, after years of competition for influence in the region, could usually agree on little, found common ground in the growing signs that Nasser represented a very real threat to their economic and political interests in Egypt, and, eventually, the wider Arab world as well. For the French there was a growing awareness that Nasser was involved in funding and supplying weapons to the FLN in Algeria who were fighting for independence from the French. Algeria was the dominant issue of the day in France, and Nasser's actions were judged as little short of a provocative act of aggression against France and its continued presence in North Africa. To some degree, Nasser's action led to closer ties between Israel and France, with the latter selling armaments to the IDF.

Whatever his original intentions towards Israel and the outside world, Nasser was finding the task of transforming Egypt extremely difficult. The need to transform the economy and the military led Nasser towards greater ties with the Soviet Union. The Soviets were looking for greater influence in the region as the Cold War started to develop into a global rush for influence in the bi-polar world of 'are you in our camp or their's?' The first product of these ties was the Czech Arms Deal, which effectively turned the Egyptian military into the powerful and modern army that Nasser had originally intended. In Jerusalem the Israeli government took Nasser's action as confirmation of his aggressive intent towards Israel – a fact that was seemingly confirmed by the closure of shipping lanes to Israeli ships.

From this point onwards a second major war was always going to be the most likely development. Ben-

Gurion had returned from retirement to finally defeat Sharett and assume the position of Prime Minister for a second time. For Ben-Gurion and the Chief of Staff of the IDF, Moshe Dayan, war with Nasser was not only unavoidable but should also take place as soon as possible. At the root of Ben-Gurion's fear was that the Czech Arms Deal had altered the balance of power in the region in Nasser's favour and that Israel must strike to restore the balance in its favour.[48] Israel was looking for a pretext to launch an attack on its own when it became clear that the French and British were proposing a joint attack after a series of meetings in Sèvres (France), at the conclusion of which a document was signed committing the parties to war.[49] Rarely in the theatre of modern warfare have three such strange bedfellows come together, and for differing reasons, to form a military alliance to go to war.

Ben-Gurion was himself extremely distrustful of British intentions. Despite Nasser's having nationalised the Suez Canal (effectively taking over the running of the Canal from Britain), checking other British economic interests in Egypt, and being viewed as posing a threat to the supply of oil to the UK and France that was dependent on transit through the Canal, Ben-Gurion was not sure whether, when the moment came, Britain would commit its forces to the operation. So the second major war in the Middle East in eight years came to be not only the second Arab–Israeli confrontation, but also a war involving Britain and France. Like most wars, the Suez War (or Suez Crisis as the British prefer to label it) had two outcomes: a military one and a political one. Crucially, the fact that the United States under President Eisenhower did not take part in the fighting played a major role in determining the political outcome of the War. In terms of the fighting, Israel achieved the vast majority of its military goals in the Sinai. Central to the Israeli war plan were two important concepts that came to play an important role in all subsequent wars with the Arabs: surprise and speed.

Near total surprise was achieved with Israeli forces being parachuted deep into the Sinai.[50] The numbers of Israeli paratroopers involved in the initial attacks were kept deliberately low in order to confuse the Egyptians. Consequently, the Egyptian military were not sure, during the crucial opening hours of the War, if indeed the Israeli force represented an invasion force, or simply another retaliation raid for the on-going *fedayeen* raids into Israel. There was an added political advantage for Ben-Gurion, in that if the UK or France did not intervene at the correct time with their own ultimatum to Nasser and subsequent entry into the war, Israel had the option of a tactical withdrawal using the cover that its military action was in fact simply a major retaliation raid, and not the start of a full-scale invasion that it really was intended to be.

Speed was essential to the Israelis, as they believed that the international community would step in quickly, through the United Nations, to try to impose order and secure a ceasefire before Israel had reached its military goals. The participation of the UK and France in the War never reached the intended levels. Ben-Gurion's scepticism, as a result, was well placed. Public and party pressure in London on Sir Anthony Eden, the Prime Minister, mixed with pressure from the United States, led to a scaling back of British participation in the military hostilities in the first instance, and eventually, its acceptance of a ceasefire proposal before the majority of its forces had become engaged in the fighting. France, in reality, was left with little choice but to follow the British lead and agree to the ceasefire that ended the war prematurely for the two ex-colonial powers and deeply dented their prestige in the region. In military terms, Israel achieved its three goals and emerged in the short-term as the clear victor in the conflict. Moshe Dayan listed these as: freedom of shipping for Israeli vessels in the Gulf of Aqaba; an end to *fedayeen* raids; and the neutralisation of the threat of attack on Israel by the joint Egypt–Syria–Jordan military command.[51] For Britain and France, their forces had achieved the majority of objectives set for them, but they had been unable to fight the decisive battle against Nasser, due to the political restraints imposed upon them from Washington. Egyptian forces under President Nasser, while having been soundly defeated by their Israeli enemies, could point to the fact that the colonial forces (UK and France) had not been able to achieve their military goals.

The political outcome of the War did not mirror the military realities on the ground. A furious President Eisenhower was loath to forgive Israel, the UK and France for instigating hostilities so close to the American Presidential election of November 1956, in which he was seeking re-election. In an interesting comparison with the US-led war against Iraq in 2003–4, the US administration in 1956 did not regard the removal of an Arab dictator from office as reason to go to war. While Eisenhower did note that Nasser was a troublemaker, the sense in Washington was that he and his ambitions could be contained with the careful use of diplomacy. Tellingly, though, it is clear that the threat posed by Nasser and his policies to the national interests of the USA was not as great as that posed to the interests of the UK and France. The key word here, and in much of modern Middle Eastern history, is oil. In simple terms, the USA was not as dependent on freedom of passage through the Suez Canal to get its oil from the region as both the UK and France.

Suez marked an important turning point for US policy in the Middle East. The conflict had illustrated the post-Second World War realities with the decline of the British and French empires and the rise of the Cold War theatres of influence and conflict. With the Soviet Union having already developed close ties with Nasser, and to a lesser degree at the time, Iraq, the USA started to become much more active in the politics of the region. The leftover business from the Suez War was dealt with by the Eisenhower Administration. Israel was strongly pressurised by Eisenhower to withdraw from all the territories that it had captured during the War. Eisenhower's attitude was summed up in a letter to Ben-Gurion, demanding that Israel withdraw its troops, stating that

'it would be a matter of the greatest regret to all my countrymen if Israeli policy on a matter of such grave concern to the world should in any way impair the friendly cooperation between our two countries.'[52]

After much diplomatic manoeuvring at the UN and between the USA and Israel, Israel announced to the UN General Assembly on 1 March 1957 that it would indeed withdraw from the Sharm el-Sheik area and the Gaza Strip.[53] Following the Israeli withdrawal in the Gaza Strip, despite the efforts of the UN to take control, Nasser soon re-established *de facto* control, appointing his own people to run the area. For Israel, therefore, the Suez War brought only short-term gain: the re-opening of shipping lanes in the Straits of Tiran to Israeli vessels, and the re-establishment of its strategic military advantage over the most powerful Arab army.

Peacekeeping duties then and now

Arguably the most significant development in the post-Suez era was the stationing of a United Nations Emergency Force that patrolled the borders between Egypt and Israel and in the Sharm-el-Sheik area (which was placed under UN control). The force successfully kept the border between Israel and Egypt quiet for a decade before they were withdrawn in 1967 in one of the biggest blunders in UN history. The deployment of UN troops in the Sinai marked the first occasion on which the UN committed soldiers on a peacekeeping mission. There is no mention of peacekeeping duties in the original UN charter, so it is slightly ironic that this has become in all honesty the major contribution of the organisation to conflict resolution in the world. A UN Special Committee outlined the UN's mandate for peacekeeping by reaffirming that the primary responsibility for the maintenance of international peace and security rested with the United Nations, and affirmed that peacekeeping continued to be one of the key instruments available to the United Nations in discharging that responsibility.[54] In 2002, for example, the UN supported some 20 peacekeeping-orientated missions, involving some 39,392 military personnel, 5,347 civilian police and 554 civilian observers at a cost of $2.63 billion.[55]

Before we all rush to make the connection between the success of this force and the potential use of such an international force along the border between Israel and a Palestinian state, several points are first worth considering. While it is fair to say that the force did prevent points of friction between Israeli and Egyptian forces, as well as largely stopping raids by the *fedayeen*, the latter started to attack Israel along its eastern and northern borders where there was no such buffer force. Also, to a large degree, the quiet on Israel's southern border was caused by Nasser's at least temporary acceptance of the *status quo* in the area, which allowed him to turn his attention to developing his own position in the wider world.

Today, the stationing of a UN peacekeeping force has been widely mooted in two areas: on the borders between Israel and the Gaza Strip, and the Gaza Strip and Egyptian border, and also along the eventual border between Israel and the Palestinian state in the West Bank. Certain specific flashpoints have also been suggested, such as between West and East Jerusalem, in the Old City of Jerusalem, and in the centre of Hebron where a small group of Jews continues to live. The Palestinian leadership would welcome the stationing of peacekeepers that, they argue, could prevent the worst excesses of the IDF and protect Palestinian citizens. The truth, however, is that the stationing of an international peacekeeping force would realise one of the key goals of the Palestinian national movement, the internationalisation of the conflict with Israel. The key thinking behind this strategy has been that only the international community can pressurise Israel into making the kind of concessions it seeks. The presence of a UN force, the Palestinians hope, would be matched by an increased attempt at intervention in the conflict by international leaders.

Some readers may be left wondering about the political context of this argument. Surely the UN peacekeepers would be in place to patrol the results of a peace agreement between Israel and the Palestinians in which a Palestinian state has already been created? Its job would be simply to keep the two sides apart and act as a viable alternative to the Israeli construction of the Security Fence. Without resorting to wild bouts of crystal-ball gazing, there is a fair chance that any so-called final status peace agreement between Israel and the Palestinians might not end the conflict. The prerequisite for the successful stationing of the force in the Sinai between 1957 and 1967 was Nasser's consent to the presence of the force. This consent might not be matched by a prospective Palestinian leader looking to find ways of securing additional political concessions from Israel by using or encouraging the use of tactical violence for political gain along the border with Israel.

Israeli leaders, in general, have always been much more cautious about the stationing of a peacekeeping force along any of its borders. In general, they cite practical reasons for their opposition to international peacekeepers. What will they do? And where will they patrol? The question of hot pursuit, they argue, is too difficult to resolve. Take a scenario where Israeli forces are chasing a Palestinian who, they believe, has just carried out an attack in Israel. Will the peacekeepers try to prevent Israeli forces from entering, for example, Arab-controlled East Jerusalem, or will they merely step aside, as did the Irish peacekeepers who were patrolling the border with Lebanon at the outset of the Israeli invasion in June 1982? From which countries would such a force be drawn? Most Israeli leaders have always voiced their objections to European soldiers who, they argue, would reflect the Israeli perception of the anti-Israeli biased nature of their respective governments' foreign policies. US soldiers would be more acceptable to Israel, but here there are two additional problems: US reluctance to commit additional forces in the Middle East in the foreseeable future, and the fact that such a force would, in all likelihood, become a target for local Palestinians or Jordanians with links to the *Al-Queda* network. There are also question marks over the sponsor of the force. With the UN's history of failed peacemaking efforts and its institutionalised anti-Israel bias, this organisation would today be unacceptable. The force would most probably have to be sponsored by NATO and drawn from key members of the alliance. Turkey, which is one of the biggest contributors to NATO, would appear to be an obvious candidate. Turkish govern-ments of various political colours – including Islamic Fundamentalist ones – have enjoyed close ties with Israel in recent years, while at the same time maintaining a good relationship with the Palestinian Authority.

Underlying the Israeli objections on practical grounds is the real reason, however, for fearing peacekeepers. Key elements in the Israeli political and military leadership fear that the stationing of international peacekeepers would either be as the result of a peace deal that the international community had imposed on Israel, or that the stationing of such a force could in fact lead to greater international pressure on Israel if, as expected, the force started to take casualties after either becoming caught in the crossfire, or as the result of direct attacks against the force by terrorist groups. The agreement of Nasser and Israel to have the peacekeepers reflected military and not political considerations. In other words, neither Nasser nor his Israeli counterparts thought that the stationing of such a force was a precursor to a political agreement between the two countries. The peacekeepers in effect formed part of an overall Armistice Agreement that had been imposed by the outside powers led by the United States. Nasser calculated that if he did want to employ a war option or threaten the use of war, he could in all probability by-pass the peacekeepers or discover a way to have them relocated or moved. For Nasser, however, quiet on the Israeli front in the decade between the stationing of the force and the June 1967 War with Israel allowed him to look to make mischief in other areas.

President Nasser's Pan-Arabist aims were put to the test during this decade, and by and large his attempts ended in varying degrees of failure. The consequences of his efforts were felt right across the Arab world during this time, with an increase in the instability of regimes and the real threat of major inter-Arab wars breaking out. The closest Nasser came to achieving his aim was the short-lived formation of the United Arab Republic, which was in reality a merger between Egypt and Syria. The ambitious merger, however, was not all it seemed to be. This was, in effect, an Egyptian takeover of Syria, with Nasser appointing a series of Egyptians to key positions in the Syrian political, bureaucratic and military elites. The trouble was that the calibre of the Nasser appointees was not great. Naturally, Egypt kept the best for themselves and this point was not lost on the Syrians, many of whom grew extremely bitter at being passed over for top jobs that were filled by inferior Egyptian candidates.

The union eventually broke up amidst much rancour, with each side blaming the other for its failure. To a large degree Nasser's vision on Pan-Arabism – Egyptian control over large parts of the Arab world – had been exposed, and his dream never really recovered from this setback. Unperturbed, however, Nasser and Egypt became involved in a bitter and bloody civil war in the Yemen – a war in which Egyptian forces, for a number of reasons, were performing badly. Consequently, not only had the shine been knocked off the great Nasser political vision, but his other major credential, the so-called might and power of the Egyptian army, which, as Egyptian history had it, had fought so bravely and cleverly against the joint might of the Israeli, British and French armies in 1956, was unable to successfully resolve the situation against opponents considered to be much inferior. These facts, taken together with continued economic problems, meant that Nasser was in a great deal of trouble both in the Arab world and even in Egypt.

If Nasser was busy attempting to transform Egypt and asserting his leadership over the Arab world, Israeli leaders were just as engaged dealing with the consequences of the Lavon Affair, that rumbled on until the point we mentioned in the Introduction, the electoral defeat of David Ben-Gurion in 1965. The other pressing issue for Israeli leaders during this era was the absorption of the Sephardim or Orientals into Israel. Both the Lavon Affair and the arrival of the Sephardim posed different, but incredibly important, questions about Israeli democracy and society.

The political fallout in Israel from the Lavon Affair came to dominate the internal political agenda, and the consequences of this sorry tale had extremely important implications for civil-military relations in Israel. It is worth reminding ourselves about the key issue that lay at the heart of the affair – the question of who gave the authorisation and order for the attacks in Cairo to take place. The Israeli chain of command would mean that for such an operation to go ahead, authorisation would have to have come from at least the Minister of Defence, and, in all probability, the Prime Minister. Pinhas Lavon claimed, in short, that he had not given the authorisation for the operation. Likewise, the Prime Minister, Moshe Sharett, claimed to know nothing about it. Indeed, the desperate message he sent to President Nasser to try to save the dialogue between Israeli and Egyptian diplomats would seem to confirm this. So the question of the day became, if Lavon did not give the order, then which person did give it? Here suspicion fell on hard-line elements in Israeli Military Intelligence (Aman). The head of Aman, however, stated that he had received oral instructions from Lavon authorising the operation. The Chief of Staff of the IDF, Moshe Dayan, also held Lavon to be responsible, but a formal committee of investigation was not able to verify the claims made by the head of Aman. Lavon did eventually resign from the government in February 1955 over the Lavon Affair and other issues relating to the defence of Israel. Lavon's replacement as Minister of Defence was David Ben-Gurion, who came out of retirement and soon after assumed the position of Prime Minister as well.

Lavon's resignation, however, did not mark the end of the affair, with Ben-Gurion never accepting Lavon's denial. In 1961, another committee of enquiry, this time consisting of seven ministers, concluded that Lavon had not given the order and knew nothing of the operation in Egypt. Subsequently, the government endorsed the committee's findings. So, end of the story – well not quite. Ben-Gurion refused to accept the decision, saying that inter-party political considerations had made the committee unable to pass judgement on Lavon. As a result Ben-Gurion resigned, and new elections were called in 1961. After the elections, Lavon was persuaded to resign from his position as Secretary-General of the influential Histadrut, in order to facilitate Ben-Gurion's return as Prime Minister. In 1963, Ben-Gurion resigned (again!) and returned once more to a kibbutz in the Negev. Ben-Gurion's replacement this time was Levi Eshkol, famed for his ability to get a consensus out of a meeting. Even in retirement, Ben-Gurion would not let things rest. In 1964 he demanded that Eshkol appoint an independent committee of enquiry to determine if the 1961 committee of seven ministers had acted in a correct manner. Eshkol refused and the struggle continued on until the 1965 Mapai Party Conference, at which 60 per cent of the participants supported Eshkol and 40 per cent Ben-Gurion. As a result, Ben-Gurion and many of his supporters left the party and formed a new party called Rafi. They contested the 1965 elections, but were no match for the electoral machine of Mapai and did very badly. In 1968 most of Rafi rejoined Mapai and another Labour-based party to form the Israeli Labour Party. Ben-Gurion did not return, preferring instead to form a new

State List that made little impact. It was a sad end to a political career that deserved something better.[56]

With the exception of destroying the political careers of Ben-Gurion and Lavon, why then was the affair so important to Israeli democracy? Here the answer lies in looking at the extremely grey area of civil-military relations in Israel. With the Arab–Israeli conflict remaining at the forefront of the national agendas of both the frontline Arab states and Israel, the role of the military in both societies has become much greater. In the Arab states, the military leadership have attempted to intervene in either replacing a civilian government with a new one, or, in most cases, replacing such a government with military rule. To this extent, the on-going conflict with Israel has helped the military, not only in maintaining a large slice of national budgets, but also by aiding them in their ambitions to rule. Though the reason cited by most military dictators in the Arab world has been that there was no alternative to their rule – otherwise known as the chaos argument – it is the underlying increased role of the armed forces in Arab civil society caused by the conflict with Israel that allows the military to seize power. Even strong men such as President Nasser, who relied on the 'I am the only man capable of holding the country together' argument, used the conflict with Israel as a means of helping to secure the legitimacy of his rule over Egypt, and for his unofficial position as leader of the wider Arab world.

In Israel, civil-military relations are meant to be different. The country is considered by many to have many of the characteristics of a typical western-style democracy (parliamentary elections, cabinet government with a ceremonial

79

style presidency, division of legislature and judiciary, etc). It is in the arena of civil-military relations, however, where Israel diverges from the norm. The charge made by both Sharett and Lavon during the Lavon Affair was that, as they had not given the order for the operations in Egypt, it must have come from either an unelected and unaccountable military figure, or from hard-line politicians outside the government with close ties to the armed forces. The latter was a polite way of accusing Ben-Gurion or one of his cohorts of giving the order. Either way, this would be a serious state of affairs in a democratic country where the military takes orders from the elected government of the day. No-one was more acutely aware of this than Ben-Gurion himself, who largely shaped the IDF, and who saw the charge of operating without the proper and correct political authorisation as a major slur on Israel's armed forces. As a result, Ben-Gurion spent the rest of his career trying to clear the name of the IDF and, indirectly, any suspicion that he had been involved.

A further complication in civil-military relations has been the increasing number of Israeli military leaders who have crossed into the political sector. Moshe Dayan, Israel's Chief of Staff during the Suez War in 1956, was one of the first cases in point. Dayan, a member of the 'young guard' of political and military leaders who were closely associated with Ben-Gurion, was clearly headed for a political career once his time as Chief of Staff of the IDF came to an end. This caused two problems. One was the charge that his actions and decisions made during his tenure as Chief of Staff were influenced by the fact that he would soon be in the political arena. The second was to use a curiously Israeli term 'political parachuting', whereby an ex-general who had recently retired from the armed forces would, in effect, be parachuted into the top-tier of political leadership, over and above other politicians who had made their careers in the political arena. The argument put forward by Ben-Gurion and others who supported this process was that Israel wanted and needed the best heads and minds in national leadership. In effect, in the arena of national security, it was perfectly normal for key civilian positions in the government to be occupied by technocrats (ex-IDF), given the continued nature of the Arab threat to the state.

As the numbers of such appointments grew, however, fears were raised about the implications for Israeli democracy. A quick look at the current Cabinet in Israel today reveals the extent of this process. Out of the 22 ministers who serve in the Cabinet, five have either held the rank of General in the IDF, or been a leading figure in Israel's internal security force (GSS).[57] The vast majority of these were parachuted into senior positions within their respective parties soon after leaving the armed forces. The notable exception to the rule is Ariel Sharon who, after leaving the army, formed his own faction before eventually joining the Likud, led at the time by Menachem Begin. Of the latest group, most concern has been raised over the appointment of Shaul Mofaz as Minister of Defence. Mofaz was appointed after only finishing his tenure as Chief of Staff of the IDF a few months before. He was also appointed before being elected to the Knesset. He was effectively parachuted in during the mid-term and kept his job following the election in 2003, in which he was placed in a lowly position on the Likud list of candidates for the election. During his time as Chief of

Staff, there were several ugly rows between himself and the government of the day, as some of his comments and statements appeared to cross into the political arena. Mofaz, in reality, was no fool. He was using his time as Chief of Staff to help prepare the ground for his future political career, in which he has made it clear that he is seeking to be the successor to the current Prime Minister, Ariel Sharon. Though there are laws in place that are meant to determine the amount of time between leaving the army and joining the government, this time period has been getting less and less, and people like Mofaz are finding ways of getting round the system. In reality, it says much about the calibre of politician in Israel, and the somewhat cynical viewpoint a lot of Israelis appear to hold them in, that there is a still a clamour for military leaders who are viewed, somewhat simplistically, as being above the fray, to join governments.

The grey lines between the civilian and military sectors do not stop here. Perhaps of greater concern has been the role that the IDF played in the negotiations of the various parts of the Oslo Accords, and the implications that this had for the political independence of the IDF. As the Israeli political scientist, Yoram Peri, points out, such was the level of the role of a group of IDF commanders in the negotiations that the IDF's ability to offer impartial security advice to the political leadership was diminished.[58] To critics of Oslo, this meant that the IDF had a vested interest in trying to make the Oslo Accords work long after they had been seen to have failed. The period of peacemaking in the 1990s consequently further blurred the civil-military relationship in Israel that had really started to become fuzzy as a result of the Lavon Affair. The

construction of the Security Fence has additionally complicated the relationship between the civilian and military
sectors, as the IDF's planning division has been responsible
for devising the route of the fence. There have been several
legal challenges by both Palestinians and Israelis about
parts of the route that cross over the Green Line. The IDF,
which claims that the route was chosen to maximise its
security value to Israelis, has been forced into having to
make alterations as a result of High Court rulings. It
would appear, at times, that the top brass of the IDF
were becoming responsible for demarcating Israel's
probable future border with a Palestinian state. Question
marks also remain over how wise it really is to allow the
IDF to determine which areas are vital to Israeli interests.
Traditionally, IDF thinking has centred on security issues
alone and not the political implications of its judgements.

Many Arab commentators use the evidence of the
increasing role of the military to suggest that Israel is in
effect a garrison state – one in which military values and
personalities dominate political ideals and leaders. To put
it another way, the military is running the show. Taking
the argument a step further, this impacts upon the chances
for peace, as, for many in the IDF, peace is not a rational
goal to obtain, as it would endanger the lofty position of
the IDF within the political system of Israel. The 'peace is
not logical for everyone' argument is also employed
against Israel's large military industry complex which, it
is claimed, is reliant upon continued conflict in order to
justify its large state subsidies and to keep its major market
(the IDF) intact. Such are the strong connections between
Israel's military industry complex, the top brass of the IDF,
and the political leadership (many of whom, as we

discussed, are retired military officers) that this prevents Israel from making any major political concessions that would potentially bring an end to the Arab–Israeli conflict.

These arguments, on the surface, appear rather seductive, and critics of Israel provide further detailed evidence to support this argument. On closer examination, despite the Lavon Affair, the high cross-over from military to political leadership, and the construction of a large military industry complex, the political leadership has always been the sovereign legislating body. There has, to my knowledge, never been the threat of a direct military coup in Israel. In terms of the military industry complex, where the argument stands up a little better is in its role in helping to shape, not internal Israeli policies, but rather Israel's military industry complex relations with the outside world. The need to sell military hardware to countries has been a direct necessity for the survival of the military industry complex for decades. This has meant that Israel has had to deal with a number of regimes that one could describe as being not particularly desirable – South Africa in the apartheid era, and Uganda under the brutal dictator, Idi Amin, to name but two. Such links have further hindered Israel's diplomatic efforts for international recognition and a place among nations.

In retrospect, the period between the Suez War of 1956 and the June 1967 War needs to be seen as a period of 'growing pains' that is natural for most new states. It should be remembered that Israel and the Arab states were fairly recent artificial creations, and that none of the states in the conflict had achieved full maturity in their respective civil societies and political systems. There were no written constitutions on either side of the divide, and an unhealthy interest in political affairs from the respective militaries. Supporters of Israel would no doubt point out that, while there are admittedly problems in this area, Israel was founded as a democratic state and remained so, even during its difficult early days of existence. The 'shining beacon of democracy in a neighbourhood of darkness' argument remains somewhat simplistic, just as it is simplistic to describe Egypt under Nasser as a brutal dictatorship. The reality was that internal developments alone probably would have prevented any opportunity for peace during this period.

Lest we forget, however, that internal political and economic difficulties were not the only obstacles to peace, the impact of the Cold War on the region could not be over-estimated. Once the Soviet Union entered the region with the Czech Arms Deals and its subsequent intensive programme of reconstruction of Egyptian forces following the Suez War in 1956, and the Americans had done likewise with the Eisenhower doctrine to check Soviet advances in the region, the full impact of the bi-polar international system was felt in the Middle East. Two areas were conditioned by the intervention of the super-powers during this era: arms sales and economic aid. Regarding the former, superpower intervention in the region helped fuel an arms race, with first the Soviets supplying the Arab world and then, during the 1960s, the USA starting to openly replace France as the major supplier of high-tech weapons to Israel. By the mid 1960s (and especially during and after the June 1967 War), the Arab–Israeli conflict was viewed as an important testing ground for weaponry by both Soviet and American manufacturers. Approximate answers were provided, for example, as to how well Soviet-built fighter aircraft would perform in aerial combat against American fighters. Much high-tech weaponry was modified on the basis of its performance in the Middle East theatre. The impact of the Cold War was also felt, both during this era and during the 1970s, in terms of not allowing any side a total victory over the other in any of the wars. This lack of a definitive defeat for one side or the other, as Bernard Lewis suggests, prolonged the conflict.

So, no major war, but no peace either, would appear to have been the logical state of affairs given the internal dynamics in the Arab world and in Israel, as well as the rise of superpower influence and the emergence of the Cold War. To be sure, there were chances for peace, but it would be difficult, after detailed examination of the circumstances behind such developments, to characterise them as serious or, indeed, realistic prospects for full peace agreements to be signed. The Middle East as a whole (the Arab world and Israel) experienced worrying developments during this period, which was characterised by the continued resentment in the Arab world of what they viewed as a colonial settler state that had been largely created as a result of Christian guilt over the Holocaust in Europe that had taken place during the Second World War. Arab populations, exposed to tightly controlled state medias that demonised the Jews and Zionist enemies, continued to talk about Israel's eventual destruction. Arab leaders, acutely aware of the populist sentiment, from time to time tapped into it by promising that Israel's defeat was coming, and, as one Arab leader promised, the Jews would be driven into the sea. Israel, buoyed by its defeat of the Arab armies in 1948 and Nasser's Egypt in

1956, appeared in no rush to come to the negotiating table. In truth, the 1960s in Israel were characterised by a sense of melancholy about the continued nature of the threat that the country was facing from the Arabs. The term 'war weariness' is often misused to describe Israeli periods of introspection, but during the 1960s there certainly existed among Israeli society a sense that the country was standing alone in an increasingly hostile region, and that another war with the Arabs was inevitable at some stage. For many Israelis, the coming war would either lead to the destruction of Israel, or would inflict the level of defeat on the Arabs that would force their political leadership to accept Israel's right to exist. The coming battle, in short, was to be the decisive one.

Notes:

[43] For more on civil-military relations and the causes of military intervention in the Arab world see: N. Ayubi (1995), *Overstating the Arab State: Politics and Society in the Middle East*, London and New York: I. B. Tauris, pp. 256–60.

[44] For an interesting example of the views of the Ben-Gurion camp, see Ministry of Foreign Affairs, Jerusalem, 'Article by Chief of Staff (Moshe) Dayan in Foreign Affairs, XXXIII, January 1955, pp. 1–18' MFA/1-2/20/V, 1947–1994.

[45] C. Herzog (1994), *The Arab–Israeli Wars*, New York: Vintage Books, p. 113.

[46] The most recent example of this in English is S. Aburish (2004), *Nasser: the Last Arab*, London: Duckworth.

[47] Ministry of Foreign Affairs, Jerusalem, 'Statement by Prime Minister Ben-Gurion to the Knesset', (18 August 1952) MFA/1-2/13/V/ 1947–1974.

48 For Ben-Gurion's public response to the Czech arms deal, see
    Ministry of Foreign Affairs, Jerusalem, 'Statement to the Knesset
    by Prime Minister Ben-Gurion', (2 November 1955) MFA/1-
    2/22/V/1947–1974.

49 For a fascinating account of the meetings at Sèvres, see A.
    Shlaim (2001), 'The Protocol of Sèvres: Anatomy of a War Plot'
    in *The 1956 War: Collusion and Rivalry in the Middle East*,
    London and Portland: Frank Cass, pp. 119–143.

50 For a detailed account of the War, see K. Kyle (1991), *Suez*,
    New York: St Martin's Press.

51 M. Dayan (1966), *Diary of the Sinai Campaign*, New York: Da
    Capo, p. 203.

52 Ministry of Foreign Affairs, Jerusalem (MFA), 'Letter from
    President Eisenhower to Prime Minister Ben-Gurion', (7
    November 1956) MFA/1-2/9/IX/1947–1974.

53 (MFA), 'Statement to the UN General Assembly by Foreign
    Minister Meir', (1 March 1947) MFA/1-2/26/IX/1947–1974.

54 UN General Assembly, 'Report of the Special Committee on
    Peacekeeping Operations, "Comprehensive Review of the
    Whole Question of Peacekeeping Operations in all their
    Aspects"', (28 March 2003) A/57/767, p. 5.

55 Figures from *SIPRI Yearbook 2003: Armaments, Disarmaments
    and International Security*, Oxford: Oxford University Press.

56 For details of the Lavon Affair and its impact on Israel, see P.
    Medding (1990), *The Founding of Israeli Democracy,
    1948–1967*, New York: Oxford University Press.

57 Profiles of Israel's Cabinet Ministers are on-line at
    www.mfa.gov.il.

58 Y. Peri (2002), 'The Israeli Military and Israel's Palestinian
    Policy: from Oslo to the Al Aqsa Intifada', *Peacework*, 47.

4

❧❧❧

Reading the Signals:
Defining Strong and Weak in the
New Middle East

Traffic lights and first strike

As the first Israeli aircraft climbed from their ground-hugging altitude towards their bombing positions high above the Egyptian airfields, any uncertainty over the outcome of the third Arab–Israeli War ended even before the first shot had been fired. The first waves of Israeli bombers had achieved total surprise as they dropped their bombs on the Egyptian planes and runways. It was early morning on 5 June 1967, and within hours the Egyptian Air Force had ceased to exist as a fighting force. The vast majority of the Egyptian Air Force's planes were destroyed on the ground – their pilots had just returned from their first sorties of the morning and were enjoying breakfast when the Israelis struck. The planes were left exposed on the runway or in makeshift hangers. There was a marked absence of concrete shelters or attempts to disguise the position of the planes. For the Israeli pilots it was a chicken shoot. Those Egyptian planes that did get off the ground were no match for the swarms of Israeli aircraft. For the Israeli pilots, the chief concern had focused on the need to achieve total surprise: something they had successfully achieved through a complex planning operation and with a degree of luck. Jordanian radar had picked up some of the attacking force, but the codes used to transmit a warning to their Egyptian colleagues had been changed the day before and so the Egyptians failed to understand the warning. Israel had achieved near total domination over the skies on its southern front on the first morning of the War. With air cover secured, Israeli ground forces were able to advance quickly against the Egyptians. The morning of 5 June 1967 was about as close as the conflict came to being ended by a single battle or action.

Conventional wisdom in Israel and the West has it that war between Israel and the Arab states was unavoidable in 1967. In supporting this argument the following evidence is generally presented. At the centre of events once more was President Nasser, whose popularity in both Egypt and the Arab world sharply declined during the 1960s. Nasser's Pan-Arabist dream had been largely exposed. There was deep resentment of his role as leader of the Arab world from the rich Gulf States, and, in particular, Saudi Arabia. The United Arab Republic (the union of Egypt and Syria) had collapsed, and the Egyptian military had been drawn into the civil war in Yemen where it was not proving to be very effective. Economically, Nasser experienced various waves of economic crisis in Egypt and was becoming ever more reliant, economically and militarily, on the Soviet Union. In truth, the one populist card left in his hand was the conflict with Israel; despite the quiet on the border between Egypt and Israel, Nasser's anti-Israeli rhetoric had been stepped up. On top of this Nasser was clearly using the conflict as a back door to try to gain a degree of control over the Arab world. So when he received intelligence reports from the Soviets that Israel was massing troops and tanks on its borders with Syria, Nasser was only too happy to start to move his troops out of the Yemen and send them to the Sinai. What still remains unclear are the Soviet motives for the false report. In a declassified top-secret memorandum from Nathaniel Davis of the National Security Council Staff to the President's Special Assistant (Rostow) on the Soviet role, Davis stated that he felt that it was probable that Soviet agents actually picked up intelligence reports of a planned Israeli raid into Syria. He went on to suggest that he would not be surprised if the reports were at least partly true. The Israelis, he argued, had made such raids before; they had been under heavy provocation; and they maintained pretty good security (so the USA might well not know about a planned raid). In short, the 'partial cock up' theory. In essence, he sensed that, with intelligence being an uncertain business, the Soviet agents may not have known the scale of the raid and may have exaggerated its scope and purpose.[59]

Whatever question marks there remain about Soviet intentions, the motives for Nasser's moves were not lost on the Israeli leadership, which was also forced to deal with attacks originating from Jordan and cycles of violent confrontation with Syrian forces in the north. Levi Eshkol, who served as both Prime Minister and Minister of Defence during much of this period, was not a military expert. Consequently, the Chief of Staff of the IDF, Yitzhak

Rabin, took on powers that went beyond the normal remit of those of his position. While it would be an exaggeration to suggest that Rabin in effect acted as the *de facto* Minister of Defence, it is true to suggest that on military matters the Prime Minister trusted the Chief of Staff's judgement. In other words, Rabin enjoyed the ear of the Prime Minister on a whole range of security issues. Rabin and his military colleagues had concluded as early as the mid 1960s that war with Nasser was highly likely, and consequently war planning in Israel was stepped up. At the centre of the planning was the debate over whether Israel should fire the first shot in the War. The relative advantage of Israel taking such action was that it was perceived that this would both shorten the War and lead to fewer Israeli casualties. The downside was that Israel would be perceived as the aggressor not only in the Arab world but among the many non-aligned nations as well. As ever, however, the central factor in Israeli decision-making on the first strike issue remained the attitude of the American Administration of Lyndon B. Johnson to such action.

As the crisis in the Middle East deepened, the Johnson Administration initially made it clear that it opposed any Israeli use of the first strike. In a meeting with the Israeli Foreign Minister Abba Eban, the US Secretary of Defence, Robert McNamara, told Israel starkly that it would stand alone if it initiated an attack.[60] It should be remembered that at the time, the Johnson Administration was under pressure from Congress not to act unilaterally, nor allow Israel to do the same. In the wider context it is worth recalling that the USA was up to its neck in a war in Vietnam that it was slowly losing, and that the Soviet

Union was looking to make mischief in the Middle East in order to try to further weaken America's position in another theatre of the Cold War. Of course, that was not the end of the story. As war grew more likely, Levi Eshkol was persuaded to broaden his governing coalition in Israel by forming a National Unity Government, which included for the first time Menachem Begin and the Herut Movement (the direct political descendents of the Zionist Revisionist movement). The inclusion of Begin was by no means a popular move among the rank and file leadership of the ruling Mapai party. Many veterans from the labour Zionist movement regarded him as a dangerous hothead – not a minister or statesman. It was, however, the appointment of Moshe Dayan as Minister of Defence on 2 June 1967 that drew most attention, and had the greatest impact on the War. Dayan had, it is true to say, walked out of Mapai with some reluctance when his mentor and patron, David Ben-Gurion, left following the Lavon Affair described above. Relations between Mapai and Ben-Gurion's new party, Rafi, had not been at all gentlemanly since Ben-Gurion and his supporters had quit. The appointment of Dayan therefore represented a rare case of the leadership of Mapai putting national over party interests (or, some would say, giving in to the popular sentiment of the Israeli public).

Eshkol, in truth, had been under pressure for sometime to appoint Dayan. Widely regarded as a peacetime leader, his lack of military experience appeared to indicate a need for a Minister of Defence with an intimate knowledge of conflict. There is also evidence that appeared to suggest that some individuals were uncomfortable with the power and influence of Rabin over the

Prime Minister. Ben-Gurion himself pushed for the creation of the National Unity Government in some degree to check Rabin's influence (Rabin, being a former officer in the Palmach, never enjoyed the confidence of Ben-Gurion). Ben-Gurion also hoped that the formation of a National Unity Government would lead to his own political rehabilitation – code for his hope that he would be asked (again) to return as Prime Minister in Israel's hour of need to face his old foe, President Nasser. Ben-Gurion, however, remained on the outside as Eshkol made it clear that he would remain in his position.

Bringing Dayan into the Cabinet led Israel to two fateful strategic decisions. Dayan did not think that international diplomacy would be able to avert war, so Israel's military and diplomatic activity was subtly altered as the crisis with Egypt deepened. It was reported that when Dayan arrived in the bear pit (the area where senior IDF planners hone their war plans) he said 'Show me your plans – if you have any.' Dayan soon made it clear that he supported the IDF's call for a pre-emptive strike, and his support was crucial in Cabinet. Knowing President Johnson's objection to such a plan, Israel once more sent military man, Meir Amit, the head of Mossad, to Washington to lobby support for an Israeli first strike. Here there are disputes as to which traffic signal Israel received from the Americans for their actions: green (go), amber (proceed with caution), or red (do not proceed). Current evidence available in the USA appears to suggest that Israel got a red light. Amit, however, suggested after meetings with Secretary of Defence Robert McNamara that Israel had in effect been given an amber light – allowed to proceed with caution by the American Administration, though here it should be stressed that the documentation does not confirm Amit's version of the key meeting with Secretary McNamara.[61]

Returning to the original statement about the inevitability of the War, it was clear that once Mossad had passed on their version of the meetings in America to the Israeli Cabinet the point of no return had been crossed. Prior to this, however, two related issues dominated the seemingly relentless march to war: the intentions of President Nasser and the mischief-making of the Soviet Union. The decision-making of the ruling Politburo in Moscow was always cloaked in intrigue, with the fine line between fact and fiction sometimes obscured by deliberate misinformation and misdirection. What is clear, however, is that elements of the Soviet leadership in 1967 accused Israel (falsely) of massing troops on the border with Syria. As a result, Nasser was persuaded to send Egyptian troops across the Sinai to mass on Israel's southern border. Prime Minister Eshkol offered to take diplomats to Israel's northern border to illustrate that nothing out of the ordinary was happening: Israel was not massing troops and the Soviet report was incorrect. This was the era when verification of such claims was much more difficult than today. Satellite technology was largely gathered by the superpowers and not shared with their client states.

What followed was depressingly predictable and needs to be viewed within the context of the Cold War and the increasing hostility between President Nasser and Israel. The crisis with Israel once more gave the Arab world an excuse to come together under Nasser's leadership and with the military backing of the Soviet Union. The last piece of the jigsaw to fall into place was the signing of a military pact between President Nasser and a somewhat reluctant King Hussein of Jordan, that effectively placed Egypt in charge of the War from an Arab perspective. Up until the last moment Israel tried to keep King Hussein and Jordan out of the War. On the first morning of the War, Prime Minister Eshkol sent a message to the King stating that Israel would not attack Jordan unless it attacked Israel, but it proved to be of no avail, as Jordanian forces soon joined the fighting.[62] While the Soviets appeared keen to create a crisis in the region it remains, as we have seen, much less likely that they actually expected – or indeed hoped – that the end scenario would be war. The United Nations, as ever not to be relied upon to solve a crisis, took perhaps the single biggest decision that led the parties to war – the withdrawal of the United Nations peacekeepers from the Israeli–Egyptian border.[63] Even allowing for the benefit of hindsight, the decision of UN Secretary General, U. Thant, to stand up to pressure from Nasser to relocate some of the force by withdrawing the whole force appears bizarre. Whatever Thant's motives, Israeli and Egyptian forces faced each other directly and war appeared unavoidable.

In victory comes defeat – in defeat comes victory
The success of the opening Israeli air strikes meant that the War was over before it had really started. By the end of the sixth day of the War, Israeli forces had secured control over the West Bank, the Golan Heights and East Jerusalem (including the Old City). The major debate within Israel centred upon whether to try to take the strategically important Golan Heights from the Syrians at the end of the War – this aim had not been included in Israel's

original war plan. Eventually Moshe Dayan won the day over a more reluctant Rabin, and an Israeli flag flew over the Golan Heights just prior to the internationally brokered ceasefire coming into effect on 11 June 1967. From a military point of view, there is little doubt that Israel was the victor. From a Jewish and Zionist perspective, the reuniting of Jerusalem under Israeli control seemed to be the fulfilment of the Zionist dream of a Jewish state with Jerusalem as its eternal capital.[64]

There were two immediate consequences of the War to which historians, correctly, draw much attention: the creation of lands that Israel could identify as 'buffer zones'; and the related issue that, for the first time, Israel became an occupying power, directly ruling over one million Palestinians. In the long-term both these issues were to prove central to any resolution of the conflict. In the short-term, however, the fundamental issue for the Arab states became how to regain the lands that had been lost to Israel in 1967, and, in truth, how to do this from a position of apparent weakness and offering only minimal concessions to Israel. What was made abundantly clear to the Israelis was that, despite the catastrophic military defeat, the Arab states would not come to the negotiating table, and certainly not from the position of weakness they found themselves in at the end of the War.

The military defeat, by all accounts, was made all the worse for the Arab leadership by the fact that this time they had promised victory, and there was a deep sense of shock among the Arab masses about what had actually happened, as opposed to what had been promised. The Jews, in short, were not driven into the sea. The Arab states were, as a result, more desperate than ever to gain a military victory of some kind over Israel. This was viewed as essential in some Arab capitals, in order both to regain a degree of honour (very important in Arab political culture), and, in some regimes, to shore up their extremely weak domestic political and economic positions.

President Nasser tried to pre-empt the criticism by resigning during the War. News of his resignation, however, led to a relatively genuine outpouring of popular sentiment calling for him to reconsider. The demonstrations at which crowds chanted for him to remain in office, however, took place before the full extent of the Egyptian military defeat had reached the general public. When this happened Nasser moved quickly to effectively shift blame on to others for the military losses. To a certain extent, this tactic came unstuck when attempts to prosecute those charged over the War led to widespread mass demonstrations that called for the 'real guilty figures' to be brought to justice. Growing difficulties at home for Nasser were matched by an extremely complex international situation. At the heart of Nasser's difficulties lay the need to retain Soviet military aid, while at the same time trying to increase overseas economic aid from other countries to shore up Egypt's economy. In truth, many of Nasser's political policies following the June 1967 War until his death in 1970 were dictated by Egypt's economic needs.

As for the other Arab leaders, Syria underwent another period of instability before President Asad and the Ba'ath party secured full control. In Jordan, King Hussein, who had reluctantly been drawn into war, faced growing threats from Palestinian groups, which were not resolved until September 1970.

As previously stated, the central debate within these three front-line states was how best to regain the lands captured by Israel during the War. All Arab leaders, including Nasser, made the usual fiery noises about Palestinian rights and the need to resolve this issue. In practice, they were far more interested in the art of political, and sometimes physical, self-preservation to offer anything more to the Palestinians than rather hollow sounding rhetoric. The Khartoum Summit of 1967 and its three 'No' resolutions of 1 September 1967 defined this era of Arab hostility towards what they termed 'the Zionist Entity':

1. No recognition of Israel.
2. No negotiations with Israel.
3. No peace with Israel.[65]

Never one to miss an opportunity to flex his Arab nationalist credentials – though he did this largely to please the hard-line Gulf States whose money he needed – President Nasser added an additional 'No' at the conclusion of the summit – otherwise known as the fourth rejection of Israel: no concessions on the legitimate rights of the Palestinian people.

With Yasser Arafat and his radical friends seizing control of the PLO and publishing a radical Palestinian National Covenant in July 1968 that called for the destruction of Israel, the inter-war years (1967–73) were to prove extremely bloody.[66] Arafat and his fighters launched a series of attacks against Israeli targets in both the West Bank and inside the Green Line. For his part, President Nasser initiated what became known as the War of

Attrition, which in reality was a continuous low-intensity war fought mainly in the area of the Suez Canal. Nasser's aims were complex, but centred on his efforts to rebuild morale in the Egyptian military, to make life difficult for the Israeli forces on the banks of the Canal, and, in strategic terms, to use the conflict as cover for moving missile batteries into forward positions. The latter proved to be of great significance for the 1973 War.

The Israeli response to the outcome of the June 1967 War and in turn its misreading of both Nasser and, following his death in 1970, his successor Anwar Sadat, says much about the failings of its military planners and intelligence services. The Egyptians, and the Soviets, quickly learned important lessons from the 1967 War, which led to a change in their respective military doctrines. At the heart of these changes lay a shift away from attempting to neutralise the Israeli Air Force by using aircraft towards the creation of nests of surface-to-air-missile batteries (SAMs), which would be able to shoot down Israeli aircraft. Crucially, and somewhat inexplicably, Israel missed this change in thinking and continued to measure the potential of an Arab attack by way of counting the number of Arab aircraft it would take to neutralise the Israeli Air Force. Planners in Tel Aviv did not think that such a point would be reached until the mid to late 1970s at the earliest. This one-dimensional thinking helped create the impression that Israel was relatively safe from a major attack until that point. Both Nasser and Sadat also devoted a great deal of time to trying to develop a united Arab front, which it was hoped would be able to liberate all the territories which Israel had conquered in 1967. The hope expressed by Nasser was that Israel must be made to fight on multiple fronts at the same time.[67]

The Golda and Moshe show

The death of Levi Eshkol in 1969 brought Golda Meir to power. A compromise candidate among the increasingly bitter power struggles between the younger generations of the ruling Labour Party, she was the last of Israel's veteran leaders drawn from its founding generation of the Second and Third Aliyahs, and, like her predecessor, was no military expert. As a result, she was highly dependent on the judgement of Moshe Dayan in the key areas of military and security issues. As these issues dominated much of the political agenda in Israel, this made Dayan central to almost all decisions of importance during this period. For Golda Meir and Moshe Dayan the status quo in relations with the Arabs was an acceptable state of affairs. Dayan helped develop the policy of 'economic functionalism' for the now occupied West Bank and Gaza Strip. This policy was in reality an attempt by Israel to develop the economic well-being of the Palestinians living in these lands to higher levels, in the hope that this would lead to a reduction in their nationalist aspirations. This variation on the 'shower them with gifts to win them over' theory of course failed. In the meantime, while not annexing these lands, successive Israeli governments started to build settlements for Jews in key parts of them. With the settlements came roads, IDF bases and checkpoints. As a result, the thorny issue of the Jewish settlers and settlements was created.

In some ways, Israel became the victim of its own success in 1967. The political inertia within the government

101

continued, with the exception to the rule being Golda's acceptance of a peace plan sponsored by the US Secretary of State, William Rogers.[68] Golda's acceptance led to the break-up of the National Unity Government when Menachem Begin and Gahal departed over the Cabinet's backing of the plan. President Nasser had previously accepted a different variation of the plan, which Israel in turn had rejected, but did not agree to what he termed the Israeli version.[69] To be fair to Nasser, the Nixon Administration appeared so keen to get the sides to agree to anything that they in effect allowed widely differing interpretations of the plan by Egypt and Israel. Central to the debate was the meaning of the infamous United Nations Security Council Resolution 242, which was passed unanimously by the Security Council on 22 November 1967.[70] The Resolution called, in part, for Israel to withdraw from territories it had captured during the 1967 War.

The ambiguity lay in the absence of the definite article (the) in the English version of the Resolution (the first language of the UN). Without a definite article the phrase can be taken to mean (as it was by successive Israeli governments) withdrawing from some of the territories. In the Arabic translation of the Resolution, the definite article is included for linguistic reasons.[71] For this reason, Nasser and successive Arab leaders have taken this part of the Resolution to mean that, for Israel to be in compliance with Resolution 242, it must withdraw from ALL the lands it captured in 1967. Both Golda Meir and President Nasser were in reality accepting very different versions of the Rogers Plan as a result. In order to get Golda to sign, the Nixon Administration, and in particular the National

Security Advisor, Henry Kissinger, had been forced to offer additional sweeteners to Israel, such as not making Israel withdraw from anywhere until full peace had been agreed. This, of course, was to prove unacceptable to Nasser and the Arabs.

The efforts of the US Secretary State, William Rogers, should not be under-estimated. True, they did not bring peace any closer, and some argue that they actually contributed to making another Arab–Israeli war more probable. What Rogers did achieve in his own small way, however, was in some form or other to get the major Arab power, Egypt, to agree to recognise Israel's right to exist with secure borders, if it agreed to take a certain number of steps (withdrawal to 1967 boundaries amongst others). The death of President Nasser on 28 September 1970, however, transformed the Arab world, and in the short-term reduced any small opportunity for a major diplomatic breakthrough.

Succession and legitimacy in the Arab world

The selection of Anwar Sadat to succeed Nasser came as a surprise to a great many people. Though he had served as a loyal deputy to Nasser he was considered to be something of a lightweight. Many viewed him as something of a Western playboy with little in the way of leadership skills or political judgement. At the time it was widely presumed that he was a stopgap appointment who would soon be replaced once the various Nasserite factions had come to an agreement over a long-term successor to Nasser. As we all know, however, stopgap appointees have a habit of becoming more permanent fixtures than was originally thought possible (just ask

Yitzhak Shamir, who took over following the resignation of Menachem Begin in Israel in 1983, and who was viewed as such an appointment, but went on to become Israel's second longest serving Prime Minister).

The issue of succession has been one of the most difficult areas in Arab states, which are effectively run by military juntas, or are in the nominal sense constitutional monarchies. In Egypt, Nasser had made no real provision for his death. The elevation of Sadat happened largely because there was no mechanism in place other than appointing his deputy. Later, when President Asad of Syria passed away in 2001 his son had already been widely trained and groomed for the job and his elevation to the Presidency passed with a minimum of fuss. Also, had the Allied Coalition not removed Saddam Hussein from power in 2003–4, both his sons appeared ready to step into their father's shoes. More recently, President Mubarak of Egypt's attempts to position his son as his anointed successor has run into greater opposition. Even in the so-called constitutional monarchies the question of succession was often problematic.

In Jordan, King Hussein had originally appointed Crown Prince Hassan as his successor, only to later remove this title and name one of his sons, Abdullah, as Crown Prince and consequently the King-in-waiting. King Hussein never fully publicly explained his change of heart, but court gossip suggested that he had become disillusioned by indirect attacks on his leadership style. Arab leaders want their regimes to continue beyond their own death, and often have to devote much of their time at the end of their lives assuring that this will happen. A major downside of this is that the new young leaders are generally heavily dependent on the very people who kept their fathers in power. In Syria, President Asad II relies on two key figures, the head of Syrian Intelligence, and the head of the Army, to keep him in power. More often than not, President Asad's tentative attempts at introducing economic and political reforms have been blocked by conservative individuals and groupings who were close to his father. In the arena of making peace with Israel, this makes it all the harder for the successor to break the mould of a past that has been characterised by the total rejection of Israel, and in which present opposition to the Zionist entity remains one of the very few genuinely unifying factors in Arab countries and across the Arab world as a whole.[72]

In the land of the blind the one-eyed man is King

With the benefit of hindsight, it is clear that there was something of an inevitability about the October 1973 Arab–Israeli War. I say this despite the near total surprise in Israel when it was first revealed on 5 October that an Arab attack was imminent the next day. The logical development of the Arab–Israeli conflict suggested that, at some stage in the relatively near future, some Arab states would try to avenge their crushing defeat in 1967. The events and difficulties that I have just described in the Arab world during this era, and the continued support of the Soviet Union for both Egypt and Syria, appear to confirm this inevitability of a major attack. What was harder to foresee was just how close these attacks came to destroying the State of Israel. Though the situation in Israel was extremely bad during the first phase of the 1948 War, this War was perhaps the closest Israel came to ceasing to exist.

THE VIEW FROM THE FENCE

Before looking at the failure of Israel's intelligence agencies to foresee the Arab attack, it is worth briefly recounting the events of the War itself. The armies of Egypt and Syria launched a co-ordinated attack on 6 October 1973. In Israel, it was Yom Kippur (the Day of Atonement), one of the holiest days in the Jewish calendar. In the Muslim world it was Ramadan, but the Egyptian and Syrian soldiers who participated in the attack received special permission from their respective religious leaders to take part at a time when they should have been fasting. The initial attacks on Israeli forces situated both on the eastern side of the Suez Canal and in the north on the Golan Heights proved to be extremely successful. Indeed, on the southern front, the few hundred Israeli soldiers who were manning the Bar-Lev Line (a series of fortified defence posts) were no match for the thousands of Egyptian soldiers who had crossed the Suez Canal using specially constructed pontoon bridges and water canons that created breaches in the sand banks next to the Canal.

The Israeli government had known about the attack, which started on time at 1.50 pm, since the previous evening. Indeed, there is evidence to suggest that prior to this, King Hussein of Jordan had tried to warn Israel that an attack was to take place. Golda Meir decided, however, that because there was no major evidence of such attack, and because the King had been somewhat vague in his warning, there were no grounds for taking the necessary action. There was much debate between Golda, Moshe Dayan and the Chief of Staff of the IDF, David Elazar, on the evening of 5 October on two fateful questions: should Israel launch a pre-emptive strike against the Egyptians and Syrians? And should the order be given for a full mobilisation of Israeli forces? Golda said 'no' to a pre-emptive strike. She later argued that, had Israel repeated its tactic at the start of the June 1967 War, the country would have been seen as the aggressor and consequently diplomatically isolated. It probably was not lost on Golda that, at some stage during the War, Israel would have to ask the United States for weapons, and that the administration led by President Nixon would be more sympathetic to an Israeli shopping list of military hardware if it had not fired the first shot in the War. Golda also noted that Israel was not sitting on its pre-1967 War borders. The initial attacks would take place far away from Israel proper in the south, and in the north Syrian forces would have to fight their way up and over the Golan Heights. On the question of mobilisation, Golda sided with Dayan, who argued for a limited mobilisation of Israel forces.

With the majority of Israeli forces away from the theatre of conflict, Egyptian and Syrian gains during the opening hours of the war were substantial. The Egyptian Generals were reported to be surprised at how low their casualty figures had been in crossing the Suez Canal and establishing a series of bridgeheads on its east bank. The fact that it was Yom Kippur in Israel when most people are at home – and therefore easily contactable – and usually heavily congested roads deserted meant that, once the order was given, Israeli forces mobilised extremely quickly. After the initial early gains of the Egyptians and the Syrians a number of factors changed the course of the war: the strategic thinking of President Sadat, counter-attacks by Israeli forces, and the airlift of US arms to Israel.

The first was the decision of President Sadat to halt the advance of the Egyptian Army in the Sinai. Sadat allowed his troops to advance only as far as the SAM batteries could shield his army from attacks. To a degree, this allowed Israel to seize the initiative once Israeli reinforcements arrived at the front and started to push the Egyptian Army back. In a counter-attack, Israeli forces led by General Ariel Sharon managed to cross the Suez Canal and set up a major bridgehead on the west bank of the Canal. Once this was achieved the outcome of the war in the south was largely determined. Freed from major threat in the south Israeli forces were able to turn their attention to the northern front where the Israeli Air Force, after destroying missile sites, launched a series of heavy raids on Syrian forces on the Golan Heights. In fierce fighting, much of it at close quarters, the IDF retook the Golan Heights and threatened to move down towards Damascus. The airlift of US arms to Israel in the middle of the War is often cited by Arab sources as having tipped the balance of the War in Israel's favour. In truth, the War had already turned. Yes, they proved to be extremely useful and helped to replace weapons that Israel had lost during the initial stages of the War. The arms lift probably shortened the War and helped increase the scope of Israel's victory, but did not directly impact upon the overall outcome.

Once more, under heavy pressure from the Soviet Union, the United States applied pressure on Israel to agree to a ceasefire before the IDF encroached further into Egyptian and Syrian territory. The Egyptian Third Army had been encircled by Israeli forces and faced imminent destruction when a ceasefire was agreed. The military outcome of the War was clear for all to see. Once more, the Arab forces had been routed and were facing the prospect of an even greater defeat if the internationally brokered ceasefire had not come into effect. For Israelis, however, the successful outcome of the War was overshadowed by the political and military failings at its outset, which had left Israel exposed to the threat of being overrun. The failings came at all levels, but much emphasis was given to two areas: intelligence, and the Bar-Lev Line in the Sinai.

Being geographically small (even post-1967), Israel has to a large degree had to rely on its intelligence services to provide early warning of Arab attacks on the State. With regard to attacks by Arab regular armies, it is the responsibility of Military Intelligence to give early warning, to provide evidence and to draw deductions and conclusions from their findings. In May 1973, there were all the signs of Egyptian preparations for war: ground troops were moved into the Canal region, new tank ramps were built and openings prepared in the ramparts; and, away from the front, there was mobilisation of civil defence, calls for blood donors, and President Sadat talking of the total confrontation with Israel.[73] Israeli Military Intelligence, however, argued to the Cabinet that the potential for war with Egypt remained low despite all the above signals. Their assessment was based on two strategic judgements: that Egypt would not go to war while the Israeli Air Force would be able to bomb advancing Egyptian troops, and that Sadat was merely sabre-rattling, and his language of war was merely a reflection of Egyptian frustration at the lack of progress in US-sponsored diplomatic efforts.

The fact that President Sadat eventually decided to postpone the War until the Autumn created the impression in Israel that the assessment provided by Military

Intelligence was spot on. Among the leadership of Military Intelligence there was a deeply held belief that its framework for making their assessments was based on accurate assumptions. In October, when there were similar indications that Egypt was about to launch a major attack, Military Intelligence in Israel, buoyed by their success earlier in the year, made a similar assessment and deduction based on the evidence it had in front of it. To be fair, there were dissenting voices within the organisation, but these voices were overruled by more senior figures. The resultant failure proved to be catastrophic for Israel. The results of the committee of enquiry, the Agranat Commission, which was set up after the War, have still not been made public. Only the introduction is in the public domain, but the committee was said to be extremely critical of Military Intelligence and called for a number of personnel changes and systematic changes in the way intelligence evidence is assessed.

The blind leading the blind

Away from all the official findings, the failings of 1973 led to what became known as the Yom Kippur Syndrome among Israel's intelligence services. In simple terms, this translates as an overcautiousness in assessing risks whereby the services have, at times, over-estimated threat levels to Israel, and at times to the western powers as well. It would be over-simplistic to argue that the current difficulties that Israeli intelligence services find themselves in is caused by Yom Kippur Syndrome alone – even among IDF Military Intelligence, which was the service most at fault in 1973. Before looking at the difficulties Israeli intelligence services faced in identifying Saddam Hussein's

Weapons of Mass Destruction (WMDs) and its failure to spot the Libyan nuclear programme, it is worth briefly summarising who is who and who does what, as well as the relationships between the organisations.

There has always been a degree of competition between the four agencies, which has from time to time broken out into outright hostility, and also within each agency.[74] IDF Military Intelligence, Air Force Intelligence, Shin Beth (sometimes known as the GSS or by their Hebrew name, Shabak) and Mossad all have on paper clearly defined roles and spheres of influence. Military Intelligence is a reactive organisation gathering intelligence about potential hostile movements by regular Arab armies, interpreting it, and reporting on their findings to the civil and military leadership in Israel. Shin Beth operates mainly in the Occupied Territories against Palestinian groups, and Mossad mounts preventative operations as well as undertaking intelligence gathering operations.[75]

Israeli intelligence services were at the heart of the presumption made by both the CIA in Washington and MI6 in London that Saddam Hussein had a substantial arsenal of WMDs, including an advanced chemical and biological warfare programme. The parliamentary committee of enquiry into Israeli intelligence services following the US–Iraq War found that IDF Military Intelligence had been over-confident in its assessment of Iraq's military capabilities and WMD capabilities following the expulsion of the UN weapons inspectors in 1998.[76] Mossad and Air Force Intelligence assessments were similar to IDF intelligence, but crucially contained clear doubts about the basis of their assessments, due to the concerns about the quality of information their deduc-

111

tions were based upon.[77] The committee of enquiry did not censure the intelligence services for the inaccurate assessments and rather provided a number of reasons for justifying the conclusions the services arrived at. These reasons included the history of Saddam Hussein's regime to try to develop such weapons, the reports of the weapons inspectors who appeared to suggest that Saddam Hussein had such weapons, the refusal of the regime to allow the inspectors to carry out full-scale monitoring in Iraq, the fact that WMDs are easily concealed, and the assessments of Western intelligence services which were extremely similar to that of the Israelis. The last two are the most interesting, reveal a lot about Israeli thinking at the time – and remain the most controversial.

The question of concealment of WMDs is extremely important, given the accusation that Israeli officials made at the start of the Iraq War in 2003 that Iraq had in effect moved the WMDs out of Iraq and into Syria. At the time, there was a great deal of scepticism about such claims from many political and intelligence leaders throughout the world. They pointed to the fact that such claims fitted in with Israeli attempts to damage the international standing of President Bashir Asad, and that there was no photographic evidence of such movements. The question of Saddam Hussein's motives was also put forward. In other words, why would he transfer his WMDs to a country that, despite some re-establishment of economic links during the mid to late 1990s, he still had not forgiven for joining the US coalition against Iraq during the 1991 Persian Gulf War, although here it should be remembered that stranger things have happened. On the eve of the Persian Gulf War, Saddam Hussein ordered his air force to fly to his arch-enemy Iran, where they sat out the War. In truth, while it is not inconceivable that the WMDs were taken out of Iraq – probably in regular looking articulated lorries – the most likely scenario, as the Israeli parliamentary enquiry implied, remains that they simply did not exist in the first place. Although, as intelligence experts suggested, if they did not exist then Saddam Hussein's behaviour in the period from the mid 1990s onwards appears extremely strange.

The case of Libya is even more intriguing. The central defence of IDF Military Intelligence was the old adage 'we were never asked, and had we been asked there would have been a detailed response'. In private, Israeli officials blamed the Americans and British for not sharing information with Israel. In reality, this charge only refers to the point just before the Libyans made their disclosure. The fundamental reason that Israeli intelligence was so off the ball on Libya was more connected with the fact that the intelligence community in Israel widely regarded Libya as more of threat to Egypt, with whom it has several long-running border disputes. In other words, Israel did not consider it to be worth investing the kind of resources into Libya that it does, for instance, in Iran. Nonetheless, there was widespread surprise in Israel at just how far advanced the Libyan nuclear programme had become. These failings of Israeli intelligence in Libya, when taken together with its failings in regard to WMDs in Iraq, led some in Israel to compare 2003–4 with the failings prior to the October 1973 War.

The findings of the committee of enquiry into Iraq and Libya called for a massive reorganisation of responsibilities within the intelligence community in Israel, with a proposal to give Mossad a much greater role at the direct expense of IDF Military Intelligence.[78] Israel has not seen proposals like this since the Agranat Commission's findings about the 1973 War were implemented. In truth, the much-vaunted Israeli intelligence services are at breaking point, and, in some areas, desperately short of good old human intelligence sources (both those turned from the enemy and Israeli agents working undercover in the Arab world). The popular image from cinema and television of superhuman Israeli intelligence carrying out James Bond style operations was in reality little more than myth-making. Indeed, the image of Mossad was severely tarnished during the 1990s due to a series of botched operations in the Middle East and Europe.

Mossad's internal sister organisation, Shin Beth, experienced difficulties in the Occupied Territories caused by the implementation of the early parts of the Oslo Accords that led to Israeli withdrawals from large parts of the West Bank and Gaza Strip. As a result of these withdrawals Israeli intelligence went blind. Palestinian sources dried up or disappeared from view altogether and it became much harder for Israeli agents (even Arab-looking Jews of Sephardic background) to operate in these areas. Successive Israeli governments had to some degree rely on Palestinian Authority sources or the CIA, which, following difficulties over the implementation of the Oslo Accords from 1996 onwards, started to play a much more active role in both the Gaza Strip and Palestinian Authority-controlled parts of the West Bank.

Arab and Israeli lessons from 1973: the shift towards a peace process

The 1973 War was a major turning point for both Israelis and Arabs alike. The Israeli feeling of military invincibility that had followed its victory in the June 1967 War had been broken. This was particularly true of the Israeli Air Force that had proved to be such a decisive factor in 1967, but had suffered very badly at the hands of the SAMs in 1973. As we have just seen, Israel's intelligence services, which play such a vital role in defending the country, were in disarray following their failures at the start of the War, and in truth, as we now know from current events, do not operate with the degree of success that their lofty image indicates. The War also was a major factor in leading to the end of the period of rule of the political elite who were drawn from the labour Zionist movement.

The defeat of the Israeli Labour Party in 1977 was caused by a number of complex factors, ranging from the alienation of the political leadership from the party and Israeli society and demographic shifts in Israeli society, to difficulties in managing Israel's economy.[79] To these long-term factors for decline we can add other short-term ones, such as poor electoral organisation, corruption and the formation of a new centre party, DASH, that took votes directly from Labour. At the very heart of the decline, however, was the failure of its political elite in 1973. The Agranat Commission of Enquiry did not call for either Golda Meir or Moshe Dayan to be removed from office, but the truth is that the bond that existed on security-related matters between large sectors of the Israeli population and the ruling elite had been broken. After

115

strong pressure from the public, Dayan resigned, as did Golda on grounds of ill-health. Their replacements, Yitzhak Rabin as Prime Minister, and Shimon Peres as Minister of Defence, inherited a difficult political situation and were able to do little to turn things around.

In Egypt, the War had quite the reverse impact upon the leadership. President Sadat portrayed the war as a political victory. Egyptian forces, he said, had regained their honour, and it had been his daring plan that had achieved this. The military outcome of the War, with Israeli forces deep into Egyptian territory, was largely glossed over for public consumption. Sadat, however, used the heavy defeat the Egyptian armed forces suffered as a pretext to help purge the army of key Nasserite personnel. As a result of the War, he not only strengthened his authority over the Egyptian public, but effectively was able to assert his full authority over the armed forces for the first time. The stopgap leader was here to stay. To outsiders from the Arab world all this might appear a little strange, for the scale of the defeat of both the Egyptian and Syrian armies was huge. Just as Nasser, however, in 1956 was able to present to his people the intervention of the imperial powers as having aided Israel, so Sadat could point to the massive US airlift of arms to Israel as having swung the tide of the War. Sadat, in short, had an excuse or seemingly rational explanation for the defeat of the Arab armies in 1973. Truth or exaggeration, it hardly mattered in a political culture which was characterised by conspiracy theories about Israel and the United States.

President Sadat used his increased authority to radically alter Egyptian foreign policy that had previously, during the Nasser era, centred upon its relationship with the

Soviet Union. As we have seen, the fact that Egypt was closely allied with the Soviet Union and Israel with the United States complicated any peacemaking efforts during the era of the Cold War between the two superpowers. Providing of course that he could strike the best deal for Egypt, Sadat concluded that Egypt's best interests lay with the USA. Central to Sadat's thinking was not, as many presume, making peace with Israel, but rather, dealing pragmatically in the international arena to best help deal with Egypt's increasing economic problems. The Soviet Union had made it clear that, while it remained relatively committed to military aid, it did not foresee writing off Egyptian debt or, indeed, offering much in the way of major new economic aid. Sadat, in truth, had started moving camps prior to the War – the expelling of the Soviet military advisors being the most tangible piece of evidence of his new thinking. After the War the pace of this process increased and, for the first time, the major Arab power of the day and Israel were both considered to be in the political camp of the United States. In peace-making terms this offered new prospects of a deal between Egypt and Israel, with the United States acting as both a mediator and paymaster in terms of agreeing the political and financial terms of the agreement. The latter of these roles arguably became the most important, with the United States being forced to make a permanent annual contribution to maintaining the peace agreement via its provision of economic aid to Egypt and military and economic aid to Israel. Today, the USA still supplies Israel with some $3 billion of aid ($1.8 billion military aid and $1.2 billion economic aid), and Egypt with nearly $1.8 billion, every year. Palestinian sources claim that the real figure of US aid to Israel is closer to $5.5 billion per year when other monies are taken into account, such as around $2 billion of loan guarantees given in 1997 to Israel (indirect aid) and funding from other US Federal agencies. This works out to around the USA giving Israel $15,139 each day. Just for the record, the Palestinians claim that the daily figure for Palestinian aid from the USA is a mere $569.[80] Though in terms of US aid to Israel it is worth noting that the $1.8 million in military aid comes with certain unofficial strings attached. Israel, in short, is expected to use this money to buy equipment from the American Military Industrial Complex. Israeli trade has become vital to the prospects of many parts of the US Military Industrial Complex, and therefore the aid really takes the form of a credit note for Israel to use with US companies.

Political upheaval in Israel
The Middle East has a funny habit of turning everything upside down just when you think all the actors and processes are in place for a real push towards some form of peaceful co-existence between Arabs and Jews. The election of Menachem Begin and the Likud in Israel's 1977 elections was not, in retrospect, a surprise. At the time, however, the electoral victory was viewed as an upheaval that moved Israel and the Middle East into new and uncharted waters. Outside of Israel, most observers took the view that the new Likud government made another regional war much more likely. Menachem Begin and the Likud assumed power in Israel for the first time after some 29 years in opposition, with what was thought to be an extremely hawkish agenda.

Those who looked a little closer at the time would have seen two grounds for optimism, however, from the perspective of peacemaking with the Arabs. The first of these concerned what to do with the West Bank, which Likudniks believed should be annexed and brought under full Israeli sovereignty. The West Bank, they argued, was part of 'Greater Israel', which drew heavily on religious legitimacy. In practical terms, this made the Likud (and its predecessor parties) opposed to any territorial compromise with either Jordan or the Palestinians that would involve sovereignty. Prior to the election, the Likud had attempted to play down this deeply-held ideological viewpoint and to emphasise a more pragmatic approach to these territories, largely to try to win the crucial centre ground voters needed to win elections in Israel. Despite fears that, once elected, a Begin government would switch back to an ideologically driven approach, it was clear that, much to the disappointment of many rank and file Likud members, the government would not attempt to annex the West Bank. The second concerned the appointment by Menachem Begin of Moshe Dayan as Minister of Foreign Affairs in the government.

As we have discovered before, Dayan could not be characterised as a lover of the Arabs. During his time in the Israeli army and in politics he had developed a reputation for being a hawk. He was, however, to coin a strangely Israeli phrase, 'a security hawk' – one who saw the strategic value of hanging on to large parts of the lands Israel had captured during the 1967 War. With the exception of David Ben-Gurion, who had passed away in 1973, and possibly Golda Meir, he was the most recognisable Israeli in the world. His distinctive eye patch and

119

confident manner made him a political hit in much of the world. His chances of becoming Prime Minister (a post for which he felt he was destined) were effectively ended, however, by the October 1973 War. Dayan had since fallen out with the Labour Party, and for the second time left to start a new party (the first was in 1965 with Ben-Gurion). The party had not proved to be a great success, and before Begin gave him the foreign ministry, his political career appeared pretty much over. Begin's chief motivation in appointing Dayan was therefore not political, but rather to reassure the outside world that there would be a degree of continuity in Israel's foreign policy and, in particular, its policies towards the Arabs.

The arrival of Begin and the Likud was viewed with deep concern by President Sadat. In 1975, Sadat and the then Israeli Prime Minister, Yitzhak Rabin, had been able to conclude an interim agreement on the Sinai – the first such agreement between Egypt and Israel, and generally viewed as a precursor to the signing of a full agreement on the Sinai within the parameters of an Egyptian–Israeli peace agreement. The arrival of Begin complicated the process. As an Egyptian official put it, as Begin took time to deal with all his ideological baggage and viewpoint of the concept of Israeli strength before moving towards a full peace agreement with Egypt. An understanding of the latter is an extremely important indicator of the Israeli mindset.

For Begin, strength for Israel lay in its military power, its ability to defend itself in a hostile neighbourhood from any type of attack. Peace would only come, as his political mentor, Vladimir Jabotinsky, argued, once the Arabs came to the conclusion that they could not destroy Israel by military force; and until the Arabs came to this conclusion,

Israel would have to live behind an Iron Wall. Added to the military concept was the idea that Israel had first to show the Arabs that economic sanctions and boycotts would not destroy the State either. Given that the Arabs, even after a crushing military defeat in 1967, had not come to the conclusion that they could not destroy Israel on the battlefield, this did not bode well for any chance of negotiations. Begin, however, for all his wrapping himself up in religious clothes, and his use of religious references and pretexts in his speeches, was essentially a security hawk – much closer to Dayan than to some in his own party. Begin took the view that, with the United States actively involved in diplomatic efforts to secure an agreement between Israel and Egypt, his government would have to become engaged in the process, but this involvement would stop well short of being pro-active in the diplomacy.

What Camp David told us about the Middle East?

The eventual outcome of the negotiations between Egypt and Israel were a victory of President Sadat's strategy of war and diplomacy, which he had conceived soon after assuming the presidency in 1970. It is worth reminding ourselves exactly what Sadat got out of the negotiations with Israel, and what he had to give up in return. In terms of the Sinai, after months of stalemate and weeks of diplomatic brinkmanship at the Camp David Summit hosted by President Jimmy Carter, Menachem Begin caved in and agreed to give back all of the Sinai, to dismantle Jewish settlements in the area, and to evacuate strategically important Israeli airbases as well. In effect, Israel agreed to simply give back all of the territory it had captured from

121

Egypt during the June 1967 War.[81] In return, Sadat became the first Arab leader to formally accept Israel's right to exist. The additional part of the Camp David Accords that dealt with the question of the Palestinians committed Israel, in theory, to implementing a limited degree of autonomy for Palestinians living in the West Bank and Gaza Strip. The signing of the formal peace treaty between Israel and Egypt took place the following year on 26 March 1979.[82]

For Sadat, the signing of the agreements with Israel brought Egypt fully into the camp of the United States. Back in Egypt, there was growing opposition to both the ties with the United States, and the peace agreements with Israel. Despite the favourable terms he had won from Israel there was unease about the extent of normalisation. The agreements had called for joint co-operation in many areas, ranging from medical research to education. The reluctance of many Egyptians to cross the divide and deal with Israel was soon apparent, particularly due to the lack of progress in implementing the Palestinian part of the agreement. Egyptian isolation in the Arab world was expected; its impact upon important sectors of the Egyptian population was severe. Sadat had touched a raw nerve by shattering the façade of Arab unity that was characterised by a total rejection of Israel's right to exist. Arab leaders charged that Sadat had weakened the Arab front against Israel, and that he had done little for Palestinian nationalist aspirations. Though there was a ring of truth about both charges, those doing the prosecuting were hardly great supporters of the PLO and the Palestinian fight for a state.

An outcast in the Arab world, and stung by criticism back in Egypt about his leadership, lifestyle and peace accords with Israel, Sadat became dangerously detached from Egyptian society and key political debates. He was assassinated in 1981 by radical Muslims who were opposed to his clampdown on religious extremism in Egypt. His legacy will always be that he was the first Arab leader to visit Israel (he did so in dramatic fashion in 1977), and the first Arab leader to agree to sign a formal peace agreement with Israel (1978). As a senior Egyptian official once told me, however, the trouble with Sadat was that he was no Nasser. There is a certain ring of truth to this statement, for Sadat, despite emerging as a strong Egyptian leader after the October 1973 War, was unable to convert this strength into leadership of the wider Arab world, a role Nasser had enjoyed for over a decade. Another official suggested that perhaps Sadat never succeeded in ruling over the Arab world simply because he was unable to screw his Arab enemies as well as Nasser did. However history remembers Sadat in the long-term, his decision to seek peace with Israel, for whatever motives, was the first real strategic decision taken by an Arab leader since 1948.

Meanwhile, in Israel, when Begin brought the accords back from America to the Israeli Knesset for ratification the criticism did not only come from the right in Israel, but also from the Labour Party.[83] Its leader, Shimon Peres, argued that Begin had returned Israel unnecessarily to the pre-1967 borders with Egypt, and this would have major ramifications for future negotiations. In the ratification vote Begin won the day, but many of his colleagues either abstained or voted against the Bill.[84] Subsequently, some members of the Likud moved to newly-created parties to the right of the Likud, and so the far or radical right in

Israeli political culture was born. For much of the rest of his period in office, Begin returned to a harder-line position towards the Arabs. After winning a bitterly fought, and at times violent, election in 1981, the second government of Menachem Begin was very different from the first, both in terms of composition and in policy. Two hawks, Ariel Sharon and Yitzhak Shamir, occupied leading positions in the Cabinet. Plans were laid for a change in military strategy, with Israel taking a more offensive posture in the region. Israel, in short, was to become more proactive rather than reactive. The link between Camp David and this new strategy is clear, in that peace with Egypt removed the need to commit large numbers of Israeli forces to its southern front. The phrase 'payback time' for the concessions made to Egypt would be putting it too simply, but there was a sense, certainly among Sharon and some senior figures in the IDF, including the Chief of Staff, Raful Eitan, that Israel should develop more grandiose schemes for securing peace with the remaining Arab states.

When strength becomes weakness: Israel's war with the PLO and Lebanon
At the heart of the strategy lay the deeply-held belief by Sharon and others that Israel's military strength, particularly in the light of Egypt's removal from the equation, meant that there was a military option to resolving the Palestinian issue. Maybe Israel's military ought to be used to defeat Yasser Arafat and the PLO once and for all. This, it was hoped, would force Palestinians living in the West Bank and Gaza Strip to develop their own leadership and cut a deal on largely Israeli terms (code for no Palestinian

124

state). From this thinking came the plans for Operation Peace for Galilee, known to the outside world as Israel's Lebanon War. Its impact on Israeli society and among key Israeli thinkers and planners was immense. The War, in short, led to levels of political polarisation in Israeli society not witnessed since the birth of the State in 1948, and led to a fundamental reassessment of the definitions of strength and weakness. The latter was to prove the starting point for the road to the signing of the Oslo Accords a decade later.

With the benefit of hindsight, Israel's plans for Lebanon were unrealistic in the extreme, and reflected a near total lack of understanding about the relationship between military and political strength. The plans also represent a classic case of a Western style democracy becoming too deeply involved in the murky world of a nation that was run, at the time, by warlords, drug traffickers and various ethnic leaders.

The context and background to Israel's Lebanon War lay in the location of a large number of PLO fighters in southern Lebanon, close to its border with Israel. The PLO units had relocated there after fleeing from Jordan in 1970 during what the PLO termed 'Black September'. In parts of southern Lebanon the PLO had effectively become a state within a state. The civil war that ravaged Lebanon during the mid 1970s had led to a breakdown in centralised control of the country. Lebanon came to be divided into zones controlled by different factions, with the divided city of Beirut at the heart of the problem. Several thousand PLO fighters were based in the capital city along with the PLO administrative headquarters, as well as Palestinian refugee camps called Sabra and Shatilla.

THE VIEW FROM THE FENCE

Tensions between the Palestinians and local Lebanese factions remained high, with atrocities being committed by both PLO fighters and local Lebanese militiamen.

From Lebanon, the PLO had been carrying out three major types of attack against Israeli northern towns, villages and kibbutzim. The first was the shelling of such areas, which at times forced many residents in the north of Israel to spend a great deal of time in bomb shelters. The second were cross-border raids, whereby PLO units would mange to cross the heavily fortified border – usually at night – in order to carry out attacks against Israeli civilians. Though many of these attacks were prevented, a number did get through, leading to moderate to heavy loss of Israeli life. The third were undertaken from the sea, whereby PLO units would sail from a port on the Lebanese side of the border and land in Israel in order to carry out either random attacks on civilians or attacks on pre-designated targets. Needless to say, the second and third forms of attack grabbed the most headlines and led to the heaviest Israeli retaliation.

The Israeli response to such attacks ranged from bombing raids by the Israeli Air Force, to shelling (from land and sea) and commando-style raids by Israeli Special Forces. Regarding the latter, in one typical attack an Israeli Special Forces officer dressed as a woman (none other than Ehud Barak – later to become Prime Minister), and several Arab-looking officers were dropped off in Beirut by navy boat in order to assassinate a PLO leader living in the city. In 1978, the Israeli Cabinet authorised 'Operation Litani' that was to prove to be a dry run for its full-scale invasion of Lebanon in June 1982. Operation Litani involved the IDF clearing an area of southern

Lebanon of PLO fighters, in effect pushing the PLO back and trying to make it more difficult for its units to shell and attack Israel's northern border. Following the successful conclusion of the operation, Israeli forces pulled back to the international border.

Part of Sharon and Eitan's thinking was to devise a 'Grand Scheme', whereby Israel would not only attempt to remove the PLO from the scene as a viable fighting force, but also attempt to end Syrian influence in Lebanon by helping to install a pro-Israel Christian Maronite government in Beirut, which would sign a peace deal with Israel. This in turn, it was hoped by Tel Aviv, would further weaken the negotiating position of President Asad of Syria, and reduce the regional influence of Syria's patron, the Soviet Union. The plan fitted with Israel's overall goals of negotiating with the Arab states in a bi-lateral rather multi-lateral fashion; and with the peace with Egypt relatively complete (Israel was still to undertake the final part of its staged withdrawal from the Sinai), it appeared a good time to turn its attention to another front-line Arab state.

Of course, Israeli tactics towards peace with Lebanon were very different to those employed with the Egyptians. Somewhat ironically, it had been Ariel Sharon whom Menachem Begin had called from Camp David about the dismantlement of the settlements in Yamit in the Sinai. Sharon gave his blessing to Begin and the deal was struck. With Lebanon, Sharon effectively intended to involve Israel directly in the internal politics of an Arab state and then try to impose a peace on the newly created Lebanese government. This loading of the cards ploy was to come disastrously unstuck. Even at the planning stage, the architects of the plan must have realised that it was, at best, a long shot. Prior to the War, Sharon and Eitan, as well as some elements of the Israeli intelligence services, were holding secret meetings with Bashir Gemayel, considered to be the most likely Christian Phalangist to emerge as a possible contender to lead Lebanon.[85]

Israeli planners could point to a number of regional and international factors, which at the time made the Grand Design appear a little more realistic. The first of these was the Iran–Iraq War, which was being fought on a huge front with enormous casualties on both sides. This war was taking much of the attention of the Arab League, which had been weakened anyway as a political instrument by its expulsion of Egypt. The Iran–Iraq War was also further exposing deep divisions within the Arab world, divisions that would reappear in the Arab world's response to the Israeli invasion of Lebanon. The importance of the election of President Ronald Reagan in November 1980 in the USA cannot be stressed deeply enough. Reagan was viewed by the Israeli government as being extremely pro-Israel, an opinion that was based on his statements while serving as Governor of California, and also speeches made during the 1980 presidential campaign.

The Israeli linkage between military might and political influence still appears today to be very crude. The recent example of American intervention in Iraq in 2004 is, in many ways, a similar illustration of this crudeness. In military terms, the US-led coalition was able to successfully invade Iraq in a relatively short space of time, suffering only light to moderate casualties in the process. Even Baghdad, which some observers felt had all the potential of a new Stalingrad fell quickly and without much of a fight. The USA, as we now know, has found life much harder in the phases of the operation after President Bush's declaration that the major stage of the military campaign was over. Indeed, the US-led coalition has sustained more casualties in the post-offensive period than during the invasion itself. The setting up of a democratic regime in Baghdad that is willing and able to protect western interests in the country has proved to be extremely problematic in a country that is deeply divided along religious lines.

Israel's plans for Lebanon were as ambitious as the US plans for Iraq. Israeli planners, however, had a problem; the United States Special Ambassador Philip Habib had pressurised both the Israeli governments and PLO leadership into agreeing a ceasefire along Israel's northern border with Lebanon.[86] What is more, the ceasefire appeared to hold, with both sides – with some exceptions – observing its terms. Israel, however, was waiting for the trigger to launch Operation Peace for Galilee, and the Palestinians soon provided one – though from an unexpected source. The Israeli Ambassador to the United Kingdom, Shlomo Argov, was shot and seriously wounded as he left the Dorchester Hotel in London. Suspicions immediately fell on the PLO, and Sharon brought his plans for the invasion of southern Lebanon before the Israeli Cabinet. Anti-Terrorist detectives in London soon discovered that the PLO was not behind the attempted assassination; rather, another Palestinian group, who were only really known for murdering other Palestinians – including members of the PLO – had carried out the attack. In Israel, this fact did not seem to matter as the invasion had been triggered.

THE VIEW FROM THE FENCE

It is worth recounting the events of Israel's complex 18 year war in Lebanon. The War started almost 15 years to the day after the start of the June 1967 War at 11 am on 6 June 1982 (the Cabinet had approved plans for a 40 km advance the previous evening), when the Israeli armoured units, together with close air support, crossed the border into Lebanon.[87] The Lebanon War came to dominate all aspects of Israeli political life between 1982 and 1984. It led to the resignation of Menachem Begin, and the architect of the War, Ariel Sharon, was forced to leave the Defence Ministry. The initial part of the fighting needs to be divided into four stages: the limited aim of the first 40 km advance forward into southern Lebanon, the push further north to surround Beirut (11 June onwards), the evacuation of the PLO from the city, and the massacres at Sabra and Shatilla Palestinian Refugee Camps (September 1982).

At first, it was not clear to Israelis, or to the outside world, if this was another operation along the lines of the Litani Operation of 1978. As previously discussed, the element of surprise is a favoured tactic of the IDF and had previously been used to good effect at the start of the Suez War in 1956. Israelis, however, soon began to realise the extent of the invasion. The residents of the north could see the tanks on their low-loaders on the way to the border, and growing numbers of reservists were called up. At first, there was a general consensus of support for the operation; Israelis believed that it would clear a 40 km zone of Lebanon and help secure Israel's northern border. There is a strong culture within all elements of Israeli society not to raise criticisms when the IDF are fighting.

On the military front, the Israeli advance was not without problems. The topography of much of southern Lebanon does not favour the invader and provides extensive cover for the defensive forces. One such example was the Beaufort Heights, at the top of which stands Beaufort Castle. Both the PLO and Syrian forces were well armed, and the former often operated from civilian areas, which made it difficult for Israeli armoured units and air power to be effective. The level of commitment and discipline of the PLO fighters in the area surprised the IDF, a fact that was to have a lasting effect on IDF planning strategies.

A central feature of the Israeli attack was to get to the Beirut–Damascus road and then turn eastwards in the direction of the Syrian border, in the hope that Syrian forces based in Lebanon's Beqa'a Valley would be in danger of being outflanked and return towards the Syrian border. Israel wanted to avoid a major confrontation with Syria that could spill over into the Golan Heights. In the end, though there were some direct clashes between the IDF and Syrian forces, they did not escalate into full-scale war. Much of this was down to President Asad who appeared reluctant to commit large-scale Syrian forces to the battleground, particularly after around 20 Syrian MiG aircraft were shot down by the Israeli Air Force, who also destroyed some 23 SAM missile sites in the Beqa'a Valley.[88] Israel, despite suffering serious casualties in heavy fighting taking the Beaufort Heights, achieved its first set of objectives within days. Speed was once more a vital factor in a Middle East war, as Israel moved quickly to prevent PLO reinforcements reaching the battle zone from the centre and north of Lebanon. It was at this stage that the Grand Scheme started to become apparent as Israel moved further north to surround Beirut. Publicly, Sharon argued that a longer-term solution to Israel's Lebanon problem was needed.

Back in Israel, opposition and concern were raised both from within the government and the opposition Labour Party. For the latter, this was a particularly difficult time – the Lebanon War was the first to be waged in Israeli history without the Labour Party in power. At times, the response by critics to the War seemed mixed and confused, due, in a large degree, to the lack of information that the Ministry of Defence was making available to the political elite, including apparently Begin himself. For much of the duration of the War the Knesset was in recess, but in appearances before the Knesset Foreign Affairs and Security Committee – that included Peres and Rabin – Sharon and Chief of Staff, Rafael Eitan, were evasive in their responses, at times misleading the Committee as to the aims and conduct of the War. The political consensus in Israel was broken for the first time during a war when the IDF entered Beirut. Some senior Labour leaders with a military background (notably Rabin) could not resist an invitation from Sharon to offer security advice to the Ministry of Defence.

In Lebanon a ceasefire was negotiated, which the IDF used to tighten its hold around Beirut. Mediation efforts took place to arrange the total evacuation of the 8,000 PLO fighters besieged in the city, along with some Syrian personnel. On 14 July 1982, the Lebanese government called for the removal of all foreign forces from Beirut, but the mediation efforts led by the USA were complex and drawn out. In Israel, the internal debate over whether

Israel should enter West Beirut had become bitter and acrimonious. Those against entry argued that the cost to the IDF and the civilian population of Beirut would be too great. Arafat, aware of the divisions in Israel, played for time in the negotiations. Heavy Israeli air raids and artillery attacks continued to apply pressure on Arafat to leave. On 4 August, Israeli forces completed the occupation of Beirut International Airport. On 12 August, in one of the heaviest attacks mounted by the Israeli Air Force, West Beirut was bombed for 11 hours, prompting the US President, Ronald Reagan, to call Begin and express his concern over the raids. At this stage, Menachem Begin issued an immediate cease-fire. In Israel, criticism of Sharon in the Cabinet grew to such an extent that he was isolated with only one minister supporting him. In the wider public, the debate on the justification of the War intensified, with Peace Now organising a series of anti-war rallies in Israeli cities.

The eventual evacuation from West Beirut of the PLO and Syrian forces took place under the supervision of a multi-national force in late August, and by the first week of September the evacuation had been completed. Arafat and his staff moved to Tunis, where they remained until his move to Gaza in 1994 following the signing of the Oslo Peace Accords. The remaining PLO fighters were evacuated to eight Arab countries. In Lebanon, Bashir Gemayel, the leader of the Christian Phalangists was elected President (he was the only candidate). However, on 14 September, before assuming office, he was murdered by a massive car bomb that destroyed the Phalangist Headquarters in Beirut. Bashir had many enemies who would have wished to kill him, but the indications are that

Syria and his Christian enemies were behind the massive car bomb. Following his death, his brother, Amin, assumed office. Amin, unlike his brother, did not favour any alliance with Israel.

Following Bashir's death, Ariel Sharon, with the Prime Minister's approval, ordered the IDF into West Beirut. The Israeli government announced that this was done to prevent revenge attacks and massacres. Sharon later admitted that the aim of the operation was to clear out the remnants of the PLO who were still hiding in West Beirut. He argued that around 2,000 fighters had stayed behind and that they were well supplied. Two days after the IDF entered West Beirut, Chief of Staff Eitan announced that all centres of West Beirut were under Israeli control and that the Palestinian refugee camps were surrounded. On 16 September 1982, Lebanese Christian Phalangist forces entered the refugee camps of Sabra and Shatilla. Their aim, according to the Israeli Ministry of Defence, was to root out the remainder of the PLO fighters who were thought to be fighting in the camps. Tragically, this was neither their aim nor their intention. For two days the Phalangists massacred anyone they came across in the camps. Israeli forces heard sounds of shooting, but presumed it to be the sounds of battle between the PLO forces and the Phalangists. On the morning of Saturday 18 September 1982, the extent of the massacre became clear, as aid workers and elements of the international press entered the camps. The scenes they found shocked the world. In Israel there were immediate calls for a State commission of enquiry and the resignation of both Begin and Sharon.

At first, both Begin and Sharon tried to resist the calls for such an enquiry, but pressure from within the ruling coalition, the Israeli opposition Labour Party, and the Israeli public left the government with little choice.[89] Public pressure culminated in a mass protest rally in Tel Aviv that was attended by some 400,000 Israelis (10 per cent of the total population), and remains the largest rally seen in Israeli history. The Kahan Commission, which had been set up to investigate events surrounding the massacres, took some four and a half months to deliberate on the events and decision-making leading up to the massacres.[90] The Commission published its report on 8 February 1983, and in its conclusions called for the resignation of the Minister of Defence and the removal of several military officials.[91] Though Begin carried out its recommendations, he retained Sharon in the Cabinet as Minister without Portfolio. Though Israel was not directly responsible for the massacres its lack of awareness of the dangers of unleashing the Phalangist forces in the camps was bordering on the idiotic. Furthermore, it became clear to Israel that the murdered Bashir Gemayel and his family did not have the kind of power base among the Phalangists or wider Christian population of Lebanon that Israel had thought. Bashir had also been hesitant about an alliance with Israel, and on the day of his death was contemplating other alternatives.[92] Israeli planners, including Sharon and Eitan, had looked for easy, clear-cut resolutions to Israel's problems with Lebanon, and once they believed they had found them in the form of Bashir, they constructed the plans for Israeli intervention in Lebanon around him. Today, there is growing evidence that Bashir, a charismatic and calculating leader, duped the

135

Israelis into supporting him during a series of secret meetings held in the late 1970s–early 1980s. It is argued that Bashir had little intention of ever openly forming an alliance with Israel, and little intention of signing a separate peace treaty with it.

Eventually, on 17 May 1983, an agreement was reached that would lead to withdrawal of the IDF from Lebanese soil, but under Syrian pressure the Lebanese reneged on the agreement.[93] What followed was a series of fruitless negotiations between Israel and the various groups in Lebanon, as Israel looked for new strategic partners in the country. The IDF had pulled back to the Awali River, principally to shorten the economic burden of the occupation and reduce the length of Israeli supply lines that were targets for attacks. Israel did not want its army to act as a policeman, standing between the feuding Lebanese factions. At the time, with the Syrians looking unlikely to withdraw their forces, a *de facto* partition of Lebanon existed between Israeli and Syrian forces with the central Lebanese government having little influence.

The 1984 Israeli elections were dominated by the debate over the Lebanon War. The National Unity Government that was formed after the inconclusive election result was led for the first two years by the Labour Party leader, Shimon Peres, a strong supporter of withdrawal from Lebanon. The Israeli Cabinet voted to withdraw from the vast majority of Lebanon on 14 January 1985. The decision was widely welcomed by an Israeli public that had become increasingly sceptical about any wider international deal to get the IDF out of Lebanon.[94] The 17 to 8 vote in the Cabinet was an illustration of the widespread belief that Israel's northern border could be protected by arrangements drawn up by the new Minister of Defence, Yitzhak Rabin, which included the setting up of a security zone inside Lebanon.[95]

How to lose friends and not influence people
Israel's problems in Lebanon, however, were far from over. Israel found it more difficult to extricate itself from Lebanon than it had done to mount a successful invasion. In the south of the country, the IDF had developed the infrastructure required to service its armed forces in the area such as military bases, new roads (complete with Hebrew road signs) and newly built prisons. These actions, together with Israel's intense security operations in the area, led the local – mainly Shi'a – population, many of whom had originally welcomed the IDF as a liberating force from the Palestinians and showered them with rice, to turn against Israel. The Shi'a population came to see the IDF as an army of occupation, and this coincided with an increase in the politicisation of the Shi'a population and the rise of Shi'a organisations such as Amal and Hezbollah. These developments had been largely overlooked by Israeli planners, who had placed too much emphasis on the Palestinian aspect of southern Lebanon, at the expense of understanding the needs of Amal and Hezbollah.[96] Consequently, Hezbollah, which is funded by Iran, but largely controlled by Syria, started a guerrilla-style campaign against Israel aimed at forcing it to leave Lebanese territory.

As a result, the Lebanon problem dogged every Israeli administration between 1985 and 2000. The withdrawal of Israeli forces and the setting up of the Security Zone in 1985 did not, as Yitzhak Rabin had hoped, solve the problem. On the contrary, it led to fears among the local population of a permanent Israeli presence in Lebanon, and an intensification of the conflict with Hezbollah. Between 1985 and 1999, Israel suffered on average around two dozen fatalities a year in Lebanon, along with several hundred wounded. A deep-rooted consensus still remained among the Israeli political and military elites – and for much of the time, within Israeli society – that the Security Zone, and the resulting cost to human life, was a price worth paying to secure Israel's northern border. The central argument appeared to be that it was better to effectively move Israel's *de facto* border with Lebanon further north than to allow Hezbollah to get any closer to the international border between Israel and Lebanon.

IDF forces were drawn more and more into patrolling the Security Zone, due to the failure of the Israeli-backed local militia, the South Lebanon Army. Syria, in turn, increasingly backed and controlled Hezbollah. The Syrian position, which one senior Israeli leader described as 'like something out of a Fellini film', was that Israel must withdraw from all Arab lands – including the Golan Heights – or be prevented from undertaking an orderly withdrawal from Lebanon. Lebanon became the stick that President Asad could use to apply pressure on Israel. This proxy war dragged on for nearly two decades, as successive leaderships in Israel argued that a unilateral Israeli withdrawal from Lebanon was too risky an option. This assessment was based on the number of casualties that the IDF might sustain during a withdrawal, and the ensuing uncertainty over the security of Israel's northern border.

Between 1985 and 1999, there were several dangerous escalations in the fighting between Israel and Hezbollah. In response to heavy fighting, the government of Yitzhak Rabin launched 'Operation Accountability' in July 1993.[97] In April 1996, Rabin's successor, Shimon Peres, launched the even less successful 'Operation Grapes of Wrath'.[98] From an Israeli perspective, both operations were far from successful in the long-term, but both Prime Ministers had little option but to instigate them, in the wake of increased Hezbollah shelling of towns in northern Israel. Indeed, by this stage, the fighting between Hezbollah and the IDF had changed character. Hezbollah were well trained, highly motivated and supplied with good quality weaponry. Their attacks, as a result, were becoming more daring and co-ordinated. Hezbollah filmed their operations, and within hours of the attacks the tapes were in the hands of Arab news agencies. Many of the tapes were shown on Israeli television, thus bringing the war directly into homes in Tel Aviv and other Israeli towns far removed from the fighting. These public relations coups came to play an important role in re-shaping Israeli public opinion towards supporting calls for a unilateral withdrawal from Lebanon that gathered pace from the mid 1990s onwards.

During the 1999 Israeli election campaign, Ehud Barak promised to get the IDF out of Lebanon within one year of assuming office, with or without the agreement of Lebanon or Syria. At the time, Barak's comments were treated with a degree of scepticism, given the fact that he was a product of the Israeli military establishment, which tends to be conservative in nature, and that he had played an active role in supporting the maintenance of the Security Zone. Critics suggested that it was merely an electoral ploy to win support from the increasing number of Israelis who favoured unilateral withdrawal from Lebanon. After assuming office, however, in the summer of 1999, Barak moved ahead with first trying to secure a regional agreement for Israeli withdrawal, and, when this failed, laying the plans for the unilateral withdrawal. In late May 2000, and with lightning speed, the IDF withdrew from Lebanon, completing the process in the early hours of 24 May.[99]

Israel's decision to leave Lebanon in 2000 reflected the realisation of the political and military elites in Israel that the country had failed to convert an initial military victory into a long-term political victory. The original aims of the invasion in 1982 were to remove the PLO from southern Lebanon (achieved within a few months), install a more favourable pro-Israel regime in Beirut (failed in 1982 and never tried again), and secure Israel's northern border from terrorist attack (failed because within a few months the PLO was replaced by Hezbollah). It took 18 years for Israel to formally withdraw, not because its leaders were slow to realise the situation, but because the alternatives to the occupation in the south were even less appealing both politically and militarily. The fact that Israel withdrew was more a reflection of the new consensus in Israeli society, and a feeling that Israel needed to assume the moral high ground even if that led to a long-term escalation of the conflict. Barak's decision would appear to have been vindicated in the year following the Israeli withdrawal. Despite many threats from Hezbollah, the northern border has been relatively quiet.

The lessons of strong and weak from the three wars
Conventional thought, as put forward by both Zionist and
Arabist writers, is that the June 1967 War (or Six Day War
as Yitzhak Rabin named it) was the most important in
changing the shape of the Middle East. Writers such as the
BBC journalist, Jeremy Bowen, suggest that the current
conflict between the Israelis and Palestinians is a direct
product of the events of 1967. On a superficial level such
writers are, of course, correct. This was the War in which
Israel captured the West Bank, the Gaza Strip, the Golan
Heights and the Sinai Desert. At a deeper level, however,
there is a strong case for arguing that the October 1973
War led to profound changes in Israel's and Egypt's
political and military thinking about the conflict. President
Sadat made peace with Israel, in part, as a result of the
1973 War – specifically the fact that the initial joint Arab
attacks on Israel had helped gain a degree of Arab military
honour. Israel developed new, more offensive, strategies as
a result of this War. The Grand Scheme of Sharon and
Eitan may, in retrospect, appear foolhardy to say the
least, but at the time it reflected a very new and aggressive
line of thinking in Israel, of taking the fight to the enemy,
rather than waiting on any border for the enemy to choose
the time and location of its attack.

If the October 1973 War proved to be the catalyst for
one last attempt by Israel to settle the Arab–Israeli conflict
by military means alone, then the Lebanon War was
merely the implementation of such strategies. Would the
Lebanon War have happened without the collective Israeli
trauma caused by the 1973 War? – the answer is almost
certainly no. Certainly not on the scale, and not with the
type of Grand Scheme which Sharon and Eitan were able

to put in place. Those looking for a starting point for the Oslo peace process and the direct negotiations between the Israeli government and the PLO need to look at the outcome of the Lebanon War. The Lebanon War was where Israel learnt, in a very painful way, the limits of its military might. From the initial stages of the War, it was faced with the fact that, despite inflicting heavy losses on PLO units, the international community – even when led by a very pro-Israel US President in Ronald Reagan – would step in in order to prevent its total destruction.[100] The PLO, in short, survived as a viable fighting force. True, its fighters were scattered around the Arab world, but its ability to hurt Israel remained in place. There were lessons for the PLO as well, who more and more came to see the military-only strategy in its struggle with Israel as unsustainable. Slowly, and only after a series of false dawns and bitter internal power struggles, a more pragmatic PLO emerged towards the end of the 1980s.

Finally, the Israeli withdrawal from Lebanon, which was conducted at night and at great speed (largely to prevent being ambushed by Hezbollah), created the impression that if an Arab army could make life as unpleasant as possible for the IDF, Israel would eventually pack up its bags and return to international borders. Though this is a gross over-simplification of events, it went down well in the Arab world. The Palestinian leadership were said to have used it as a rationale for launching the low intensity war with Israel in the Occupied Territories in 2000. Just as Vietnam, and possibly eventually Iraq as well, made the United States appear weak and vulnerable, so Lebanon made Israel appear disunited, war-weary and ready to settle with the

Arabs at almost any price. Though the reality might have been very different, sometimes in the Middle East perception about strength and weakness matters as much as the actual picture.

Ariel Sharon, in presenting his Disengagement Plan to the Knesset in October 2004 that contained plans for the Israeli withdrawal from the Gaza Strip, made reference to strength and weakness, stating that he was aware that some thought that disengagement would be interpreted as a shameful withdrawal under pressure, and would increase the terror campaign, present Israel as weak, and show that Israelis were unwilling to fight or to stand up for themselves.[101] Sharon went on to reject this idea, arguing that Israel, in reality, has the ability to strike at its enemies; but it remains to be seen how the Arab world come to view the withdrawal from Gaza. Sharon's comments rang contrary to Yitzhak Rabin's vision of a unilateral disengagement. Speaking in a major interview on Israeli television in December 1992, Rabin stated, in response to a question about Israel's future role in Gaza:

'To the best of my knowledge, any Israeli unilateral withdrawal under a reality of terrorism will be interpreted only as yielding to terrorism, and it will not put an end to it, but the opposite: it will increase terrorism. I believe in the following policy: yes to negotiations, to a severe war against terrorism, but no to withdrawal, not even one centimeter, if at all, without any agreement.'[102]

Though Rabin's comments were made in a different context, and without the kind of political pressure that Israeli deaths in 2001–3 placed Sharon under, they are nevertheless illuminating. Clearly the internal debate in Israel about strong and weak is far from resolved, and the Arab world will no doubt be watching with great interest. The withdrawal from Lebanon, and the forthcoming one from Gaza, were both undertaken without political agreement, in effect meaning that Israel got little in return for leaving Arab lands. This fact, whatever the reality, will be seen by the Arab world as Israeli weakness, and conversely a sign of Arab strength.

Notes:

[59] Memorandum from Nathaniel Davis of the National Security Council Staff to the President's Special Assistant (Rostow)/1//1/ (2 June 1967), Johnson Library, National Security File, Country File, Middle East Crisis, Vol. III. Top Secret; Nodis, Washington.

[60] Foreign Relations 1964–1968, Volume XIX, Arab–Israeli Crisis and War, 1967, 72. 'Memorandum for the Record/1/ Washington', (26 May 1967), Johnson Library, National Security File, Country File, Middle East Crisis, Miscellaneous Material.

[61] 'Memoranda of Conversations Between Secretary McNamara and Heads of State (Other than NATO)', Washington National Records Center, OSD Files: FRC 330 77-0075.

[62] Ministry of Foreign Affairs, Jerusalem, 'Message from Prime Minister Eshkol to King Hussein', (5 June 1967) MFA/1-2/16/XI/1947–1974.

[63] For an explanation of the actions of the Secretary General, see 'Report of UN Secretary General on the Withdrawal of the Emergency Force', (26 June 1967) A/6730/Add.3.

[64] For a balanced military account of the War see, M. Oren (2003), *Six Days of War: June 1967 and the Making of the Modern Middle East*, London: Penguin.

[65] Ministry of Foreign Affairs, Jerusalem (MFA), 'Resolution

Adopted by the Arab Summit Conference in Khartoum', (1
September 1967) MFA/1-2/31/XI/1947–1974.

66 (MFA), 'The Palestinian National Covenant', (17 July 1968)
MFA/1-2/33/XI/1947–1974.

67 Protocols of Nasser's meeting with President Al-Atasi of Syria
on 15 August 1969, and Nasser's meeting with King Hussein of
Jordan on 31 August 1969, published in A. M. Farid (1994),
Nasser: the Final Years, Reading: Ithaca Press, pp. 143–6. Also
the three sessions of the Quadrilateral Conference on 1–3
September 1969, pp. 146–152.

68 Ministry of Foreign Affairs, Jerusalem (MFA), 'Israeli
Government Statement on the United States Initiative', (31 July
1970) MFA/1-2/18/1947–1974/XII. See also, 'Israeli Cabinet
Reply to the United States', (4 August 1970) MFA/1-2/19/
1947–1974/XII.

69 (MFA), 'Israeli Cabinet Statement', (22 December 1969)
MFA/1-2/10/1947-1974/XII.

70 UN Security Council, 'Security Council Resolutions', (22
November 1967) S/242.

71 On legal and political aspects of Resolution 242, see M.
Mazzawi (1997), *Palestine and the Law: Guidelines for the
Resolution of the Arab–Israeli Conflict*, Reading: Ithaca Press,
pp. 199–238.

72 For attitudes towards the peace process with Israel since the
Madrid Peace Conference, see 'Interview with President Bashir
Asad', *Syria Times*, 15 December 2003.

73 C. Herzog (2003), *The War of Atonement: the Inside Story of
the Yom Kippur War*, London: Greenhill Books, p. 42.

74 *Ha'aretz Magazine*, 18 February 2005, pp. 8–12.

75 E. Kam (2004), 'Exceeding the Boundaries: the Parliamentary
Report on Israel's Intelligence System', *Strategic Assessment*, 7
(2), p. 7.

76 'The Committee of Enquiry into the Intelligence System in Light
of the War in Iraq', Report –Volume 1 (unrestricted section),
The Knesset Foreign Affairs and Defence Committee Report,
The Knesset, March 2004, p. 11.

77 *ibid.*, p. 19.

[78] *ibid.*, pp. 69–73.

[79] See M. Shalev (1992), *Labour and the Political Economy in Israel*, Oxford: Oxford University Press, pp. 285–90.

[80] Figures from the Palestinian Authority, Ministry of Foreign Affairs, based on a study by R. H. Curtiss: 'The Cost of Israel to U.S. Taxpayers: True Lies About U.S. Aid to Israel', *Washington Report on Middle Eastern Affairs*, 1997.

[81] Ministry of Foreign Affairs, Jerusalem (MFA), 'The Camp David Agreements, Annexes, Exchange of Letters', (17 September 1978) MFA/4-5/192/1977–1979.

[82] (MFA), 'Treaty of Peace between Israel and Egypt. Protocols, Annexes Letters'. MFA/4-5/251/1977–1979.

[83] (MFA), 'Statement to the Knesset by Prime Minister Begin on the Camp David Accords', (25 September 1978) MFA/4-5/200/1977–1979.

[84] (MFA), 'Reply by Prime Minister Begin in the Knesset at the close of Debate on Camp David Agreements', (28 September 1978) MFA/4-5/201/1977–1979.

[85] On the planning of the War and the thinking behind it, see (MFA), 'Interviews with Defence Minister Sharon in Ma'ariv and Yediot Aharonot', (18 June 1982) MFA/8/23/1982–1984.

[86] (MFA), 'Statement by Ambassador Habib on the Ceasefire', (24 July 1981) MFA/7/41/1981–1982.

[87] (MFA), 'Israel Cabinet Decision', (5 June 1982) MFA/8/3/1982–1984.

[88] (MFA), 'Excerpts from Press Conference with Defence Minister Sharon', (9 June 1982) MFA/8.10/1982–1984.

[89] (MFA), 'Statement in the Knesset by Defence Minister Sharon', (22 September 1982) MFA/8/83/1982–1984; *ibid.*, 'Statement in the Knesset by Prime Minister Begin', (22 September 1982) MFA/8/84/1982–1984.

[90] (MFA), 'Cabinet Communiqué on the Appointment of a Commission of Enquiry', (28 September 1982) MFA/8/86/1982–1984.

[91] (MFA), 'Report of the Commission of Enquiry into the Events at the Refugee Camps in Beirut', (8 February 1982) MFA/8/104/1982–1984.

92 For early signs of Bashir's thinking, see (MFA), 'Interview with Bashir Gemayel on ABC Television', (27 June 1982) MFA/8/35/1982–1984.

93 (MFA), 'Agreement between Israel and Lebanon', (17 May 1983) MFA/8/114/1982-1984. See also (MFA), 'Statements by Director General Kimche at the Two Ceremonies Marking the Signing of the Israel-Lebanon Agreement', (17 May 1983) MFA/8/115/1982–1984.

94 (MFA), 'Cabinet Communiqué on the Withdrawal from Lebanon', (14 January 1984) MFA/9-10/36/1984–1988.

95 For Rabin's rationale, see (MFA), 'Comments by Defence Minister Rabin on Israel Television (Mabat)', (14 January 1985) MFA/9-10/37/1984–1988. See also(MFA), 'Interview with Defence Minister Rabin on Israel Television', (17 February 1985) MFA/9-10/47/1984–1988.

96 (MFA), 'Interview with Minister of Defence Rabin in Yediot Aharonot', (15 March 1985) MFA/9-10/57.

97 (MFA), 'Statement in the Knesset by Prime Minister Rabin on Operation Accountability', (28 July 1993) MFA/13-14/93/1992–1994.

98 (MFA), 'Statement in the Knesset by Prime Minister Peres on Operation Grapes of Wrath', (22 April 1996) MFA/15/144/1995–1996.

99 (MFA), 'Defence Ministry Statement Regarding the Redeployment from Lebanon', (24 May 2000) MFA/18/116/1999–2001.

100 (MFA), 'Remarks by Ronald Reagan at the White House', (21 June 1982) MFA/8/28/1982–1984.

101 'Address to the Knesset by Prime Minister, Ariel Sharon', (25 October 2004).

102 Ministry of Foreign Affairs, Jerusalem, 'Interview with Prime Minister Rabin, Israeli Television', (14 December 1992) MFA/13-14/40/1992–1994.

5

The *Intifada*: The Rise and Fall of the PLO, and Israeli Responses

Getting the terminology right

The Arabic term *Intifada*, meaning 'uprising', is one of the most misused terms in the lexis of Middle Eastern vocabulary. The term itself has taken on a new meaning and use not normally associated with the word. Within Palestinian circles, it has been used as part of their narrative for two distinct periods of time: December 1987 to December 1992, and September 2000 to the present day. If we took the Palestinian leadership's use of the term at face value, then we would conclude that we were talking about two popular uprisings that had a degree of spontaneity and were organised from the bottom up. While this might have been the case in 1987, it certainly was not in 2000. The use of the term *Intifada*, therefore, is meant to lead us to believe that the blame for the uprising can be laid firmly at the door of the Israelis – after years of economic, political and military persecution the Palestinians snapped and started to demonstrate. Again, this may have been largely true in 1987, but was certainly not the case in 2000. We have to conclude, therefore, that the term is used for political purposes in order to mask what, certainly from 2000 onwards, has been a centrally orchestrated, low-intensity war by well-armed Palestinian groups against Israeli targets.

The post 2000 War, which some traditional Israeli scholars refer to as the Arafat War, was most probably, they argue, pre-meditated by the leadership of the Palestinian Authority. The use of the term *Intifada* in 2000 was merely a smokescreen to help shift the blame for the War away from Arafat towards the Israeli government. To be fair to Arafat and his lieutenants, this tactic was a resounding public relations success in 2000, as most non-Israelis immediately fell into line and started referring to either the Second *Intifada* or the Al-Aqsa *Intifada* in their dispatches, articles or books. From a Palestinian perspective, the latter of these terms is the best, as it implies that the violence started as a result of the walk by the then leader of the Likud opposition in Israel, Ariel Sharon, to the Temple Mount and the Dome of the Rock. This trip, undertaken by Sharon and his large entourage of Shin Beth bodyguards, was ill judged, to say the least; but to argue that it led to the start of the violence is both a highly simplistic and politically-coloured narrative of events. If Sharon was intent on antagonising someone that day it, was not the Palestinians, but rather his arch-rival for the leadership of the Likud, Benjamin Netanyahu, who was thought to be about to launch a leadership challenge against Sharon from the right. Sharon's walk was, in effect, a gamble to out-manoeuvre Netanyahu and prevent the former prime minister from trying to outflank Sharon from the right.

Last man standing: the Intifada *1987–1992*
Just as Israel's Lebanon War woke up important elements in Israel's political, economic and military elites to the fact that the country could not impose a military solution on the Palestinian issue, so the *Intifada* played an important role in shaping which Palestinians Israel would eventually have to talk with. Though the uprising lasted until the end of 1992, its significance was at its greatest during its initial months. From an Israeli point of view, the *Intifada* led to a substantial worsening of its image in the Arab world, the United States and in Europe. The nightly news programmes became dominated by images of Palestinians throwing rocks and stones and being shot or beaten up by Israeli soldiers. The mass Palestinian demonstrations that characterised the initial months of the uprising usually ended in running battles with Israeli soldiers who were trained for war, not riot control. Even many strong supporters of Israel felt a great deal of unease over what they were seeing. By controlling the West Bank and Gaza Strip, Israel may have moved the conflict away from its own centres of population, but the images being shown nightly on Israeli television caused a great deal of unease as well about the price of Israel's continued occupation of these lands.

The two key figures at the start of the *Intifada*, Yitzhak Rabin (then serving as Minister of Defence in an Israeli National Unity Government) and Yasser Arafat, were both far removed from the scene of events. Rabin was on a visit to Washington and Arafat was based in Tunis. The start of the uprising took both by surprise and neither initially understood the full impact of events, this despite warnings from the UN of growing unrest in the territories if no political progress was made.[103] Speaking in the Knesset some two weeks into the *Intifada*, Rabin still did not fully comprehend the true nature of the unfolding events in the West Bank and Gaza Strip. Rabin talked in typically bullish Israeli terms stating that Gaza and Hebron, Ramallah and Nablus were not and would not become Beirut, Sidon and Tyre. He went on to remind the Palestinians that Israel would fight with all its might against any element that attempted to, through violence, undermine Israel's complete rule in Judea, Samaria and the Gaza District.[104]

The catalyst for the start of the *Intifada* happened on 9 December 1987, when four Palestinian workers from the Gaza Strip were run over and killed by an Israeli truck. Rumours soon started to spread that the deaths were not accidental and, during the funerals, violent demonstrations broke out in refugee camps and other parts of the Gaza Strip, which soon spread to the West Bank. In response to the events, Rabin failed to cut short his visit to Washington, arguing that he had seen such events before and that his deputy could adequately deal with them. For Arafat and the other PLO leadership based in Tunis the events also came as something of surprise. In truth, a closer examination of the regional and international background would have revealed to both Rabin and Arafat just how probable this uprising had been.

Major diplomatic shifts had taken place earlier in the year that would, in the long-term, help bring Israel and the

PLO to the negotiating table. The first of these was what became known as the London Agreement, which was negotiated in January 1987 by the Israeli Foreign Minister, Shimon Peres, and King Hussein of Jordan. The Agreement called for there to be Palestinian elections in the territories, followed by an international peace conference sponsored by the United States and the Soviet Union. The results of such a conference would not, according to Shimon Peres, be binding on Israel – though here King Hussein appeared to beg to differ in the interpretation of the Agreement.

The major problem with the Agreement, and it was a large one, was that Peres had decided to negotiate in secret and had not informed the Prime Minister, Yitzhak Shamir, or the rest of the National Unity Government in Israel. Ignoring for a moment ethical questions about the legitimacy of Peres choosing to come to what was in effect a private agreement with King Hussein, the lone wolf style of negotiation appeared extremely naive for a politician famed for his political judgement and skill. It was hardly surprising, therefore, that when Peres announced the Agreement with the King to Yitzhak Shamir, he was horrified and instructed his Likud colleagues in the Cabinet to veto the plan.[105] The Israeli governing coalition, following the inconclusive elections in 1984, was a National Unity Government that included both the Likud and Shimon Peres's Labour Party. Due to the expanded size of the Cabinet, the key to policymaking (or not – as in this case) was the Inner Security Cabinet, which comprised ten ministers (five from the Likud and five from the Labour Party). It will come as little surprise to the reader that when the Inner Cabinet voted on the Agreement on 13 May 1987 it split 5:5 on the issue.[106]

152

In one of those key moments whose significance is only appreciated by politicians in hindsight, Peres had to choose between staying in the coalition, or forcing new elections at which the Labour Party would place the London Agreement at the top of their manifesto. For a number of complex reasons that centred upon fears over a speeding up in the settlement programme in the Occupied Territories if Labour left the coalition, and very real concerns over a leadership challenge from Yitzhak Rabin if the Minister of Defence found himself out of a job, Peres, after some debate, chose to remain in the coalition.[107] The London Agreement, as a result, was effectively consigned to the dustbin of history. King Hussein was said to be furious about the failure of the Israeli Cabinet to approve his agreement with Shimon Peres.

Whatever the reasons, the political vacuum, the continuing inertia in the Israeli government over the Palestinian issue, and worsening economic conditions led many Palestinians to believe that they had little to lose. Consequently, the killing of the four Palestinians in what looked like an extremely sad, but typical, road accident, lit the fuse wire that led to first violent funerals. Unlike in previous outbreaks of violence during such events, this time the demonstrations and violence increased in the subsequent days and weeks. During the initial weeks and months of the uprising, Rabin tried to crush it by using strong-armed tactics. There was a lack of understanding in Israel about the political dimension to the violence and it was really only at the end of the first year of the *Intifada* that the Israeli government fully understood what was going on.

Tensions, divisions and new movements: Palestinian politics during the Intifada

For Arafat and the PLO, events in the West Bank and Gaza Strip were welcome in terms of damaging Israel's public image in the world – pictures of Israeli soldiers shooting stone-throwing Palestinian youths made for good television the world over. Within a year of the start of the *Intifada*, the PLO pushed home its diplomatic advantage over Israel by publicly announcing that it accepted a two-state resolution to its conflict with Israel, and that it renounced violence and would seek such a state through diplomatic means only. As we saw in the previous chapter, this decision was very much the product of Israel's Lebanon War.

Prior to Arafat's declaration, King Hussein, frustrated at the Israeli failure to embrace the London Agreement and the lack of diplomatic progress in general, announced on 31 July 1988 that Jordan was ending all its territorial claims on the West Bank, which it had run from 1948 to 1967. The King's actions meant that Israel would no longer have a chance of finding a solution to the Palestinian issue through Jordan. Israel would now have to seek a resolution to the Palestinian problem by talking to the Palestinians directly, a fact that took some time to dawn on the Israeli leadership.[108] In short, by removing his claim on the land, the King made the creation of a Palestinian state more likely. The short-term impact of the King's decision among Palestinians, however, was extremely negative. Most now sensed that there was little opportunity for any political progress in the foreseeable future. With the King removed from the scene, and with an Israeli government that had caught a heavy dose of inertia, things in the West Bank and Gaza Strip were becoming desperate.[109]

The internal PLO debate between the second part of 1982 up to the announcement of its acceptance of the two-state solution in 1988 was extremely bitter, with those wishing to maintain the old ideological position of wishing to destroy the State of Israel increasingly matched by pragmatists who saw a two-state solution as the best means to securing some type of state. There were other divisions among the pragmatists, notably on whether the establishment of such a state would mark the end of the conflict or serve merely as the end of part of a phased strategy to create a single Palestinian state. Such debates, however, were kept away from the public and the media. Only when it became clear that the pragmatists were in the ascendance over the ideologues did Yasser Arafat finally commit to their viewpoint. This was, of course, a vintage example of the Arafat leadership strategy of wait and see what is going to happen and only then attach his badge to that cause.

If the pragmatists thought that Yasser Arafat standing up at the General Assembly of the United Nations and making the announcement in dramatic style would lead to an immediate opening of doors they must have been sorely disappointed. The outgoing administration of President Ronald Reagan remained extremely distrustful of Arafat and the PLO, and was slow to respond to the initiative, though it did call for the State Department representatives to enter into a substantive dialogue with the PLO.[110] This was particularly true about the announcement of the renunciation of violence, towards which the USA, under strong Israeli pressure, appeared to adopt a wait and see strategy. A letter from outgoing Secretary of State, George Shultz, confirmed, however, that despite all the misgivings about the sincerity of the PLO, the USA was entering into a dialogue with the PLO which would bring Arafat into the diplomatic fold.[111] In Israel, Arafat's speech had not gone down well. Prime Minister Shamir called it the great deception and moved to lobby the international community not to deal with the PLO.[112]

Among the local West Bank and Gaza Strip Palestinian leadership there was some resentment that Arafat appeared to be negotiating on their behalf without proper consultation – and who was he anyway to agree to a two-state solution? Among the 1948 Palestinian refugees and their descendents, there was deep concern that Arafat had just abandoned them by, in effect, accepting Israel's right to exist. In response to the fears of the refugees, Arafat followed up his UN speech with speeches in Arabic, which stated that he would never give up the right of return for such refugees, and that his concessions to Israel were merely tactical, made in order to gain the diplomatic initiative. Arafat's tactics on making a conciliatory speech in English and following it up with a couple of speeches in Arabic in which he outlined the Palestinian maximalist position became a typical feature of this period, and, more importantly, during the period of the Oslo Accords. Back in 1988, the Reagan Administration were quick to pick up on the discrepancies in Arafat's various speeches, and this further slowed down his entry to the White House and American acceptance of a PLO role in its Middle East diplomatic efforts.

In 1988, on a strategic level, the uprising posed nearly as much a threat to the PLO leadership in Tunis as it did to Israel. One of the greatest fears of the PLO-in-exile was always the emergence of a strong, well-organised and heavily supported local West Bank and Gazan Palestinian leadership. Such a leadership could present a viable alternative partner for negotiations for an Israeli leadership that was still intent on talking to anybody other than Arafat. Conversely, the *Intifada* also provided an opportunity for Arafat, as it soon became clear that if the uprising was to be maintained, it would require money and political organisation. While the local Palestinian leadership had proved itself to be efficient in terms of maintaining the initial impetus, it was clear that they lacked the support structures to keep it going indefinitely. Arafat and the PLO leadership decided that they would have to assume direct control over the *Intifada* and moved to put their own people on the ground in the West Bank and Gaza Strip. This, of course, led to tensions between these agents of Arafat and the local leadership, but it was the former who controlled the purse strings and the necessary political training, and were able to direct events.

The schism between the PLO Tunis Brigade and the local Palestinian leadership is important in understanding domestic Palestinian politics, not only during the era of the first *Intifada,* but also during the Oslo peace process, when the majority of the Tunis leadership moved to the Gaza Strip and West Bank to assume senior positions within the political, economic and military structures of the Palestinian Authority. Often their appointment blighted the career prospects of local Palestinians who, by the end of the Arafat era, were growing increasingly resentful about this process – particularly as many members of the Tunis Brigade were seen as not being very effective in the positions they had been given. When Arafat died in 2004, it was noticeable that the old guard from Tunis moved quickly to select a candidate to replace him, before the local leaders had a real chance to put forward one of their own leaders as a serious candidate. It should be noted that many of these home-grown leaders are not well known outside Palestinian circles – they do not seek, nor are they sought out by, foreign journalists, who prefer a high profile interview with one of the big names from the Tunis Brigade. With the exception of Marwan Barghouti, who is currently in an Israeli jail, other members of the home-grown Palestinian leadership have had to attach themselves to a leading member of the Tunis Brigade for patronage and career advancement.

In completing this picture of the changing Palestinian domestic political scene from the uprising onwards, it is important to mention the non-secular groups or movements – most notably Hamas. To a certain degree, the development of Hamas fits in with the sense of unease over the PLO-leadership-in-exile we have just outlined. Hamas was founded essentially by local Palestinians who had grown tired of the PLO or who, for religious reasons, did not wish to submit themselves to the more secular brand of Palestinian nationalism espoused by the PLO. Given what came later during the Oslo era, it might appear strange to learn that Israel initially helped fund Hamas. The Israeli Minister of Defence, Yitzhak Rabin, sensed an opportunity to employ the old trick of divide and rule in the Occupied Territories. Israel's aim was, therefore, not to build a powerful Islamic movement among the local Palestinian community, but rather for Hamas to act as a check on the growing direct influence of the PLO leadership in Tunis in the Occupied Territories during the *Intifada*. It should be made clear, however, that Israel was never the major sponsor of Hamas. That position was occupied by the oil-rich Saudi Arabians (both state funding and generous sponsorship from shadowy Saudi individuals).

The leadership of Hamas saw an opportunity to develop support across the Occupied Territories by employing a tactic used heavily by the labour Zionist movement during the British Mandate in Palestine. This involved the development of strong 'dependency ties' between the movement and the local population, which could be translated into political support. With Saudi funding, Hamas was soon able to create an infrastructure of social services ranging from hospitals to schools, whose standards were much higher than the existing levels of social services. Many Palestinians soon became heavily reliant on such hospitals and voiced their support for the political movement. From an outsider's perspective, what made this process all the more interesting was the fact that the vast majority of Palestinians were secular in nature and did not adhere to the more radical forms of Islamic teachings that Hamas espoused. Over the years, Hamas has taken on an interesting characteristic, whereby its leadership is much more committed to the cause of radical Islam than its supporters, who are more interested either in social services, or, in more recent years, its public rejection of the Oslo peace process and Israel's right to exist.

The development of Hamas in the Occupied Territories, and its funding by Saudi Arabia during the *Intifada*, caused anxieties in both the Egyptian and Jordanian leaderships. Both President Mubarak and King Hussein of

Jordan feared an Islamification of 'Palestine', and showed a much greater willingness to engage in the peacemaking. Both leaders were concerned that the rise of a populist Islamist movement in the West Bank and Gaza Strip would have ramifications for their own rule. Mubarak, while not under direct threat from such groups, foresaw such a development leading to increased tension in Egypt. For King Hussein, the threat was much more real and direct. Hamas was not only making gains in the Occupied Territories, but in Jordan as well. Both Mubarak and Hussein, as a result, swallowed hard and started to re-engage with the PLO and Yasser Arafat. Make no mistake: there was still no hiding their respective dislikes of Arafat, and vice versa; but all three leaders found common ground in moving to check and weaken Hamas.

From the outset, Arafat's relations with Hamas and his strategy for dealing with it were complex, and when Arafat moved to Gaza as part of the Oslo Accords in 1994 the relationship became even foggier. What is clear is that Arafat, from an early stage, attempted to avoid direct confrontation with the Hamas leadership. Unsurprisingly for a man as politically sharp as Arafat, he sensed that Hamas was, in effect, serving a purpose or a role in his own long-term strategy. Arafat, to be precise, was acutely aware that the Western powers, the front-line Arab states, and, yes, even Israel, preferred the secular PLO to Hamas. At the start of the 1990s when Hamas commenced military operations against Israel, Arafat was quick to exploit the relative quiet from PLO units as proof that he was a more reliable partner than Hamas. The real story of Hamas's involvement in the Arab–Israeli conflict does not begin until the signing of the Oslo Accords, when its relationship with the PLO and Israel disintegrated to new lows.

Shifting to the right: increasing divisions in Israel
The *Intifada* led to two important political shifts in Israel. In the short-term it led to a marked shift towards parties of the right, including the parties of the far right – some of whom supported the idea of the transfer of the Arabs out of the Occupied Territories. The question of transfer had always been an issue for those on the margins of Israeli democracy, but its support here said much about the degree to which many Israelis felt threatened by the violence in the Occupied Territories. The medium-term impact of the *Intifada* on Israel was that it led to an increase in support in general for the parties on the edge of the political scale: far left and far right. The support for such parties was especially strong among young first-time voters, who appeared to favour some type of solution to the problem of the Occupied Territories – the far left wanted to give them back, and the far right wanted to keep them and get rid of the Palestinian Arab population living in them.

Just as the 1984 Israeli elections had been dominated by the issue of the Lebanon War (and Israel's spiralling hyper-inflation), so the decisive issue of the 1988 campaign was the *Intifada* and the wider question of the future status of the Territories. In a close run race the Likud won. The Prime Minister, Yitzhak Shamir, decided to form yet another National Unity Government, but this time the Labour Party was a junior and not a full partner.[113] Internal tensions within the ruling coalition were never far from the surface, especially during times when Israel

161

attempted to become a little more pro-active in its diplomatic efforts. The development of the major Israeli peace initiative during this period, the Rabin–Shamir Plan of 14 May 1989, illustrated these internal tensions.[114] The Plan – also known as the Shamir–Rabin Plan (depending on your political loyalties) – was like something out of a Shakespearian tragi-comedy. As Labour and Likud ministers fought among themselves, it appeared at times that Israel had two quite separate governments, with very different agendas, and to some degree this was the case. Perhaps if they had listened to the total rejection of even the most Palestinian-friendly version of the Plan by the PLO, they could have saved a lot of time and trouble. Things really were that bad.

The peace initiatives put forward by President Mubarak of Egypt on 11 September 1989,[115] and by the US Secretary of State James Baker on 1 November 1989,[116] brought matters in the National Unity Government to a head, with the US-sponsored plan leading to the eventual collapse of the government in Israel in March 1990. The Likud was concerned that the US administration was trying to move the National Unity Government too far from its agreed positions. Shamir, who had supported the Rabin–Shamir Plan, was against the two external initiatives, strongly arguing that no Palestinian representatives from East Jerusalem be allowed to take part in the Palestinian electoral process that was to precede formal negotiations.[117] Shamir feared that by agreeing to such a demand, he would in effect be putting the future status of Jerusalem on the table for negotiation.

Yitzhak Rabin attempted to find a compromise formula that allowed Palestinians from East Jerusalem to take part in the process but not vote. Shamir, however, rejected the compromise, a decision that led Rabin to conclude that there was little point in remaining in the government. In a last-ditch attempt to solve the crisis, the Minister of Foreign Affairs, Moshe Arens (Likud), came to a private agreement with Secretary of State Baker. They concluded that Israel would consider the Palestinian participants on a name-by-name basis, and accept that the list would include people who were not officially resident in Jerusalem but who merely had a second address there. When Arens took the plan to Shamir he rejected it out of hand and this proved to be the final nail in the coffin of the National Unity Government, and, as it turned out, any chance of progress in Israeli–Palestinian negotiations for over two years.

Eventually the seemingly inevitable happened, and the coalition collapsed when Shimon Peres and the other Labour Ministers left; with the help of the Ultra-Orthodox party and movement, Shas, they were able to bring down the government during a vote of no confidence in the Knesset. Then after weeks of tense, bitter and financially costly negotiations, just as Shimon Peres was about to present a new governing coalition, with himself and the Labour Party at the helm, it all fell apart, as Shas withheld its support in a vote of confidence tabled to ratify the new coalition, as did another religious party. In one of the darkest periods for Israeli democracy, Rabbis – one of whom did not even live in Israel – had effectively given instructions to scupper Peres's coalition. Instead, the Israeli President, Chaim Herzog, turned to the Likud and within a couple of weeks, on 8 June 1990, Israel had its most hawkish coalition ever, with the Likud joined in government by the religious parties, and, for the first time, the parties of the far right.[118] As one sulking Labour party official suggested, 'the Likud made this mess: let them clear it up instead of coming to us to do it for them.'

So what use are the buffer zones now? The Persian Gulf War and question marks over the value of the Occupied Territories

From an Israeli perspective, the Iraqi invasion of Kuwait on 2 August 1990 postponed the inevitable clash between the new Shamir government and the international community, particularly the US administration. Saddam Hussein's invasion deflected attention away from the Palestinian issue, and even two such divisive events as the killing of 19 Palestinians by Israeli Border Guards at the Temple Mount in Jerusalem (8 October 1990)[119] and the assassination of the extreme Jewish Kach Party leader, Rabbi Meir Kahane, (5 November 1990) received scant international attention, due to the impending war in the Persian Gulf.

The period following the Iraqi invasion and prior to the Allied attacks was dominated by two key factors: international diplomatic efforts to avoid the War, and growing US pressure on Israel to stay out of the conflict, even if attacked. For his part, Saddam Hussein made crude attempts to link an Iraqi withdrawal from Kuwait to an Israeli withdrawal from the lands it captured in 1967. There was concern among the Israeli elite, especially Yitzhak Rabin, that the USA may, as he speculated, 'try to buy off Saddam using Israeli currency'. By this he meant that the USA would, in return for a deal to get Iraq out of Kuwait, be willing to apply more pressure on Israel to withdraw from the Territories it had captured during the June 1967 War.

This linkage proved to be extremely popular among Palestinians who, in general, were supportive of the Iraqi invasion on Kuwait. This support had little to do with the Arab–Israeli conflict, and was based on the poor treatment of tens of thousands of Palestinians who worked in Kuwait by the Kuwaiti authorities. The Palestinians, like other foreign workers in Kuwait, were denied any form of Kuwaiti citizenship, which would have brought immense benefits in the form of health care, housing and education. The Kuwaitis had a very low regard for these Palestinian workers, who tended to be employed in menial jobs such as rubbish collection. With the exception of Israel, Kuwait hosted more Palestinian workers, desperate to find work and send payments back to their loved ones in the West Bank or Gaza Strip, than any other country. Sectors of the Palestinian economy were highly dependent on such funds being subsequently spent in shops and markets, though it should be stressed that there is a downside to this, with the economy more vulnerable to loss of jobs and wages during times of external political crisis.[120] The Palestinians in Kuwait, therefore, greeted the Iraqi soldiers as liberators (a fact that would come back to haunt them when the Iraqis were driven out of the country and the local population took their revenge, killing many Palestinians; many more still remain unaccounted for in Kuwait City).

In Israel, the public had to get used to carrying newly issued gas masks wherever they went. Saddam Hussein's promise of chemical weapons raining down on Tel Aviv was taken seriously. For many young Israelis, the cases for the masks became fashion accessories, to be decorated in chosen styles; but for many older residents the masks were a terrible reminder of the horrors of the Second World War. For their part, Israel's leaders let it be known that any use of chemical weapons would be seen as crossing a red line, and that Israel would respond with a tactical nuclear strike on Iraqi targets. In the same way as the threats of Nasser and Radio Cairo had had a profound impact on the Israeli national mood in the 1960s, so the threats from Saddam Hussein had much the same impact. In 1990, this feeling of depression was compounded by an Israeli sense of exasperation at Palestinian support for Saddam Hussein – and, in particular, the glowing endorsement offered by Arafat and the PLO of the Iraqi invasion. Even the left in Israel – who were calling for direct talks with the PLO – were taken aback by Arafat's actions. In their eyes, he appeared to have come so far and then regressed into his old hard-line ways. For Arafat, however, his support for Saddam Hussein proved to be disastrous and almost led to the bankruptcy of the PLO.

Israel braced itself for a new kind of warfare: one in which its coastal cities and population centres became the front-line for the first time. The War was the first of the high-tech era – smart missiles that could fly for several hundreds of miles before landing more often than not on target. The only consolation for Israeli planners was that the Iraqi SCUD missiles would be right at the end of their range over Tel Aviv, therefore their accuracy was thought to be poor. As it turned out, this factor proved to be of vital importance, with many Iraqi missiles landing in unpopulated areas in the desert.

Away from the media spotlight, and the ongoing international diplomatic efforts, the Israeli Prime Minister Yitzhak Shamir held a secret meeting with King Hussein near London, the outcome of which changed the course of the War. The meeting took place on 4–5 January 1991 at the King's private residence.[121] Three top Israeli officials accompanied Shamir. The King outlined his dilemma of why he was driven to publicly support Saddam Hussein, his lack of trust in the Iraqi leader, and his fears that a war would be a disaster for Jordan. He responded to detailed questions from the top Israeli military official, Ehud Barak, and reassured Israel that he would not let a third party (Iraq) use Jordanian territory to mount attacks against Israel. In return, Shamir promised the King that Israel would not use Jordanian sovereign territory to launch attacks against a third country (both land and air space). As any attack by the Israeli Air Force on Iraq would have to fly over Jordan, Shamir was in effect severely limiting his hand to respond to any Iraqi attacks on Israel. Shamir did not inform the USA of the outcome of the meeting, a deliberate oversight to ensure that the USA continued to lobby Israel to stay out of the potential war. In effect, Shamir wanted to extract the maximum political and economic price possible from the USA for Israeli restraint.

The War started on 17 January 1991, when the Coalition forces' aircraft attacked Iraqi targets. On the following day Iraq launched eight SCUD missiles at Israel with varying accuracy. Though they caused extensive damage to property, Israeli preparations meant that casualties were minimised. Some residents of Tel Aviv and the coastal plain simply left their homes and went to Eilat or even to Jerusalem which was thought to be safe. Saddam would not

167

risk bombing the holy city. The majority who stayed spent nights in bomb shelters wearing their gas masks and listening to news broadcasts.

The missiles that landed were of a conventional nature and this continued throughout the War. From the outset, pressure was applied on Shamir from two different directions. President Bush called and asked for continued Israeli restraint, as did James Baker and US Secretary of Defence, Dick Cheney. The USA was becoming increasingly alarmed that any Israeli action would lead to the withdrawal of the Arab forces from the Coalition before the ground offensive had even started. To help bolster Israeli defence systems, the USA rushed batteries of ground-to-air Patriot missiles to Israel to shoot down the incoming missiles. This was done more to reassure the Israeli public. Indeed, an Israeli report published after the War concluded that, at most, the Patriot batteries had been successful in shooting down one missile and the Patriots themselves had caused collateral damage as they fell to the ground.

From within the Israeli Cabinet, Shamir came under intense pressure to make a military response to the Iraqi attacks. Leading hawks such as Ariel Sharon and Rafael Eitan, both ex-military men, argued passionately that such a response was vital to the long-term system of Israeli deterrents. Even more moderate forces such as Minister of Defence, Moshe Arens, favoured a response. Shamir argued that Israel was gaining much sympathy from the USA and the international community, and that Israeli forces could not do anything that the Coalition forces were already doing in Western Iraq.[122] Shamir's decision not to retaliate proved to be extremely popular with the Israeli electorate, with around three-quarters of them supporting the policy.

Members of the Israeli Cabinet were not aware of Shamir's commitment to King Hussein. At times, Shamir had to relent and order that missions be prepared, but low cloud over Iraq meant that the Israeli Air Force was not able to commence such sorties. The swift success of the Coalition ground offensive against Iraq meant that Israel was not subjected to a longer-term threat of attack, thus making Shamir's restraint appear all the more prudent. There was, however, disquiet in both the Israeli military and political leaderships that the USA had, in effect, allowed Saddam Hussein to remain in power, and that the Coalition forces had not gone on to Baghdad.

Following the ending of the War, Shamir's popularity both at home and abroad soared. He was able to negotiate a substantial compensation package from the USA for damage to Israeli property and lost earnings during the War. His political opponents in Israel from the left had been placed in a difficult position by the PLO support of Saddam Hussein during the crisis. Prior to the Iraqi invasion, there were signs of a growing realisation within the Israeli left and centre-left that Israel would have to talk with Arafat and the PLO, particularly given the failure of the London Agreement and the withdrawal of Jordan's claim of the West Bank. By the end of the War this appeared to have been rather hasty. The feelings of the left at the time were perhaps best summed up by the darling of the Israeli left, Yossi Sarid, who told the Palestinians, 'don't call us; we will call you.'

The Persian Gulf War was very different from Israel's previous wars. No IDF personnel took part in it; Israel did not fire a shot in anger, but rather relied on the efforts of

169

others to prevent attacks on Israel. Two of the strands of Israeli military doctrine were broken: the use of retaliation, and self-reliance on security issues. The Persian Gulf War became Israel's first television war, with round-the-clock coverage on the cable networks. As a result, public relations and getting the message across became almost as important as the attacks themselves. Fortunately for the government, it had a telegenic spokesman in Benjamin Netanyahu, who put Israel's case to the world.

In the longer-term, the War had a strong impact on the arguments that both the doves and the security hawks used to support their positions on the future status of the Territories. The doves argued that the maintenance of buffer zones using the West Bank did not stop the missiles from reaching their targets. The security hawks argued that, without the West Bank under Israeli control the Iraqis may have been more tempted to move troops westwards through Jordan and pose a direct threat to Israel's eastern borders. It is also clear that no fence would be able to stop the threat of missiles. Opponents of the Security Fence argue that its use is one-dimensional, in that it is designed only to stop attacks from Palestinians, which, they argue, will be very short-term. The medium-to longer-term picture is much more likely to be dominated by missile threats to Israel, either from hostile states or, increasingly from terrorist groups that have acquired WMDs or chemical weaponry. The fence, they argue is not worth the cost and Israel should be investing more in missile defence shields.

For the Palestinians, the War had proved to be a complete disaster. Arafat and the PLO's support of Saddam Hussein meant that the PLO had backed a leader which the vast majority of the Arab world went to war against. King

Hussein of Jordan had shown a great deal of political skill in manoeuvring his way around, given the extremely difficult position the War put him in – though it would still take years, and extensive lobbying on his behalf by the Israelis, for America to forgive him and end his diplomatic isolation. Arafat, in truth, had been dealt an equally difficult hand, given Saddam Hussein's undisputed popularity among Palestinians, and his albeit crude attempts to expose Western hypocrisy over his actions in Kuwait and Israel's in the Occupied Territories. Arafat, of course, lacking the subtlety, bravery and political nuance of the King, had blundered his way through the crisis, managing to alienate even many who were well-disposed to his cause. The result was that by the end of the War, the PLO was in its weakest position politically and economically since its creation. There were increasing signs of challenges to Arafat's rule and authority, but he was probably saved by the lack of a viable alternative at this stage. The only Palestinian beneficiary of the War was Hamas, which, as the economic well-being of the PLO nose-dived, gained many new Palestinian supporters who were desperate to use its Saudi-sponsored social services. Also, as an indirect punishment for the PLO, wealthy Saudis increased their contributions to Hamas. There appeared a real chance that Hamas would one day supercede the PLO as the major political force among Palestinians living in the Occupied Territories.

From Madrid to Oslo: learning the meaning of 'never say never'
In the months that followed the end of the War, the USA started a process of intense diplomatic activity aimed at

using its military victory over Iraq as a basis for developing a political solution to the Arab–Israeli conflict. The chosen mechanism for achieving this aim remained an International Conference and direct talks between Israel and the Arab states. Between March and October 1991 the US Secretary of State, James Baker, visited the Middle East eight times, shuttling between Jerusalem and the Arab capitals, and employing his considerable Texan charm to persuade the various leaders to attend. Baker's major political asset was the strength of the USA, which, following the collapse of the Soviet Union, had emerged as the single dominant power in the region. The end of the Cold War had changed the strategic balance of power in the Middle East, but what remained unclear at the time was whether the USA would be able to use its newly acquired position of 'international policeman' to be able to bring a degree of stability to the region that had previously been absent. Cold War or not, the problems of the region remained the same: the Arab–Israeli conflict, increasing inter-Arab disputes which erupted into localised wars or the threat of war, and decreasing natural resources mixed with rising population numbers.

In truth, nobody wanted to disappoint the Americans at this stage. James Baker cleverly wielded both the stick and carrot at just the right time, and eventually the key figures of President Asad and Yitzhak Shamir agreed to take part in such a conference. Shamir, though, took some persuading, given his dislike of the international conference mechanism for peacemaking. He was, however, given enough reassurances by the USA that the PLO would not be represented at the Conference, and that its findings would not be binding.

In Israel, Shamir's popularity peaked at the start of the Madrid Peace Conference on 30 October 1991. He was seen as having successfully neutralised the Conference before agreeing to attend, by removing the East Jerusalem representation (the issue that had brought down the Israeli government the previous year). He had effectively sidelined the PLO by only allowing Palestinian participation as part of a joint Jordanian–Palestinian delegation. Importantly, the results of the Conference were not binding on Israel – it would serve only as a preamble to the bi-lateral talks that would take place in Washington some five weeks later. Shamir described the Conference as an historic achievement, arguing,

'It was the first time that Israel met together with representatives of all its neighbours without any preconditions. This was an achievement in itself even if you do not take into account the results of it. It was important for us (Israel); it gave us more standing and prestige. It was clear that we would have to get peace with negotiations one day; also it was very clear according to the Camp David agreements that we would have to find a solution for the unresolved questions.'[123]

The opening days of the Conference itself were full of high political drama, with Presidents Bush and Gorbachev making the opening speeches calling for a dialogue leading to peace. Shamir had insisted upon attending the Conference himself, despite the fact that the Arab states were represented at Foreign Minister level.[124] In truth, Shamir's decision to attend said much about his lack of trust in his political foe and Minister of Foreign Affairs,

173

David Levy. Shamir took his own foreign policy team with him, along with Benjamin Netanyahu, the Deputy Minister of Foreign Affairs, who acted as the spokesman for the Israeli delegation.

With the world's media in attendance, the parties made their opening statements, addressing their comments more to their respective domestic audiences rather than offering any new sign of compromise. Shamir's statement, though not particularly popular with his hosts, reflected the Israeli national consensus of steady, unspectacular progress in the peace process. Despite its attendance at the Conference, it was clear that the Israeli government had no intention of opening a direct dialogue with the PLO, and indeed, coming so soon after the Persian Gulf War, it was apparent that there was little support in Israeli society for such a dialogue. The statement of the Syrian Foreign Minister, Faruq al-Shara, was particularly hard-line, and his holding up of a 'Wanted' poster from the days of the British Mandate for Yitzhak Shamir added little to the proceedings. Some of the Palestinian members of the joint Jordanian–Palestinian delegation wished to show Shamir and the world that, despite pre-Conference assurances to the contrary, they were in fact members of Fatah and the PLO. One such delegate went as far as putting on the traditional headdress in the colours of Arafat's Fatah movement. Though this action was lost on much of the US delegation, Mr Shamir could not fail to notice, but did not respond. The showboating of the first days disappointed the US hosts, but Shamir's advisor to the talks, Dore Gold, described it as totally expected.[125] The fact that no-one walked out was viewed as a success by many of the participants, with lower expectations than the Bush Administration of any substantial progress coming from the public sessions.[126]

Once the talks moved to Washington – and the various committees got down to business – the extent of the task was clear for all to see. At this point, the US administration was becoming increasingly concerned about the Israeli government's settlement plans for the Territories. Ariel Sharon, now Minister of National Infrastructure, had prepared an ambitious plan entitled 'The 2010 Plan' that aimed to increase the Jewish population in the Territories by 2.6 million before the year 2010. The decline of the Soviet Union had led to widespread Jewish immigration by the Soviet Union's Jews to Israel. During the early 1990s thousands of new immigrants arrived each month in Israel, and it was hoped that they could be settled in the Territories. As it transpired, few of this new Aliyah wanted to move there, with the exception of the housing projects in the Jerusalem area that were beyond pre-1967 borders. If this was the reality, however, the perception that Israel was creating was very different. Each time James Baker arrived in Israel on a shuttle mission he was greeted with the announcement of the creation of a new settlement. Both Baker and Bush grew increasingly despondent with the Israeli government, partly due to the settlements issue, but also due to the lack of progress in the peace talks in Washington.

The Israeli government was struggling to deal with the absorption of the new immigrants from the Soviet Union. As a result, it requested $10 billion of loan guarantees from the Bush Administration, which it felt was necessary for the successful integration of the new immigrants into Israeli society. The Bush Administration was quick to exploit the request, and argued that the award of the guarantees should be tied to the suspension of settlement building in the Territories. Bush's decision to effectively intervene in Israeli politics was brave given the power of the Jewish groups in Washington. It was also a highly calculated move. Bush believed that many members of the US Jewish community were growing increasingly concerned about the Shamir government, and argued that it was important for the USA to take a stand on the issue.

The second calculation Bush made was that the Shamir government was in clear decline in Israel. The personal popularity of Shamir had fallen since it became clear that there would be no quick breakthrough following the Madrid Peace Conference. The Israeli elections had been brought forward from November 1992 to June 1992, and the Labour Party had a new leader, Yitzhak Rabin, who looked like he might be able to secure a victory over the Likud. The Likud charged that Bush was attempting to intervene in Israel's election.[127] In short, Bush wanted the loan guarantee issue over before the US Presidential election campaign entered its final phase. He planned to have the issue closed before it could do any harm to his prospects with Jewish voters in the November election in the USA. Rabin, for his part, appeared to agree to the criteria that the Bush Administration had laid down for the award of the loan guarantees. As a result, Israeli voters were faced with a real choice in 1992 between land and people. Retain the Territories (put more settlements in place), or have the $10 billion to integrate the new immigrants from the Soviet Union. It could not have both. What followed was much more complex, but the overall question remained the same: land or immigrants – two issues that went to the very heart of Zionism.

Notes:

103 UN Secretary General, 'The Situation in the Middle East', Report of the UN Secretary General', (13 November 1987), p. 11 A/42/714/S/19249.
104 Ministry of Foreign Affairs, Jerusalem (MFA), 'Statement in the Knesset by Defence Minister Rabin', (23 December 1987) MFA/9-10/312/1984–1988.
105 For Shamir's thoughts on the Agreement, see (MFA), 'Interview with Prime Minister Shamir in Ma'ariv', (3 May 1987) MFA/9-10/243/1984–1988.
106 (MFA), 'Statement by the Prime Minister's Spokesman on the Inner Cabinet Decision', (13 May 1987) MFA/9-10/247/1984–1988.
107 (MFA), 'Interview with Vice-Premier and Foreign Minister Peres on Israeli Radio', (7 August 1987) MFA/9-10/265/1984–1988.
108 (MFA), 'Reactions by Prime Minister Shamir and Defence Minister Rabin to King Hussein's Speech', (1 August 1988) MFA/9-10/384/1984–1988.
109 (MFA), 'UN General Assembly Resolution 43/21/Palestinian Uprising', (3 November 1988) MFA/9-10/395/1984–1988.
110 (MFA), 'Statement by Ronald Reagan', 14 December 1988) MFA/9-10/420/1984–1988.
111 (MFA), 'Letter from Secretary of State Shultz to Vice Premier and Foreign Minister Peres', (15 December 1988) MFA/9-10/424/1984–1988.
112 (MFA), 'Reaction by Prime Minister Shamir to Arafat's Speech', (13 December 1988) MFA/9-10/415/1984–1988.
113 (MFA), 'Coalition Agreement between the Likud and the Alignment (Labour Party)', (22 December 1988) MFA/11-12/2/1988–1992.

114 (MFA), 'Israel's Peace Plan', (14 May 1989) MFA/11-12/54/1988–1992.

115 (MFA), 'Ten Point Peace Proposal by President Mubarak', (11 September 1989) MFA/11-12/101/1988–1992 (officially proposed to Israeli government on 15 September 1989).

116 (MFA), 'Five Point Election Plan of Secretary of State Baker', (1 November 1989) MFA/11-12/107/1988–1992.

117 (MFA), 'Address by Prime Minister Shamir to Likud Central Committee', (12 February 1990) MFA/11-12/132/1988–1992.

118 (MFA), 'Guidelines of the Government's Policy', (8 June 1990) MFA/11-12/144/1988–1992.

119 For more details on the events, see (MFA), 'Summary of a Report of the Commission of Enquiry into the Events on Temple Mount on 8 October 1990', (26 October 1990) MFA/11-12/165, 1988–1992.

120 World Bank (2002), 'Long Term Policy Options for the Palestinian Economy', *World Bank Report*, (December 2002), p. 4.

121 M. Zak (1996), 'Israel and Jordan: Strategically Bound', *Israel Affairs*, 3, (1), 39–60.

122 Ministry of Foreign Affairs, Jerusalem, 'Statement in the Knesset by Prime Minister Shamir', (4 February 1991) MFA/11-12/185/1988–1992.

123 Interview with Yitzhak Shamir by the Author.

124 Ministry of Foreign Affairs, Jerusalem, 'Speeches to Madrid Peace Conference, 30 October 1991–1 November 1991', MFA/11/12/244/1988–1992.

125 Interview with Dore Gold by the Author.

126 Interview with Yossi Ben-Aharon, Director of Prime Minister Shamir's Bureau, by the Author.

127 Interview with Minister of Defence, Moshe Arens, by the Author.

6

Rabin's Choice: The PLO versus the Unknown: An Outsider's Narrative of the Oslo Era

The election of Yitzhak Rabin in June 1992 (or 'the Labour under Rabin' as it was officially listed on the ballot papers) provided a major change of direction in Israeli policy towards the Arabs. The period between 1992 up to the failed Camp David summit in the summer of 2000 is often referred to in Israel as 'historic' with what is more often than not termed as the Oslo peace process – though here again this term is not strictly accurate given the fact only the initial Declaration of Principles and Mutual Recognition Agreement were actually negotiated in Oslo. In dealing with this relatively short period of time, there has been a natural strong tendency to focus on the nuts and bolts of the relationship between Israel and the Palestinians (both those living in the Occupied Territories and the PLO leadership in Tunis). Hence there are four different narratives of this period which resulted in the signing of the Oslo Accords and their eventual failure to end the conflict between Israel and the Palestinians: two Israeli, an American and a Palestinian. In simple terms, the narratives can be categorised in the following somewhat crude way:

1. The traditional narrative of the Israeli right argues that the Oslo Accords were a terrible mistake. This group tends to focus on Arafat's motives for signing the Accords, and argues that his rejection of the generous concessions offered by the Israeli Prime Minister, Ehud Barak, at the Camp David summit in the summer of 2000 provides conclusive proof that Arafat was never really interested in peace. He duped successive Israeli leaders into thinking he was interested in ending the conflict, but was all too eager to return to a strategy of using violence in order to gain political concessions and was happy to die before having to fully accept Israel's existence.

2. The Israeli left, particularly leaders such as Yossi Beilin, who was instrumental in getting the original Accords signed, and who is subsequently one of the authors of the Geneva Accord, focus on the structural failings of the Oslo peace process. Their reasons range from the failure of interim staged agreements to difficulties caused by the use of constructive ambiguity (whereby the parties can interrupt the agreement in ways to suit their own constituents). For this group, Arafat's motives for dealing with Israel could be defined as pragmatic realism. His motives for not accepting Israel's terms at Camp David were complex and more

connected with his instinct for political survival – maintaining his own position in office over the needs of the wider Palestinian population.

3. The American narrative has been largely constructed by Dennis Ross's account of his time as the US Special Ambassador to the region and his role as the major mediator between the Israeli government and Palestinian Authority throughout the 1990s.[128] Ross, in his detailed blow-by-blow account of what was effectively the complete period of the Oslo process and also of the Clinton Administration, has made several important and controversial judgements. Ross's views are seen as all the more important, given his master's somewhat vague account in his memoirs, which were published in 2004. Central to Ross's argument are two key junctures in the process – the election of Benjamin Netanyahu in 1996, and the Camp David summit in 2000. Regarding the former, Ross clearly places a good deal of the blame for the crisis in the Oslo process between 1996 and 1999 on Netanyahu and his political manoeuvrings on the peace process – largely for domestic consumption. In terms of what Ross clearly viewed as the one chance to close the deal and bring an end to the conflict, at the Camp David summit, Ross places the blame for the failure to reach an agreement squarely on Arafat's shoulders. The Oslo process failed for a number of reasons, but the one real chance to turn failure into success was effectively vetoed by Arafat. This view is re-enforced by Ross's boss, President Clinton, who reserved some of the most damning pages in his memoirs for Arafat. President Clinton speculates that Arafat could

never really make the jump from revolutionary to statesman, and that most of the other Palestinian leaders wanted to accept what was put on the table at Camp David and the subsequent follow-up meetings. Clinton's frustration is clear when he argues that Arafat never said no, but rather just couldn't bring himself to say yes. In perhaps the most 'damning' sentence of the whole book, Clinton concludes on Arafat by claiming that Arafat's rejection of the American bridging paper at Camp David, which the Israeli PM accepted, was an error of historic proportions.[129]

4. The major Palestinian narrative charges that the Oslo Accords represented an attempt by Israel to try to impose an agreement on the Palestinians from a relative position of strength. In effect, the Accords were dominated by Israeli concerns over security, and did not address the core issues of Palestinian nationalism – statehood and the right of return for the Palestinian refugees. Israeli security concerns meant that for long periods during the era of the Oslo Accords the Occupied Territories were closed, which led to a further weakening of the Palestinian economic position. Some Palestinian writers point to the Palestinian Authority as effectively being collaborators with Israel and the United States in the process of weakening the Palestinian position. Palestinian Authority leaders in effect used the Oslo process to line their own pockets with the silver and gold that came their way in the form of international aid.

All the narratives concentrate on the relationship between Israel and the Palestinians, and the American mediation efforts to push the process forward that followed the signing of the Declaration of Principles in September 1993. There is a growing case, however, to suggest that the Oslo process failed because it represented a bi-lateral attempt to end the conflict when a multi-lateral solution was needed. This was particularly true given the economic weakness of the Palestinian position and the need for co-operation from Egypt and Jordan if a Palestinian state was to prove economically viable. The question of the Islamic holy sites in Jerusalem was another area which the Arab world was extremely nervous about making a Palestinian, rather than an Arab, issue. Egyptian officials were fond of saying, 'what right does Arafat have to negotiate over Jerusalem when it's an Islamic issue?' Consequently, when looking at the period 1992 to 2000, it is important to look at the regional context of events for the increasingly difficult relationship between Egypt and the Palestinian Authority under Arafat; and likewise Jordan and the Palestinian Authority played an important role in preventing any chance of a permanent deal.

Political change in Israel: the upheaval that never was
The election of the Labour Party under Yitzhak Rabin on 23 June 1992 was hailed as a victory for the peace block in Israel. The subsequent formation of a dovish-looking government that included the newly formed left-of-centre Meretz and the Ultra-Orthodox party Shas, appeared to indicate a major change of direction in Israel's positions towards the peace process. The reality was very different: the left-wing block actually won fewer popular votes than the Likud-led block in the election. The Labour Party's victory was a technical one; the formation of small,

splinter, right-wing election lists fragmented its vote, with two of the lists not crossing the electoral threshold – thus their votes were effectively wasted. The peace process was not the only determining issue during an election campaign that was based more on socio-economic issues and the failure of the Likud to deliver to key voting groups. In short, the election did not amount to a rejection of the Likud's polices towards the peace process, neither was it a mandate to dramatically alter Israel's positions on the peace process. This fact was not lost on Rabin as he moved at first cautiously, and then more dramatically, on the peace process.[130]

Rabin had set himself a tight timetable during the election campaign, hoping to reach a deal with the Palestinians within nine months of assuming office, though once he came to office he started to backtrack slightly on this commitment.[131] It soon became clear to Rabin, however, that the Washington peace talks with the Palestinians had reached a stalemate. The *Intifada* continued – albeit at a lower level – so he turned his attention to trying to reach a peace accord with Syria. His close advisors, including the Chief of Staff Ehud Barak, favoured an agreement with Syria, which they saw as less complex and divisive than the Palestinian track.[132] Barak, in particular, pushed Rabin towards the Syrian track, arguing that a deal with Syria would open up the Middle East to Israel, and place it in a stronger position to deal with the Palestinian track at a later date. For Barak there was more at stake: he was slated for national leadership and saw the completion of an agreement with Syria as a means of parachuting into the Prime Minister's office after Rabin retired. Consequently, throughout the negotiations, Barak kept one eye on what effect they would have on his future career.

At this stage, Rabin was very much a product of the traditional school of Israeli foreign policy-making. He felt that Israel could only make compromises on one track of the peace process at a time. So he chose the Syrian track that would mean Israel's having to return the majority or all of the Golan Heights to Syrian control. During the second part of 1992, Rabin sent signals to Damascus, but it soon became apparent that, even if President Asad had made a strategic choice to reach a peace treaty with Israel, he was driving a hard bargain. The internal restraints on Rabin were considerable. He had stated during the election campaign that Israel would not come down from the Golan; the Israeli inhabitants of the Golan are, in general, Labour Party supporters with strong representation and support within the party. In short, the negotiations with Syria looked like being long and drawn-out and, in the wake of increasing domestic difficulties, Rabin needed some tangible success in the short-term.

Timing is everything in politics. On other occasions, had a rather nervous looking Shimon Peres, the man Rabin had reluctantly made Minister of Foreign Affairs, and Peres's deputy Yossi Beilin, entered Rabin's office and informed him that they were holding secret talks with the PLO in Norway, Rabin would have asked for their resignations on the spot. In this instance, the so-called secret channel was an ideal way out of the difficulties that the government found itself in. Consequently, from this point on Rabin shifted his interest away from the Syrian track and towards the Palestinian track.

Several months before the meeting with Rabin, Yossi Beilin and a Norwegian scholar, Terje Larsen, together with Yair Hirschfeld, a senior lecturer in Middle East politics at Haifa University, had initiated a process that became known as the Oslo secret channel.[133] Once it became clear that both Arafat and Rabin were involved in the channel, its importance rapidly increased. The formal talks in Washington continued with the members of the various delegations having no idea about the Oslo channel. The talks were upgraded to include Uri Savir, the Director General of the Foreign Ministry, and an Israeli lawyer, Joel Singer, who had been recalled from the USA to undertake the drafting of Israeli position papers. The Oslo negotiations were complex, often in a state of crisis, but with both sides away from the media and their domestic constituencies, appeared to be more pragmatic.

As the negotiations developed, it was clear that the Palestinians favoured a series of interim agreements with the difficult issues left until later. This also suited the Israelis, though there were calls from Beilin to try to use this opportunity to resolve all the issues in one go. Beilin argued later that the interim stages allowed the rejectionists from both sides ample opportunity to destroy the process. The initial agreement dealt with the question of mutual recognition: the PLO as the representatives of the Palestinian people by the Israeli government, and the State of Israel by the PLO. This alone was a major step for both leaderships to take. The law banning contacts with the PLO by Israelis had only been rescinded the previous December, and only after strong pressure from Beilin and Peres. For the PLO the recognition of Israel was a great step, especially as the overall deal fell well short of the previous stated positions.

In truth, the PLO was in a terrible mess: desperately short of funds following the withdrawal of Arab support after the PLO had backed Iraq in the Persian Gulf War, it was close to bankruptcy. There were also signs of a decline in popular support for the PLO in the Territories, where rival groups such as Hamas, with generous financial backing from countries such as Saudi Arabia, were mobilising support though the setting up of hospital and other welfare programmes. The deal that emerged from the negotiations was not a marriage based on love, but rather one based on the mutual weakness of the two parties: the Rabin government and the PLO. That said, it transformed the political map of Israel and the Middle East.

Smiles and handshakes on the White House Lawn?
There were two signing ceremonies: the first of the mutual recognition document, and the second the Declaration of Principles on the White House Lawn. There was high drama and diplomatic manoeuvring to the very last, with the Palestinians introducing new clauses. Rabin signed the recognition document in his office in Jerusalem in front of the assembled international media. He signed the document with a standard issue ballpoint and made only the briefest of statements. It appeared to all watching that this was not a pleasurable experience for him. The Declaration of Principles (also known as the Oslo Accords) was signed on 13 September 1993 after a last minute crisis over terminology had threatened to cancel the ceremony.

The ceremony itself contained an element of high drama. On a sunny autumn day, President Clinton led

187

Rabin and Arafat out onto the White House Lawn to witness the signature of the document. Until a few days before the signing it was not even clear if Rabin would attend the ceremony. It was Shimon Peres who, as Minister of Foreign Affairs, would formally sign the document, along with Mahmoud Abbas, Peres's opposite number in the PLO. After the many speeches came the moment that Rabin had dreaded. Arafat's outstretched arm was being offered for a handshake. President Clinton in an apparent act of spontaneity gently pushed the two leaders together (Clinton later admitted that he had practiced the manoeuvre beforehand with his aides). Clinton's real fear was not that Rabin would refuse to shake Arafat's hand – the Israeli PM had agreed to do this deed in a private meeting with Clinton before the ceremony – but rather that Arafat would attempt to kiss Rabin on the cheek, a big no for Rabin.[134] When the moment came, Rabin appeared to hesitate, not only for personal reasons but also for political reasons. Before attending the ceremony, Rabin had hoped to maintain his Mr Security image by allowing Peres to undertake the pleasantries, while Rabin remained above the fray. Eventually, Rabin relented and shook the hand of the beaming Arafat, and at that moment the Israeli–Palestinian conflict changed beyond recognition.[135]

On the way back to Israel Rabin stopped off in Morocco and held talks with King Hassan, and it was clear that Israel's isolation in the Middle East, though not over, was undergoing change. Upon his return to Israel, Rabin's reception reflected the highly polarised nature of Israeli society following the signing of the agreement with the PLO in Washington. Opinion polls conducted in Israel on the day of the White House ceremony indicated that around two-thirds of Israelis supported the agreement with the PLO. The minority that opposed it, however, was very vocal, and started a campaign to oppose the agreement, claiming that Rabin had no clear mandate to sign it. In the Knesset, the deal with the PLO was ratified only after a stormy debate by 61 votes to 50 (8 MKs abstained), in which the right accused Rabin of negotiating with terrorists and argued that the deal would lead to a PLO state in the Territories.[136]

Benjamin Netanyahu, who had been elected leader of the Likud in January, led the opposition. His public opposition to the Accords was based more on pragmatic political rationale than any ideological grounds. Attempting to end the fragmentation of the right and far right in Israel, Netanyahu seized on this issue as a rallying call for the Likud block to unite under his leadership. Publicly, this led the Likud to shift to the right and oppose any deal with the PLO. Privately, as early as late 1993, Netanyahu accepted the deal with the PLO and knew that if he came to power he would have to continue down the path marked out in the deal. Many in the leadership of the Likud were relieved that it was the Labour Party and not themselves that had been forced to make the first deal with the PLO.

The second deal with the PLO was signed in Cairo on 4 May 1994, and dealt with more specific issues such as Israeli troop withdrawal from the Jericho area and the setting up of the Palestinian Authority. There was an element of drama in this signing ceremony, as Rabin noticed that Arafat had not initialled the agreed maps and so refused to sign the agreement. With the international media broadcasting the event, TV audiences were treated to the spectacle of the leaders arguing with each other, with a somewhat peeved host, President Mubarak, looking on.[137] The deal was eventually signed and formed the basis for the arrival of Arafat in Gaza on 12 July – he chose Gaza over the West Bank apparently in order to show solidarity with the poorer areas under Palestinian Authority control.

The peace process came under threat in 1994 with the launching of attacks by individuals and groups that were opposed to the agreements. On 25 February, a settler from Kiryat Arba, Barukh Goldstein, fired indiscriminately at Palestinians praying at the Makhpelah Cave in Hebron, killing 29 Palestinians and wounding many others in an apparent act of madness against the peace process. Goldstein was eventually overpowered and beaten to death by surviving Palestinians. The massacre led to a period of unrest in the Territories. In Israel, in April, two bombs exploded in Afula (6 April) and Hadera (13 April), signalling the start of the campaign by Palestinian rejectionists. In October, two incidents provided the major crisis between the Israeli government and the newly created Palestinian Authority. An Israeli solider who had been kidnapped by Hamas was thought to be held in Gaza, and Rabin demanded that Arafat act. It turned out that the soldier was held in a part of the West Bank that Israel still controlled. As a result, the IDF launched an unsuccessful attempt to rescue him on 14 October. Ironically, as Rabin was helping to prepare the rescue mission he learnt that he, Shimon Peres and Yasser Arafat had been awarded the Nobel Peace Prize.

The following week the peace process came under even more pressure. On 19 October, a Palestinian suicide bomber blew himself up on the Number 5 bus near Dizengoff killing 22 and wounding many more. It was the largest single loss of Israeli life in a terrorist attack since the 1978 attack on a coastal road bus. The Dizengoff attack shocked Israelis; Tel Aviv was previously considered a relatively safe city. In 1995 there were three other major suicide attacks by Islamic Jihad (Beit Lid, 22 January 1995) and Hamas (Ramat Gan, 24 July 1995 and Ramat Eshkol in Jerusalem, 21 August 1995), that resulted in the deaths of over 30 Israelis.

The criticism of Arafat and the Palestinian Authority was that they were not doing enough, or were not able to fight terrorism, as was demanded in the Oslo Accords.[138] Relations between Rabin and Arafat became ever more strained as the Israeli Prime Minister demanded more action by Palestinian Authority forces. The right in Israel saw it as proof of the non-workability of the Accords. Netanyahu argued that it was reckless to sub-contract Israel's security to the Palestinian Authority. Many in Israel felt the same way as the Likud leader who, by early 1995, enjoyed a consistent narrow lead over Yitzhak Rabin in opinion polls. The issue that the Oslo Accords had damaged the personal security of Israelis became the central focus of the debate, with Rabin replying that Israelis also died from terror attacks during the period of Likud rule. From early 1995 onwards, the debate in Israel became highly charged, with the right and far right holding regular rallies, at which the anti-government rhetoric became stronger and more personalised. For his part, Rabin accused the radical right in Israel of working with Hamas against the peace process. Rabin argued,

'The radical right is dancing on the blood of the victims of the radical Islamic murderers, trying to turn these victims into a lever against the peace agreement... The fanatic murderers of the Islamic Jihad and Hamas are the means of the Israeli radical right. There is an evil and wicked circle of partnership between Hamas murderers and the Israeli radical right wing.'[139]

These remarks were made following a demonstration organised by the Likud and other opposition groups to the peace deal, in Jerusalem on 2 July 1994. The demonstration, which was addressed by Netanyahu, Sharon and Shamir, ended in violence, with a Jewish mob attempting to enter the Old City with the intention of destroying Arab property. The rally itself was characterised by the chant of 'Rabin, traitor', which became the slogan and rallying cry of opposition groups in subsequent demonstrations against the Peace Accords up to Rabin's assassination in November 1995.

Despite all the problems, a third deal between Israel and the Palestinians that came to be known as Oslo II was signed at the White House on 28 September 1995, dealing with further Israeli withdrawal from the West Bank and the setting up of Palestinian elections. In his speech Rabin concentrated on the issue which was by now defining Israeli attitudes towards the peace process – terrorism.[140] Back in Israel, the debate on the Peace Accords was getting out of hand. The divisive debate on the future status of the Territories led to a level of polarisation of Israeli politics not seen since the early days of the State, with the battle between the labour Zionist movement and the Revisionists. The conflict then became highly person-alised, and was characterised by the bitter relationship between the leaders of the two movements, Ben-Gurion and Begin. In 1994 and 1995 a similar situation arose. Netanyahu's motives were clear: in order to rebuild the right-wing block in Israel, he had to unite the Likud with the radical right parties and extra-parliamentary groups.

Rabin's adversarial style of politics also contributed to the polarisation. Shamir, who had worked closely with Rabin in the National Unity Government, argued that Rabin's major political failing was his inability to debate issues. With his army background, Shamir argued, Rabin was used to being surrounded by soldiers who simply followed his orders, and this was reflected in his political life where he surrounded himself with military advisors. Consequently, Rabin attempted to run the government in a similar manner. He did not tolerate criticism.[141] Whenever Netanyahu attacked his policies in the Knesset, Rabin would simply walk out or continue a conversation with a Cabinet colleague. In effect, both Rabin and Netanyahu were unable to set a proper example for their supporters to follow, and indeed actually inflamed the increasing bitterness and rancour between the left and right in Israel. From this perspective both failed as leaders.

The murder of Yitzhak Rabin by an extremist opponent of the Oslo Accords on 4 November 1994 was one of the most traumatic moments in Israeli history. At the time, Israelis were shocked that another Jew, a fellow Israeli, could murder their leader. In retrospect, there were many warning signs in the weeks before the assassination that gave an indication of what was to follow. The levels of violence in Israeli political life had reached intolerable levels. The tone of the rhetoric had gone beyond the boundaries of democratic debate. On occasion Minister's cars were attacked – and in one instance badly damaged – by a mob. Death threats had been made against specific individuals, and security around Rabin, Peres, and figures such as Yossi Beilin, was tightened. Not since the fiery election campaign of 1981 had Israel witnessed such scenes. In 1995, however, the violence seemed to be worsening. A famous Israeli writer wrote that fiery debate was a sign of good political health and democracy. The truth was very different. It was against this background, and the threat of more suicide bomb attacks by Islamic militants, that a pro-peace rally was organised in Tel Aviv.

In the weeks leading up to the rally Rabin had been rather non-committal about it. His advisors had informed him that the opponents of the Oslo Accords had seized what is termed in Israel 'the street'. On his travels around Israel, Rabin could not have failed to notice the posters at every major road interchange; he saw the TV images of the mass rallies organised by the right and far right, and the dummy of himself dressed in an SS uniform. Even upon his return home there were vocal demonstrators camped on his doorstep. Pro-government rallies were notably absent. An attempt to organise a rally in support of the government in front of the Prime Minister's Office in Jerusalem collapsed when only a handful of people turned up. The rally on 4 November 1995 was to mark the start of the campaign to seize back 'the street' and win popular support for the Peace Accords. Rabin's concern was based partly on a fear that only a few thousand people would attend the event, and a reluctance to so openly embrace the left-wing dominated peace movement. The fact that the rally was organised in part to demonstrate against the increasing levels of violence in Israeli politics helped convince Rabin to attend. Indeed, Rabin referred to this very subject in his speech,

'Violence is undermining the foundations of Israeli democracy. It must be rejected and condemned. And it must be contained. It is not the way of the State of Israel. Democracy is our way. There may be differences, but they will be resolved in democratic election.'[142]

Rabin was murdered shortly after making his speech. Just before he entered his car a lone gunman approached him from behind and shot him in the back. Rabin was pronounced dead in hospital soon afterwards. After the initial shock wore off, Israel went into deep national mourning. Thousands of Israelis filed past Rabin's coffin lying in state at the Knesset, others privately mourned not only the loss of Rabin but also the loss of innocence. Israeli politics after Rabin's death would be very different. There would be a distance between the leadership and the people, imposed by the large security presence that would now accompany the movements of Israeli leaders. Leaders from around the world attended Rabin's funeral: an indication of how far Israel had come under his leadership.

In the short-term, the murder of Rabin did not derail the peace process as his assassin had intended. Yossi Sarid articulated this clearly on the night of the assassination when he stated, 'Mr Rabin has been assassinated, not his policies.' On the contrary, the murder initially had the opposite effect. Shimon Peres, who succeeded Rabin, speeded up the implementation of Oslo II by withdrawing the IDF from the Palestinian cities, towns and villages covered by the agreement either ahead of schedule or on time. This allowed the Palestinian elections to take place on time on 20 January 1996, producing the expected victory for Yasser Arafat and his Fatah Party. Peres was following the advice of his protégé, Yossi Beilin, who argued that Israel should make as much peace as possible before the elections scheduled for November 1996.

In assessing the short-term political impact of Rabin's death there are two clear consequences. It severely reduced the level of support for Netanyahu personally, and for the parties of the right in general. The centre-ground voters, outraged by the murder, clearly shifted back to the Labour Party. Many, including Rabin's widow, held Netanyahu personally responsible for creating the atmosphere that led to his murder. Such allegations reflected Israeli's search for a scapegoat for the murder, rather than having to address the very serious issue of the failings of Israeli democracy. For his part, Netanyahu attempted to deal with the more profound issue of Israeli democracy, and stated that he would not oppose the new government when it was presented in the Knesset. As he put it, 'in Israel, ballot boxes decide elections, not bullets.' The Labour Party that had been in a state of near-permanent crisis itself, caused by the deep divisions over the peace process, pulled itself together and united around Peres and the peace agenda.

As it turned out, the shift in Israeli public opinion proved to be fragile, and a series of suicide bomb attacks in late

February–early March 1996 by Islamic militants re-drew the political map of Israel once more. The attacks on buses (the same bus route was targeted twice in one week) shifted Israeli public opinion back towards the right. In essence, the question of Israeli personal security became the dominant issue at the heart of the political process. Peres's policy, as outlined in the Knesset, of continuing with the peace process while fighting terror with all Israel's might came under intense pressure.[143] In political terms all the capital from Rabin's death was used up. As one Israeli commentator noted, it was as if Rabin's death had never happened. Benjamin Netanyahu, whose career had seemed close to finished after Rabin's death, led the criticism of the government. He started to reveal his strategy for dealing with the peace process if elected. He now suggested that he would honour the Oslo Accords, but try to improve them for Israel. He also started to detail his programme of demanding more compliance from the Palestinian Authority before any further concessions from Israel would be forthcoming. In reality, the process was designed by Netanyahu's strategists to seize back the centre ground of Israeli politics. Netanyahu had already ensured that the right would enter the election united under his leadership and that there would be no repeat of the fragmentation of the 1992 vote that gave Rabin his mandate.

For Peres, the bombs were a political disaster. Following Rabin's murder, several Labour Party leaders had urged him to call a snap election to maximise the strong support of Israeli society for the peace camp – and the disarray of the right in Israel. Peres, however, had chosen the strategy of trying to make as much peace as possible before going to the electorate. In effect, the bombs cancelled out the huge lead that both Peres and the Labour Party had over Netanyahu and the Likud. Despite the intervention of Clinton and the international community to show solidarity with Peres at an International Peace Conference in Egypt, it was clear from this point onwards that the 1996 elections would be close. The key issue would be the question of which candidate could ensure Israeli's personal security. To make things worse for Peres, it was becoming abundantly clear that the negotiations between Israel and Syria were not going to produce a peace treaty in time for the election. In the end Peres suspended them after the wave of suicide attacks and tacit Syrian support for the attacks. They were not to formally resume again until 1999. Faced with few alternatives Peres moved the election forward to 29 May 1996.

The murder of Rabin had a profound impact upon the 1996 election campaign style, but little impact on the result. There was only minimal contact between the candidates and the public, due to the increased security. This was a campaign fought on TV, with the right accusing Peres of planning to divide Jerusalem and failing to protect the children of Israel. Peres and the left claimed that the Likud would destroy the peace process, but refrained from any direct attacks on Netanyahu. There was a feeling among Peres and the Labour Party's campaign chiefs (Chaim Ramon and Ehud Barak) that, if they could prevent another suicide attack before the election, they would prevail by a narrow but decisive margin.

In the end, Netanyahu won the narrow but decisive victory by under 1 per cent in Israel's first direct election for Prime Minister. In the Knesset, both the Likud and Labour Party did badly, largely as a result of the election system, but the overall balance between left and right remained relatively unchanged. Netanyahu's shift back to the political centre had proved to be successful, and he became Israel's youngest Prime Minister some six months after his political career had appeared finished. There was widespread dismay among Labour Party circles over the result. Leah Rabin declared in an emotional moment that she was packing her suitcase to leave Israel. The reality was that it was Netanyahu and the Likud who were charged with trying to reach a final status agreement with the Palestinians and a peace agreement with Syria.

The death of Rabin had a profound impact on both Israeli society and political life. In a country like Israel, however, where living with trauma is part of everyday life, people tend to internalise the feeling of loss and never really come to terms with it before the next set of traumatic events takes over. Clearly, the bombings in February and March 1996 changed the course of events. Even today, a decade after Rabin's death, there is a sense that Israelis still have not come to terms with it, dealt with the implications of the murder, or learnt the lessons of it. In short, it is conceivable that it could happen again when an Israeli leader makes difficult concessions in order to secure peace. In retrospect, from Peres's point of view, he should have gone to early elections, and reduced the potential for the rejectionists to intervene. It is perfectly possible, however, that even if he had done so there would have been attacks during the campaign whenever he decided to hold it.

THE VIEW FROM THE FENCE

From Hebron to Wye

The era of the Netanyahu government, 1996–1999, was one of near-permanent crisis in the peace process. The collapse of the peace process, however, that so many forecast in the immediate aftermath of his election victory in May 1996, did not happen until 1999. This resulted, in part, from the resilience of the Oslo Accords, but also from the ability of Netanyahu to push his coalition and Cabinet into making concessions when the time called. The Prime Minister was faced with dealing with the complex and difficult negotiations that were left over from the Rabin–Peres era, and, in effect, the most problematic issues such as Jerusalem, refugees and the issue of a Palestinian state remained to be dealt with in the framework of final status negotiations. In addressing the issues, Netanyahu had to deal with contradictory pressures: from the international community to make concessions, and domestically, a series of internal pressures from his Cabinet, party and wider coalition not to make further concessions. In numerical terms over two-thirds of his coalition had at best severe reservations about the Oslo process; many were strongly opposed to the agreements with the PLO. During his entire three-year period of office the Prime Minister started from a position of weakness each time he brought an agreement before the Cabinet.

On a personal level, Netanyahu felt that the Oslo Accords had severe limitations; he once argued that the security clauses had as many holes as a Swiss cheese. Politically his pragmatism, and deep sense of attachment to power, caused him to actively make the Oslo process work. He summed up his attitude in a key-note speech to a joint session of the US Congress on 10 July 1996, in which he talked of the three pillars that came to define his peacemaking efforts: security, reciprocity, and democracy.[144]

During his period of office, and despite all the difficulties of continued attacks by Islamic radicals, there was a broad consensus of support in Israeli society for the Oslo process. This was Netanyahu's barometer, rather than any ideological views previously stated while he was in opposition. On top of this, he developed and put in place a strategy of attempting to weaken the Palestinian Authority before final status talks started – and reducing Palestinian aspirations of what they would receive at the end of the process. Palestinian negotiators claimed that their understanding of the original negotiations was that there would be a Palestinian state that included all of the Gaza Strip and 96–98 per cent of the West Bank. Netanyahu was concerned about the Interim Agreements and preferred to go straight to final status talks, but the Palestinian Authority rejected this move. As a result, Netanyahu was faced with having to first negotiate the one issue that Peres had left over from the previous interim agreement, the future of Hebron – where, since the late 1960s, a small but vocal group of Jewish settlers had lived in the middle of the densely Palestinian populated area.

The negotiations that led to the Hebron Accord were lengthy, often acrimonious, and drew the USA far further into the process than had previously been the case. Several personal obstacles had to be passed before the serious negotiations got underway. First, David Levy, Israel's new Minister of Foreign Affairs met with Arafat, becoming the first leader from the right to meet openly with the Palestinian Authority leader. This cleared the way for a meeting between Netanyahu and Arafat that was brokered with the help of the USA and the Norwegians. For Netanyahu it was a difficult personal barrier to cross: his older brother Yonathan (Yoni) had been killed during the operation to free the hostages at Entebbe in 1976. Netanyahu, who was very close to his brother, held Arafat responsible for his brother's death. The meeting that took place on 4 September 1996 was characterised by a business-like atmosphere, but there was an absence of any warmth between the two delegations. Many members of Netanyahu's entourage regarded Arafat and the Palestinian Authority as unreformed terrorists. The handshake between Netanyahu and Arafat illustrated the lack of warmth, and the picture of the unsmiling leaders dominated the front pages of the world's press.[145]

In the absence of any substantive talks, the continued closure of the Territories imposed after the February/March bombings, and the absence of any further Israeli troop withdrawals or release of Palestinian prisoners, tensions were high.[146] The spark that triggered the resulting violence was the decision to open an exit to a tunnel that ran parallel to the Western Wall of the Temple Mount on 24 September 1996. It was claimed that the exit would make life easier for tourists, but both the Rabin and Peres governments had put off its opening in the realisation that it would be contentious. The subsequent Palestinian protests soon turned to serious outbreaks of rioting in East Jerusalem and Ramallah. During the rioting in Ramallah, a Palestinian fired an automatic weapon at IDF soldiers who returned fire. At this point, Palestinian policemen joined in, and for the first time the IDF was involved in a direct firefight with Arafat's policemen. The violence soon spread to Nablus, Bethlehem and parts of the Gaza Strip. The fighting only ended when Israel threatened to send its tanks into the Palestinian cities, and with the help of US mediation. Three days of fighting had left around 70 Palestinians and 15 IDF dead.

Once the negotiations at a lower level got underway they immediately hit problems. Netanyahu was busy flexing his hawkish muscles to his domestic constituency, while Arafat was busy attempting to win Arab and world sympathy for the Palestinian cause in the light of Netanyahu's new framework for dealing with the Palestinian Authority. Even when an agreement was reached, the Egyptians put pressure on Arafat not to accept too hastily while the international community was busy condemning Israel. The deal that was eventually agreed upon bore a remarkable resemblance to the agreement Peres had negotiated with Arafat, but had failed to sign. The deal itself was reached only after the last minute intervention of King Hussein, who mediated a compromise. On 12 January 1997, the King flew to Gaza and Israel and, in a frantic round of diplomatic activity, succeeded where the USA had failed. Netanyahu and Arafat met on the Gaza–Israel border and initialled the agreement at a low-key summit around midnight on 14 January 1997.

Netanyahu needed to employ all his political skills to get the Hebron Agreement – and subsequent troop redeployment deal – past the Cabinet and the Likud. It was only after a hotly contested debate that the Israeli Cabinet approved the Hebron Accord by eleven votes to seven.[147] Netanyahu's decision, however, to preceed with the Har Homa construction project in East Jerusalem, and the smaller than expected transfer of land to the Palestinian Authority, indicate what needs to viewed as the payback to the party and coalition. The extent of the difficulties that he faced over the ratification of the Hebron deal were shown in what became known as the Bar-On affair. Netanyahu, his Director of the Prime Minister's Office, Avigdor Liberman, and the Minister of Justice, Tzachi Hanegbi, were all placed under investigation over an alleged plea bargain deal with the leader of the religious party Shas. The deal would have seen Shas ministers in the Cabinet supporting – or abstaining – in the vote over the ratification of the Hebron deal, in exchange for a plea bargain for Aryeh Deri. Deri, the leader of Shas, was eventually convicted of corruption charges in 1999 and sent to prison in 2000. Central to the strategy that Netanyahu employed towards the Hebron Agreement was that the previous Labour-led government had already committed Israel to withdrawal, and that international pressure compelled him to make the agreement. Initially, this strategy was far from successful. The Labour Party had made it clear that they would provide Netanyahu with a safety net in the Knesset vote – and so its ratification the next day in the Knesset was relatively straightforward (87 to 17 with 16 abstentions). As a result, the IDF pulled out of most of Hebron, marking the first occasion that a Likud-led government had withdrawn from a part of 'Greater Israel'.

The decision to build at Har Homa was an illustration of Netanyahu's relative political weakness in Israel. His original strategy of playing to his right-wing constituency by handing over only nine per cent of the West Bank had clearly failed (Netanyahu won Cabinet ratification, but only after agreeing a package with the Ministers from the religious parties that included the decision to build a new Jewish housing project at Har Homa). Consequently, he gave the go-ahead for the project, for which there was strong support, not only from his coalition but also from some Labour Party leaders. There was, however, an international outcry over the decision, and Palestinian demonstrations against the project. Arafat, in effect, stalled the peace process, stating that there would be no progress until work stopped on the site.

Once more, there was rioting in the West Bank. Suicide bombers returned to Jerusalem, now operating in twos and threes to ensure maximum casualties. Suicide bombs planted by Islamic militants in Mahane Yehuda Market on 30 July 1997, and in the main shopping street, Ben-Yehuda, on 4 September 1997, caused large-scale loss of life and further slowed down the peace process. Other issues surfaced, such as the failure of the Palestinians to remove articles from their Covenant that called for Israel's destruction. The Israeli government insisted on a higher degree of Palestinian compliance in general to the details of the Peace Accords that Arafat had signed. Central to all these facts was the charge by the Netanyahu government that if Arafat wanted to advance the peace process he would have to undertake to do more about dismantling the terrorist infrastructure of Hamas and Islamic Jihad.[148]

The USA continued to attempt to mediate, at times threatening to withdraw from the peace process if there were not more signs of progress. President Clinton, however, was largely tied up with the Monica Lewinsky scandal, so it was left to the State Department team led by Secretary of State Madeleine Albright – and Special Envoy Dennis Ross – to continue to attempt to bring the sides together. By the Fall of 1998, the US administration believed that there had been enough progress to set up a Camp David style summit that began at the Wye River Plantation on 15 October 1998. After eight days, a deal was eventually hammered out, thanks largely to US officials who had worked to narrow the gaps between the sides. Even an appearance by a gravely ill King Hussein during the talks had failed to bridge the gaps. The King died soon after on 7 February 1999.

Netanyahu's conduct of the lengthy negotiations that culminated in the Wye Memorandum of 23 October 1998 once more illustrate how acutely aware he was of the internal restraints imposed upon him.[149] Prior to the negotiations at the Wye Plantation, Netanyahu had been able to resist strong US pressure to agree to further West Bank troop redeployments. During this period his coalition had held firm, but the peace process veered towards total collapse. At the same time, US–Israeli relations became increasingly strained, as US officials argued that the Prime Minister was putting his domestic restraints ahead of moving the peace process forward.

Upon his return from Wye, Netanyahu on the one hand attempted to reassure the hardliners in his coalition that, as the deal called for the Palestinians to keep their side of the bargain before Israeli conceded any more territory, they should not worry because Arafat would not do so. On the other hand, he argued to the more moderate members of his coalition that he had made difficult concessions and that the peace process was back on track. By this stage, however, the Netanyahu administration was already at an advanced state of destruction. It survived votes of no confidence in the Knesset on the grounds that the opposition could not muster the required 61 seats. The opposition Labour Party sensed victory and, despite its assurances to once more act as a safety net for Netanyahu's peace agreement, it moved to bring the government down. In effect, Netanyahu was forced to bring the ratification of the Wye Memorandum into an already hostile political environment.

On 17 November, two days before the Cabinet ratified the agreement, the Knesset met and approved the agreement itself by 79 to 19 votes. At Cabinet level, ratification proved even more difficult than it had with respect to the Hebron Agreement, with the Cabinet equally split, and, eventually, on 19 November, only narrowly approving ratification by seven votes to five with many Ministers abstaining or not attending the Cabinet meeting.[150] Clearly, many Ministers sensed the demise of the government and were positioning themselves for the expected election campaign. Other Ministers simply could not bring themselves to support a deal that made difficult territorial concessions to the Palestinian Authority. Finally, in a last ditch attempt to keep his coalition together, Netanyahu froze the implementation of the agreement, citing Palestinian non-compliance as the reason.

As it became clear that there would be no final agreement with the Palestinians before the Israeli elections that were originally due in 2000, Netanyahu attempted to reach a peace agreement with Syria in late 1998. Recent papers made available from the Prime Minister's Office in Jerusalem (by the Barak administration) suggest that

Netanyahu offered a full withdrawal from the Golan Heights to 4 June 1967 borders in return for peace. President Asad rejected Netanyahu's offer. Asad either felt Netanyahu's administration was too weak, or was receiving better offers from Barak, or simply did not want to sign a peace agreement with Israel. In the absence of any dramatic breakthrough – and with a coalition that had ceased to function – Netanyahu came to the conclusion that he had little choice but to support a bill to dissolve the government and set early elections.

It is still too premature to detail the successes and failures of the Netanyahu era from an historical perspective. Such was the divisive nature of Netanyahu that there are two polarised academic perspectives on the period. The first concentrates on 'the wasted opportunities' between 1996 and 1999, and argues that Netanyahu nearly destroyed the peace process. The second suggests that the Netanyahu era was a vital stage in laying firm foundations for peace in Israel. In effect, the period saw a necessary stage of consolidating the process after the spectacular (but divisive) agreement reached by Rabin and Peres. Proponents of the latter concentrate on the structural problems of the Oslo Accords and emphasise that any Israeli government would have encountered serious difficulties. In short, a fair judgement of the Netanyahu administration will have to wait until the final outcome of the peace process is known.

The rocky road to Camp David (again!)
The road to the Camp David summit in the summer of 2000 bore some resemblance to that of its 1977 predecessor. As in 1977, both invited parties were experiencing

increasing domestic difficulties. There were question marks over whether they could deliver their constituents, and the extent to which the leaders could make the difficult concessions required to reach an agreement. The domestic political needs of the umpire and mediator, the US President, remained constant. Presidents Carter and Clinton both required a foreign policy triumph to bolster either their long-term political career or their legacy. Crucially, here the comparisons stop. While Carter had time on his side (over two years of his presidency to run), for Clinton time was fast running out. The timing of the 2000 summit, as a result, was determined more by the needs of the US President than other factors. The failure of the summit proved to be devastating for the Middle East. Though it is too early to fully analyse the successes and failings of the Clinton Administration in the Middle East, it is clear that the summit and its timing were not its finest moment. To be fair to Clinton, there is evidence to suggest that the Israeli Prime Minister, Ehud Barak – who had soundly beaten Netanyahu in Israel's 1999 elections – was extremely keen to go to final status agreements and had been pressurising the President to initiate such a summit. Arafat and the Palestinian leadership were always consistent in their opposition to such a summit, fearing that they could not deliver on the kind of concessions required.

On 5 July 2000, US President Clinton announced his invitation to Prime Minister Ehud Barak and Palestinian Authority Chairman Yasser Arafat to come to Camp David to attempt to reach agreement on the core issues of the peace process known as the Final Status Issues. On 11 July, the Camp David 2000 Summit convened at the

President's country retreat. As in 1977, a news blackout was put in place and the President's spokesmen controlled all contacts with the outside media. Following a walk in the grounds for the benefit of the cameras, an apparently relaxed Barak and Arafat moved behind closed doors to start what turned out to be two weeks of intensive negotiations. It soon became clear, however, that the negotiations were not making the progress hoped for. Arafat appeared to have hardened his position on key issues, probably due to his increasing domestic problems that limited his room to manoeuvre. There were demonstrations in Gaza and the West Bank calling on Arafat not to make further concessions to the Israelis. If things were bad at home for Arafat, then they were worse still for Barak. He arrived at Camp David only after key coalition partners had quit his administration over his decision to attend the summit. He had survived a vote of confidence in the Knesset only because the opposition parties could not raise the 61 members needed to pass such a motion. On the Israeli 'street' the opponents of further compromises were becoming increasing vocal.

Much to his credit, Barak attempted to override the natural tendency of leaders in a weak domestic position to retreat to established policies. Prior to attending the summit, Barak had outlined his red lines in the negotiations to the Israeli Cabinet: no return to 1967 borders; a united Jerusalem under Israeli sovereignty; no foreign army west of the River Jordan; a majority of the major Israeli settlement blocks will remain; and no Israeli recognition of legal or moral responsibility for creating the Palestinian refugee problem.[151] Once he arrived in Camp David, Barak offered significant concessions that went well beyond some of these red lines in the hope of returning home with a peace agreement that would bring to an end the Israeli–Palestinian conflict. It soon became clear that the first major divisive issue was the question of Jerusalem, specifically, the status of East Jerusalem and the holy sites in the Old City that the Palestinians demanded full sovereignty over. Though the media created the impression that the talks stalled on the Jerusalem question, in reality there was little agreement on other divisive issues such as the right of return of the Palestinian refugees, and water rights. Jerusalem became the issue that symbolised the stalemate at the summit. Barak surprised many from the Israeli delegation by effectively offering to re-divide Jerusalem, with the Palestinians controlling East Jerusalem. Barak's offer was not direct, but came as the result of his acceptance of an American bridging plan. He balked, however, at the idea of awarding the Palestinian Authority sovereignty over the Dome of the Rock, as Arafat had resolutely demanded.

Unfortunately, details of Barak's proposals on Jerusalem, and Arafat's demands, were leaked to the waiting press. There is some evidence that the Israeli Prime Minister himself may have encouraged the leak in order to help prepare Israeli public opinion. In Israel, there was an outcry from both the right wing and from elements within Barak's own centre-left Labour Party. There was also a sober realisation, perhaps for the first time, of what the price for reaching an agreement with the Palestinians would entail for Israel.[152] In the Arab world there was widespread criticism of Arafat, stating that he had no right to negotiate over the status of Jerusalem with Israel, as it was an Islamic issue – not a solely Palestinian one. The subsequent reporting of the criticisms against both Barak and Arafat in effect hardened their negotiating positions, and after seven days the talks were effectively over.

As neither party was keen to be portrayed as 'the spoiler', both delegations agreed to remain at Camp David while President Clinton temporarily left in order to attend a pre-arranged engagement. During the second week of the talks there was little contact between the Israeli and Palestinian delegations, with US officials working on another ' bridging paper' aimed at getting the parties to resolve their remaining differences. It became clear, however, after President's Clinton's return, that the question of Jerusalem had at this stage become an intractable issue. From this point on, the summit entered the damage-limitation stage. Barak suggested a partial deal that did not include Jerusalem. Arafat preferred an all-or-nothing agreement. He was reluctant to commit to agreeing to any partial deal that would mark a formal end to the conflict as the Israelis demanded.

The summit ended on 25 July, without any agreement being reached. At its conclusion, a tri-lateral statement was issued defining the agreed principles to guide future negoti-ations. The drawn, downbeat expressions on the faces of Arafat, Barak and Clinton told the true story: a high-risk summit that had attempted to bring two domestically weakened leaders together to end a historical conflict had failed. At the end of the summit, President Clinton held a press conference at which he praised Barak for the courage and flexibility he had shown during the summit, stating that the Israeli Prime Minister had understood the historical importance of the moment. As Clinton later conceded, his statement was aimed at trying to give Barak as much political cover as possible in Israel.[153] Clinton also gave an extended live interview to Israel's Channel One Television News, in which he supported Barak and the concessions he had been willing to make at the summit.[154] Clinton's post-summit statement did not contain such similar praise for Arafat and from this, and other comments by US officials, it was deduced that the USA held Arafat responsible for the failure to reach an overall agreement. From this juncture, events became determined by the consequences of both Barak and Arafat exercising their exit strategies from the summit.

For Barak, there were few negative ramifications from the international community. As well as praise from Clinton, the leaders of EU countries and Arab leaders such as King Abdullah II were quick to compliment him for his apparent flexibility at the summit, and his courage and commitment to the peace process.[155] Domestically, Barak's minority coalition survived a few difficult days in the Knesset until its summer recess; a period that gave the Israeli Prime Minister three month's breathing space from the threat of being brought down by a vote of no confidence. His speeches at the time were characterised by the theme of 'I tried but the Palestinians were not ready at this time for a permanent deal.' The majority of the Labour Party he led was supportive of his conduct of the negotiations during the summit, although some remained uneasy over his offer on Jerusalem. In general, the dissatisfaction of the party was directed towards Arafat and the Palestinian Authority who, they believed, had missed a great opportunity for peace. For senior figures such as Yossi Beilin there was an even deeper sense of frustration.

A private diplomatic paper agreed upon by a senior Palestinian Authority member, Mahmoud Abbas, and himself in 1995 had formed the framework for the negotiations at the summit. Arafat was said to have embraced the paper in 1995, but did not feel able to support its contents at the summit, despite the fact that Barak's position on Jerusalem was more generous than the stated position in the original paper.

A farewell to Oslo: the return to arms

For Arafat, the exit strategy from the summit was much more complex than Barak's, as the resulting outbreak of violence in the Territories in October 2000 confirmed. Before the summit Arafat had threatened a unilateral declaration of a state for the Autumn of 2000. Following the summit, during extensive travels in Europe and the Middle East, it became clear that there was little international support for such a course of action – even the French, the Palestinian's major European ally, were not keen on the idea.[156] Indeed, within the Arab world, Arafat's already low standing had been further eroded by his attempt to negotiate a deal on Jerusalem. As a result of this lack of international support, the Palestinian Authority was forced to postpone its decision to declare a state.

The visit of the Likud leader Ariel Sharon to Temple Mount on 28 September was, as we mentioned previously, used as the excuse for the events that followed, although it should be stressed that the violence did not erupt immediately following the visit. The following day, however, as Muslims filed out of the Temple Mount following prayers, Palestinian youths began throwing stones at Jewish worshippers praying at the adjacent Western Wall. Israeli police who were already located on the scene in numbers intervened with devastating effect. Seven Palestinians were shot dead and many wounded. For Arafat this was the opportunity he had been looking for. Arafat's central aim was to change the image of the Palestinians from being the obstacle to peace to that of being the victim of Israel's military might. Palestinian youths were dispatched to military points of friction, notably on the outskirts of Ramallah and in Hebron to throw stones at the IDF.

On the diplomatic front, Arafat shifted from defending his behaviour at Camp David to arguing that the Palestinians were the victims of an illegal occupation. The highly effective public relations machine of the Palestinian Authority stressed his point in countless interviews on TV and in the print media. The Israeli public relations machine was not so effective. Barak's spokesmen appeared taken by surprise at the eruption of violence and were soon put on the defensive with the increasing number of Palestinian, and Israeli, casualties. Israeli leaders, including Barak himself, failed to articulate their arguments effectively. Speaking to the Israeli public on 7 October 2000, Barak warned about the likely intensification of the struggle.[157] Once more, as in 1987, however, with the outbreak of the first *Intifada*, Israel's international image was being tarnished, as TV pictures of Palestinian youths being shot by Israeli soldiers were shown around the world.

As Arafat had achieved his initial aim of moving from the defensive to the offensive, two more aims emerged. First, Arafat's strategy of damaging Israel's international standing was aimed at improving the Palestinian position in any future peace negotiations. Second, a hope that the violence would escalate and lead to an international force, preferably UN, being sent to the area. Arafat hoped that such an organisation would then attempt to impose a solution on Israel. In order for Arafat to have a chance of achieving his aims, there was a need to escalate the violence further, and therefore Palestinian policemen joined the fray, and armed groups of Fatah militiamen launched attacks against Jewish settlements and a suburb of Jerusalem. In short, Arafat hoped that there would be a massive Israeli retaliation that would subsequently lead to a high number of Palestinian casualties. Specifically, he hoped for a single large-scale incident that would lead to an international outcry, such as an attack of revenge on Palestinians from a Jewish settler along the lines of the Hebron massacre of 1994.

Barak and his senior generals were acutely aware of Arafat's manoeuvrings, and attempted to devise a strategy to counter Arafat. During the first weeks of the conflict the IDF attempted to avoid points of confrontation and, although Palestinian casualties remained high, there was not the single large-scale incident that Arafat had allegedly hoped for. Despite this restraint there was an expected degree of international condemnation that manifested itself in the UN Security Council Resolution 1322 that was adopted on 7 October 2000 and condemned Israel for its excessive use of force.[158] The Clinton Administration did not intervene to veto the Resolution, as is normal in the case of such resolutions. Later that month, however, 94 US Senators signed a letter that expressed solidarity with Israel and condemned the Palestinian leadership for encouraging violence.

A key turning point came with the lynching of two Israeli soldiers in Ramallah by a Palestinian mob. The two reserve soldiers had strayed into Palestinian Authority-controlled Ramallah and were arrested by Palestinian Authority policemen. An angry mob gathered, and the police station was broken into; the soldiers were beaten and the body of one of the soldiers was thrown out of a second floor window to a jubilant mob gathered below. An Italian film crew captured the horrific scenes on film and the images were transmitted to a world shocked by the intensity of the hatred. In Israel the spread of revulsion over the killings increased the pressure on Barak – who also held the defence portfolio – to retaliate. Barak, aware of the dangers of a massive response, decided to target only two buildings: the police station in Ramallah and a Palestinian Authority propaganda office in Gaza. Aware of the need to avoid casualties, the IDF informed the Palestinian Authority of its intended targets before launching the attack, thus limiting any international opposition to Israel's attacks.

The sobering events in Ramallah were a disaster for Arafat and the Palestinian Authority. This was always the risk when unleashing violence as Arafat did in October. Despite this, there was little change in the Palestinian Authority strategy in the subsequent weeks. Arafat claimed that he had no control over the violence, but the Israeli public viewed such claims with extreme scepticism, and within the Israeli leadership there was almost unanimous agreement from the left and right that he did. President Clinton, in the hope of being able to negotiate a ceasefire, arranged an emergency summit. After two days of talks at Sharm el-Sheik, an agreement was reached, but was not implemented by Arafat who still saw the use of selective violence as the best strategy for the Palestinians and himself.

On top of the violence in the West Bank and Gaza, there was widespread violence among the Israeli Arabs. This took the form of attempts to block roads, serious outbreaks of rioting in Israeli Arab areas, and attacks on Israelis such as the stoning of motorists on the main Tel Aviv–Haifa road. The levels of violence reflected both the growing feeling of political alienation of this group from Israeli society and a 'Palestinianisation' of Israeli Arabs that has developed in the last ten years. This marked the first time that the Israeli Arabs had reacted violently to events across the border. In previous times, during Arab–Israeli wars or the *Intifada*, they had remained calm. In 2000, the heavy-handed tactics of the Israeli police did not help matters. Badly trained, and without the proper non-lethal equipment for dealing with serious outbreaks of unrest, casualties among the Israeli Arabs were high from the outset. This tended to worsen the cycle of violence. The long-term consequences of the unrest may lead to calls for the further deepening of ties between the Israeli Arabs and their Palestinians brothers living in Palestinian Authority-controlled areas.

At this stage, it is difficult to gauge the successes and failures of Arafat's strategy from an historical perceptive. In the short-term it secured his very weak domestic position, but the price of the improvement in Arafat's domestic political position has been great in terms of Palestinian casualties and the cost to the Palestinian

Authority economy. In terms of loss of lives, more Palestinians died in the first six weeks of the violence than died during the entire first year of the *Intifada* in 1987–8. At the start of 2005, the numbers of Palestinians who had been killed since 29 September 2000 had reached 2,546 with a further 23,930 injured in the fighting. These figures compared with some 892 Israelis killed and a further 5,973 wounded during the same period.[159]

By the end of 2000, the Palestinian Authority economy, which was in a weak position before the October violence, was on the point of bankruptcy, with Arafat barely able to pay the wages of his security organisations. In terms of damage to the Palestinian economy, the figures are devastating. Using the World Bank poverty line of $2.10 per day, the World Bank estimated that on the eve of the second so-called *Intifada*, 21 per cent of the Palestinian population were poor. By December 2002, however, this figure had increased to 60 per cent. The number of poor had tripled from around 637,000 to just under 2 million. Around 75 per cent of the Gaza Strip were classified as poor in 2002, a frighteningly high figure nearly a decade after the first of the Oslo Accords were signed. The United Nations predicts that, even after a slight improvement in 2003, the rate of poverty in Gaza in 2006 will be 72 per cent.[160] What is worse is that the poor in the West Bank and Gaza Strip are getting poorer. In 1998, the average daily consumption of a poor person in the West Bank and Gaza Strip was $1.47 per day, but by 1992 this figure had slipped to just $1.32 per day.[161] The Palestinian Authority economy was prevented from collapse by donor aid, which in 2002 provided about $315 per Palestinian, per year. Much of this money was paid directly to the

Palestinian Authority, which employs around 26 per cent of those still working in the West Bank and Gaza Strip, and pays around 40 per cent of all domestic wages.[162] The international community, as a result, simply could not let the Palestinian Authority go out of business, for fear of the resulting social unrest – a fact that was not lost on Arafat when Israel and the USA attempted to marginalise him from the diplomatic process.

In Israel, Barak's administration came to an effective end with the decision of the Knesset on 29 November 2000 to call for early elections. Barak supported the measure himself, in the realisation that he did not have the majority to oppose it. More in hope than anything else, Barak made it clear that, until the elections, he would continue to attempt to reach a peace deal with Arafat. On 30 November, Barak presented another proposal for a partial deal with the Palestinian Authority. The proposal included a public commitment to recognise a Palestinian state: the first such statement from an Israeli leader. Both internal pressures and a further hardening of the Palestinian position led Barak to eventually give up the search for any agreement before the Israeli elections.

At the polls, Barak suffered the heaviest defeat in Israeli history to the Likud leader, Ariel Sharon. The violence in the Territories had been the dominant issue at the expense of nearly all other issues of the campaign, with Sharon promising to restore security to Israel. Sharon's 25 per cent victory margin appeared to provide him with a strong mandate. The coalition National Unity Government that he put together made it clear that they would not be bound by the offers that Barak had made. Final status agreement between the Israelis and the Palestinians appeared further away than ever.

Notes:

128 D. Ross (2004), *The Missing Peace: the Inside Story of Middle East Peace*, New York: Farrar, Straus and Giroux.

129 B. Clinton (2004), *My Life*, London: Hutchinson, pp. 944–5.

130 For Rabin's caution, see Ministry of Foreign Affairs, Jerusalem (MFA), 'Address to the Knesset by Prime Minister Rabin Presenting his Government', (13 July 1992) MFA/1/13-14/1992.

131 (MFA), 'Interview with Prime Minister Rabin on Israeli Television', (15 July 1992) MFA/1/13-14/1992–1994.

132 (MFA), 'Interview with Prime Minister Rabin in Ma'ariv', (27 September 1992) MFA/19/13-14/1992–1994.

133 For an Israeli account of the Oslo negotiations, see U. Savir (1999), *The Process: 1,100 Days that Changed the Middle East*, New York: Vintage. For a Palestinian account of the same talks, see M. Abbas (1995), *Through Secret Channels: the Road to Oslo*, Reading: Garnet.

134 B. Clinton, *My Life*, p. 543.

135 Ministry of Foreign Affairs, Jerusalem (MFA), 'Declaration of Principles on Interim Self-Government Arrangements –Texts and Speeches', (13 September 1993) MFA/108/13-14/1992–1994.

136 (MFA), 'Statement in the Knesset by Prime Minister Rabin on the DOP', (21 September 1993) MFA/110/13-14/1992–1994.

137 (MFA), 'Agreement on the Gaza Strip and Jericho Area', (4 May 1994) MFA/182/13-14/1992–1994.

138 (MFA), 'Remarks by Prime Minister Rabin on Israeli Television Following an Attack on a Bus in Tel Aviv', (19 October 1994) MFA/239/13-14/1992–1994.

139 Address by Prime Minister Rabin to Labour Party Central Committee, Beit Berl, 3 July 1994.

140 Ministry of Foreign Affairs, Jerusalem, 'Address at the Signing

ceremony of the Israeli-Palestinian Interim Agreement, Washington', (28 September 1995) MFA/15/82/1995–1996.

[141] Interview with Yitzhak Shamir by the Author.

[142] Ministry of Foreign Affairs, Jerusalem, 'Excerpts from Speech by Prime Minister Rabin at Peace Rally', (4 November 1995) MFA/15/94/1995–1996.

[143] (MFA), 'Address to the Knesset by Prime Minister Peres on Hamas Attacks in Jerusalem and Ashkelon', (26 February 1996) MFA/15/126/1995–1996.

[144] (MFA), 'Address by Prime Minister Netanyahu to a Joint Session of the US Congress', (10 July 1996) MFA/16/14/1996(MFA)1997.

[145] (MFA), 'Joint Press Conference with Prime Minister Netanyahu and PA Chairman Arafat', (4 September 1996) MFA/16/20/1996–1997.

[146] Before the Oslo Accords were signed in 1993, there were some 419 Palestinian prisoners in Israeli jails. By 2004, this number had increased to 6,324. Source: The Palestinian Authority Ministry of Foreign Affairs, 2004. It should be noted that Israel does not accept these figures, arguing that many of these prisoners are criminal and not political.

[147] Ministry of Foreign Affairs, Jerusalem (MFA), 'Cabinet Communiqué on Hebron Protocol', (15 January 1997) MFA/16/71/1996–1997.

[148] (MFA), 'Cabinet Communiqué on Bombing in Jerusalem', (30 July 1997) MFA/16/129/1996–1997.

[149] (MFA), 'The Wye Memorandum: Time Line and Letters of Assurance', (23 October 1998) MFA/17/75/1998–1999.

[150] (MFA), 'Cabinet Communiqué', (19 November 1998)MFA/17/93/1998–1999.

[151] (MFA), 'Briefing to the Israeli Cabinet by Prime Minister Barak, regarding the Camp David Summit', (9 July 2000) MFA/18/139/1999–2001.

[152] (MFA), 'Statement by Prime Minister Barak on his Return to Israel from Camp David', (26 July 2000) MFA/18/149,1999–2001.

[153] B. Clinton, *My Life*, p. 916.

[154] Ministry of Foreign Affairs, Jerusalem (MFA), 'Interview with President Clinton on Israeli Television Channel One', (27 July 2000) MFA/18/150/1999–2001.

[155] (MFA), 'Summary of a Meeting between Prime Minister Barak and King Abdullah, Tel Aviv', (22 August 2000) MFA/18/154, 1999–2001.

[156] (MFA), 'Summary of Meeting between Acting Foreign Minister Ben-Ami and French Foreign Minister Vedrine', (28 August 2000) MFA/18/158/1999–2001.

[157] (MFA), 'Statement to the Israeli People by Prime Minister Barak', (7 October 2000) MFA/18/175/1999–2001.

[158] (MFA), 'UN Security Council Resolution 1322 – End of Violence', (7 October 2000) MFA/18/176/1999–2001.

[159] Figures from the Palestinian Ministry of Foreign Affairs, 2005.

[160] UN, 'Gaza on the Edge', *Report by the United Nations Office for the Coordination of Humanitarian Affairs*, (1 October 2004), p. 1.

[161] World Bank (2003), 'World Bank Report on the Impact of the Intifada', *World Bank Report*, (April–June 2003), p. 3.

[162] *ibid.*, pp. 3–4.

7

Fences and Separation: An Outsider's View of the Future of the Arab–Israeli Conflict

At the start of this book, we looked at the reasons why the Arab–Israeli conflict remains unresolved – and specifically, why, when it appeared that peace was so tantalisingly close during the the 1990s, the peacemakers ultimately did not succeed in ending the conflict. To say that peace-making attempts failed, however, is simply not enough. It is vitally important for the future that we learn from these mistakes as well as exploring how the region, and its conflicts, will develop over the next decades. True, predicting the development of the Middle East is no easy task. Just a few years ago it would have been difficult to imagine that Saddam Hussein would be dragged out of a foxhole by US troops in Iraq, his rule of terror brought to a dramatic and conclusive end. Who would have dared hope that the succession to Yasser Arafat would be carried out in such an orderly, and by Middle Eastern standards such a democratic, way? And few people foresaw that Libya was close to being able to build a nuclear bomb (certainly not the American and Israeli intelligence services by all accounts).

Defining aims and needs

'Peace' is another term in the Middle East lexis that is more often than not misused – or at the very least, referred to in a generalist and non-specific way. When we talk about 'peace in the Middle East', or speculate on the outcome of the peace process, we appear not to know what we really mean by peace. Yet the definition of peace has had – and will have – a profound impact upon the negotiations and agreements that precede it. Let us take, for example, the state of peace between Israel and Egypt that has existed since the signing of the Camp David Accords in 1978. To some experts, the state of affairs between these two countries represents a model definition of peace: one that is characterised by the absence of organised political violence directed against the other party.

It is worth considering for a moment the implications of this most basic form of peace. It implies that there will be little in terms of the normalisation of relations between the parties involved. In practical terms, this usually translates into a lack of co-operation on most issues, with the exception of keeping or maintaining the peace. There is little in the way of economic co-operation (either at state level or between private entrepreneurs from the two countries) between Israel and Egypt. This form of peace is considered to be a starting point, one that will be built on later.

Writing in defence of the Geneva Accord signed on 12 October 2003 by a group of leading Israelis and

Palestinians, the Israeli scholar Menachem Klein argued that diplomatic agreements do not conclude the process of conciliation and peacemaking between peoples, but rather, as he puts it, should form the start line of such a process.[163] Klein went on to say that the Geneva Accord is merely the first stage of a long journey that will change the relationship between two distinct sets of peoples. Crucially, the end of the conflict at a legal and diplomatic level does not mean an ending of personal enmity, discrimination, injustice, etc. A diplomatic agreement stops the conflict and these individual feelings can be addressed at cultural and personal levels in the years to come.[164]

If we agree with Klein's definition on the role of peace agreements, then we can argue with a little more conviction that some type of agreement can be reached between the respective political leaderships (or elders of the tribes). It is clear, however, that any solution to the Israeli–Palestinian conflict in the short-term will not lead to a total end of violence between the two sets of people. Indeed, there is evidence that a peace agreement might actually lead to a short-term increase in violent attacks, as the radical elements on both sides vent their frustration at the terms of the deal and try to destabilise the implementation of any final status agreement. In theory, this is where Israel's Security Fence comes in. The conceptual idea of separation, devised by Rabin and executed by Sharon, that has been the driving force behind the construction of the wall appears to confirm that policy-makers believe that there is little prospect of peace ending all the violence; so, as Rabin put it, it is best to reduce the friction points between Israelis and Palestinians. In the short-term, the fence will achieve its purpose of limiting the violence either in the current era of limited warfare or in times of future peace. The fence, however, will act as a barrier in the medium- to long-term, in terms of addressing the need for feelings of personal enmity, and discrimination and injustice, to be addressed through cultural and personal levels. The fence, by its very existence, will make it harder for the longer-term process, of forming new ties between Arab and Jew to take place. While protecting a fragile peace agreement, it will in all likelihood stifle any chance of meaningful reconciliation between the wounded parties.

On the broader horizon, as a region, the Middle East is likely to see an increase in the number of inter-Arab conflicts and a deepening in the complexity of such conflicts. In the coming decades, wars are likely to shift away from being caused by simply political nationalist aspirations towards disputes over the decreasing amount of natural resources available for increasingly large populations. Here, Israel can play a role in perhaps protecting an infant Palestinian state from outside attempts to destabilise it, politically or economically. Such developments present both an opportunity and a potential pitfall for Israel. Even with a formal ending of the Arab–Israeli conflict, Israel is likely to remain a potent scapegoat for leaders looking to blame anybody but themselves for the problems of the region. On the other hand, the weakening of inter-Arab ties presents Israel with the opportunity to develop closer economic and political ties with parts of the Arab world that to date have remained formally averse to such ties.

For any chance of peace to succeed in the Middle East, and in particular between Israelis and Palestinians, then a number of issues need to be addressed which the building of the Security Fence will impact upon. It is worth looking at perhaps the two most important of these, both of which involve debates about the role of the outside world in the conflict. The creation of peace dividends, and the role of mediation, remain the two key areas in which we outsiders can contribute to the peace-making efforts.

Making peace dividends work
In many people's minds there is a superficial under-standing of what is meant by 'peace dividends'. Politicians, keen to sell their wares, often refer to this without ever going into detail. Most studies on the subject argue that peace dividends are essentially good – and play an important part in establishing or securing peace. In simple terms, once key sectors of society see the economic value of peace such as a new car, better living conditions, work, etc., they will turn their back on a conflict that threatens to rob them of all this seeming progress.

In areas ruled by regimes where corruption is rife, peace dividends in the form of loans or aid can, however, actually have a detrimental effect by helping to maintain such administrations in office. Often, funds that were earmarked to help improve the position of lower income groups are used to pay the wage bill for the large security services that these regimes maintain. The Palestinian Authority is a clear case in point. Despite the absence of a major peace dividend, there has nevertheless been a steady trickle of aid, particularly from Europe, aimed at shoring up support for peace among the population. Recent research, however, has highlighted the alarming drop in the living standards of Palestinians since the Palestinian Authority was created in 1994. On average, Palestinians have seen the value of their salaries drop by nearly one-third. However, the percentage of GDP that is spent on the security forces is one of the highest in the world, indeed, the ratio of policemen to citizens is one of the lowest in the world. Despite this ratio, crime is spiralling out of control as increasing numbers of Palestinians are forced to turn to petty crime such as car theft (one of the most lucrative industries is the re-plating and selling of cars stolen from Israel in Palestinian areas).

It is important, therefore, that the wider Palestinian population see very real benefits from making peace with Israel, and quickly. One of the main challenges that lies ahead for Mahmoud Abbas is the restructuring of the Palestinian economy, at the centre of which lies the need to break up cartels, reduce levels of corruption, and cut back the spending of the Palestinian Authority Security forces. The development of a peace dividend must not only come from the receipt of donor aid, but also from within the Palestinian economy itself. As we have discovered in this book, this will be made all the harder by Israel's Security Fence and the lack of access of Palestinian workers to the Israeli labour market, as well as a similar lack of access to the Israeli economy for Palestinian products. Without economic improvement, the feelings of envy, resentment and hostility that many Palestinians continue to harbour towards Israelis will continue and deepen regardless of any political agreement at governmental level.

THE VIEW FROM THE FENCE

Finding a neutral umpire

In many people's minds, there is no such thing as a neutral umpire or mediator for any given conflict. Just as no writer – or even the top academic – can claim to be totally objective in their work, so no single nation can satisfy the demands of the various actors in conflicts for neutrality. If, as a result, the arbitrator and enforcer of agreements is not seen as impartial, what chance do agreements have of being successfully implemented?

Presently there are two forms of international mediation available. The first is from individual states – the superpowers or ex-major powers. Following the demise of the Soviet Union and the ending of the bi-polar international system that characterised the period of the Cold War, the USA emerged as the sole superpower. Consequently, during the last ten years the USA has been involved in attempting to mediate all the major areas of conflict. This was, in part, due to the highly interventionalist policies of the Clinton Administration, which often used peacemaking as a means to distract the US public away from the financial and sexual scandals that dogged the Administration. It could also be put down to the USA fulfilling its self-created moral role as international policeman that was so central to the largely undefined 'new world order' of the 1990s.

The use of the USA as a mediator in the Middle East, as we have discovered, has not been without problems. The USA has a set of national interests, and each administration has a list of specific goals it wants to achieve in the foreign policy arena. Moreover, the relationship between domestic politics and foreign policy is becoming ever closer. With state control of the economy reduced, foreign policy is where leaders can leave their mark – or secure their legacy. As President Kennedy, in a telephone conversation to Richard Nixon following the Bay of Pigs fiasco in 1961, put it somewhat crudely,

'It really is true that foreign affairs is the important issue for the President to handle, isn't it? I mean who gives a shit if the minimum wage is $1.15 or $1.25, in contrast to something like this?'[165]

Foreign policy is also often viewed as an opportunity to distract attention away from domestic troubles. The negative impact of this is that, at times, US leaders apply pressures on the parties involved in a conflict in order – to put it bluntly – to get a result for the President. Such pressures can affect the judgement of its mediators. There was a perfect illustration of these pressures in the Spring of 1994. Warren Christopher, the Secretary of State, took a 'hypothetical offer' from the Israeli Prime Minister, Yitzhak Rabin – on a potential Israeli withdrawal from the disputed Golan Heights – directly to President Asad of Syria. Christopher was under pressure to wrap up the second phase of Middle East peace before the mid-term Congressional elections, and had clearly allowed the Administration's self-interest to override his role as trusted mediator between the two parties.

The second group of mediators are the international agencies. At present, the United Nations remains the major international forum for conflict resolution. In recent years, however, many leaders have come to see the UN as little more than a talking shop. Scandal and spiralling financial costs have led many to question the worth of the organisation. The USA has shown itself willing to bypass the UN at times of crisis and to work to actively keep out the UN from active peacemaking in areas of strategic interest to the USA – nearly everywhere. Today, as we have seen, the major role of the UN is in the supplying of peacekeeping forces to act as buffers between Israel and the Arab world.

The European Union regards itself as a major player in Middle East peacemaking. In economic terms this might be true. Between 1994 and 2001 (the era of the Oslo Accords), the EU and its member states provided some €3.81 billion in aid to the Palestinians.[166] Between 1995 and 2000 the EU provided the Middle East with some €5 billion in aid.[167] Other bi-lateral figures indicate the potential for a major EU role, particularly the fact that EU member states are the destination for some 31 per cent of total Israeli exports.[168] As recent research has confirmed, however, the EU has been unable to convert any economic influence into political weight. To a large extent, this has been caused by the fact that the national interests of the member states have not merged together to create one viable set of European political interests. In one study, the national interests of the two recent colonial powers, France and the UK, were compared. The results were very revealing, illustrating that the national interests of both countries are, in reality, moving further apart. Such differences make it difficult for Europe to talk with one voice and offer consistent mediation. Europe has a long way to go before it can rival the ability of the United States, or even the United Nations, in Middle East peacemaking.

In the absence of a strong international forum to solve regional conflicts, the United States has had to develop its role as international policeman to such an extent that old alliances are coming under increasing strain. For example, Israel, once the sole ally of the USA in the Middle East, now fears antagonising its patron so much that its political leaders have shown a willingness to make concessions that were previously unthinkable. Research tends to agree on one issue: the so-called 'new world order,' as outlined by President Bush at the start of the 1990s, has led to more complex international security systems. Perhaps here, Israel's decision to build the Security Fence has given the Untied States an opportunity to develop the potential for a more even-handed role in the Israeli–Palestinian conflict. There exists within the State Department a strong consensus that Israel must not be allowed to build the fence over the Green Line, and that it should face political and economic sanction for any lands that it effectively annexes into Israel proper. The fence, as a result, might just provide US politicians with a ticket to greater credibility among the Palestinians and wider Arab world.

A warning from history

Finally, the search for peace will become ever more complex as competition increases over ever-decreasing natural resources – particularly the case of water. In the Middle East, we can already see the consequences of this with the increasing number of inter-Arab conflicts that are essentially about control over the diminishing natural resources in the region. More states competing for fewer resources is a recipe for continued unrest. How long before a newly created Palestinian state with no real natural resources starts to make aggressive noises about obtaining such resources from other countries? There is a great deal of truth in the idea that if there is to be another major war in the Middle East, it will be fought over control of natural resources. The challenge for all those involved in peacemaking today is first and foremost to clearly define what is meant by the term 'peace'. Let us hope that the Israelis and Palestinians will not only be able to sign a formal peace agreement, but that one day they will be able to reduce the level of hatred and suspicion that currently exists between the two sets of peoples. The tearing down of Israel's Security Fence, at some point in the future, would be the greatest sign that the process of bringing an end to the conflict had eventually succeeded.

Notes:

[163] For more on the Geneva Accord, see Y. Beilin (2004), *The Path to Geneva: the Quest for a Permanent Agreement, 1996–2004*, New York: RDV/Akashic.

[164] M. Klein (2004), 'A Response to the Critics of the Geneva Accord', *Strategic Assessment*, 7, (2), JCSS, Tel Aviv University, p. 10.

[165] Quoted from R. Dallek (2003), *John F. Kennedy: An Unfinished Life, 1917–1963*, London: Penguin, p. 370.

[166] Figures from the European Commission Technical Assistance Office to the West Bank and Gaza Strip.

[167] *European Commission Technical Assistance Office to the West Bank and Gaza Strip* (2004), 'EU-Med Partnership Regional Strategy Paper, 2002–2006', p.16.

[168] This figure is for 2003 in, Central Bureau of Statistics, Jerusalem, *Statistical Abstract of Israel 2004*.

Bibliography

Primary Sources

Archival Material

Bank of Israel, Jerusalem.
British Public Records Office (National Archives), Kew.
Central Bureau of Statistics, Jerusalem.
Central Zionist Archives, Jerusalem.
European Union, Brussels.
International Monetary Fund, Washington DC.
Israeli Defence Forces, Tel Aviv.
Jabotinsky Archives, Tel Aviv.
Knesset Archives, Jerusalem.
Library of Congress, Washington DC.
Mapai Archives, Beit Berl, Israel.
Ministry of Finance, Jerusalem.
Ministry of Foreign Affairs, Jerusalem (MFA).
Ministry of Defence, Tel Aviv.
Palestinian Central Bureau of Statistics, Ramallah.
Palestinian National Authority, Ramallah.

BIBLIOGRAPHY

Presidential Libraries: Clinton, Bush, Reagan, Carter, Nixon, Johnson, Kennedy, Eisenhower, Truman.
Prime Minister's Office, Jerusalem (PMO).
State Department, Foreign Relations Series, Truman to Nixon, Washington DC.
State Department Library, Washington DC.
The World Bank, Washington DC.
UN General Assembly – Official Records, New York.
UN Secretary General – Official Records, New York.
UN Security Council – Official Records, New York.
UN Security Council – Supplementary Records, New York.

Memoirs:

Abbas, M., (1995), *Through Secret Channels: the Road to Oslo*, Reading: Garnet Publishing.
Albright, M., (2003), *Madam Secretary: a Memoir*, London: Macmillan.
Arens, M., (1995), *Broken Covenant: American Foreign Policy and the Crisis between the US and Israel*, New York: Simon and Schuster.
Beilin, Y., (2004), *The Path to Geneva: the Quest for a Permanent Agreement, 1996–2004*, New York: RDV/Akashic.
Boutros-Ghali, B., (1997), *Egypt's Road to Jerusalem: a Diplomat's Story of the Struggle for Peace in the Middle East*, New York: Random House.
Clinton, B., (2004), *My Life*, London: Hutchinson.
Clinton, H. R., (2003), *Living History: Memoirs*, London: Headline.

Dayan, M., (1966), *Diary of the Sinai Campaign*, New York: Da Capo Press.

———, (1981), *Breakthrough: a Personal Account of Egypt–Israel Negotiations*, London: Weidenfeld and Nicolson.

Farid, A. M., (1994), *Nasser: the Final Years*, Reading: Ithaca Press.

Herzog, C., (1997), *Living History: The Memoirs of a Great Israeli Freedom-Fighter, Soldier, Diplomat and Statesman*, London: Weidenfeld and Nicolson.

Kissinger, H., (1994), *Diplomacy*, New York: Touchstone.

———, (1999), *Years of Renewal*, London: Weidenfeld and Nicolson.

Peres, S., (1995), *Battling for Peace: Memoirs*, London: Weidenfeld and Nicolson.

Rabin, Y., (1996), *The Rabin Memoirs*, Berkeley: University of California Press.

Ross, D., (2004), *The Missing Peace: the Inside Story of the Fight for Middle East Peace*, New York: Farrar, Straus and Giroux.

Weizman, E., (1981), *The Battle for Peace*, London: Bantam Books.

Newspapers:

Ha'aretz, Tel Aviv.
Independent, London.
Jerusalem Post, Jerusalem.
Ma'ariv, Tel Aviv.
Middle East Times, Cairo.

BIBLIOGRAPHY

New York Times, New York.
Syria Times, Damascus.
The Times, London.
Washington Post, Washington DC.
Yediot Aharonot, Tel Aviv.

Secondary Sources: Books and Articles

Abu-Amr, (1993), 'Hamas: a Historical and Political
　Background'. *Journal of Palestine Studies*, 22, (4)
　pp. 5–19.
Aburish, S., (2004), *Nasser: the Last Arab*, London:
　Duckworth.
Al-Haj, M., (1993), 'Strategies and Mobilisation
　Among the Arabs in Israel', in K. Keith and J. Peters
　(eds.), *Whither Israel: the Domestic Challenges*,
　London: I. B. Tauris, pp.140–160.
Al-Khazender, S., (1997), *Jordan and the Palestine
　Question: the Role of Islamic and Left Forces in
　Shaping Foreign Policy-Making*, Reading: Ithaca
　Press.
Allen, R. and Mallat, C. (eds.), (1995), *Water in the
　Middle East*, London: British Academy Press.
Arian, A., (1995), *Security Threatened*, Cambridge:
　Cambridge University Press.
———, (1998), *The Second Republic: Politics in Israel*,
　Chatham: Chatham House.
———, (2003), 'Israeli Public Opinion on National
　Security 2003'. Memorandum Number 67, JCSS, Tel
　Aviv University.
Arian, A. and M. Shamir (eds.), (1999), *The Elections*

in Israel 1996, Albany: State University of New York Press.

Aronoff, M., (1991) *Israeli Visions and Divisions*, New Brunswick: Transaction Books.

Aronson, S., (1999), *Israel's Nuclear Programme: the Six-Day War and its Ramifications*, London: Kings College London Mediterranean Studies.

Ayubi, Nazih N., (1995), *Over-Stating the Arab State: Politics and Society in the Middle East*, London and New York: I. B. Tauris.

Azmon, Y. and Dafna, I. (eds.), (1993), *Women in Israel*, New Brunswick: Transaction Books.

Bailer, U., (1990), *Between East and West: Israel's Foreign Policy Orientation, 1948–1956*, Cambridge: Cambridge University Press.

Bailey, S., (1990), *Four Arab-Israeli Wars and the Peace Process*, London: Macmillan.

Bar-On, M., (1994), *The Gates of Gaza: Israel Road to Suez and Back 1955–1957*, New York: St Martin's Press.

Bavly, D. and E. Salpeter, (1984), *Fire in Beirut: Israel's War in Lebanon with the PLO*, New York: Stein and Day.

Begin, M., (1952), *The Revolt: the Story of the Irgun*, Tel Aviv: Steimatzky.

Beilin, Y., (1992), *Israel: a Concise Political History*, London: Weidenfeld and Nicolson.

———, (1999), *Touching Peace: From the Oslo Accord to a Final Agreement*, London: Weidenfeld and Nicolson.

Ben-Meir, Y., (1993), 'Civil-Military Relations in Israel', in K. Keith and J. Peters, *Whither Israel: the*

Domestic Challenges, London: I. B. Tauris, pp. 223–243.

———, (1995), *Israeli Public Opinion, Final Status Issues: Israel–Palestinians, No.6*, Tel Aviv: Jaffee Centre for Strategic Studies.

Ben-Zvi, A., (1993), *The United States and Israel: the Limits of the Special Relationship*, New York: Columbia University Press.

———, (1998), *Decade of Transition: Eisenhower, Kennedy and the Origins of the American–Israeli Alliance*, Chichester: Columbia University Press.

Bernstein, D. (ed.), (1992), *Pioneers and Homemakers: Jewish Women in Pre-State Palestine*, Albany: State University of New York Press.

Biswas, A. K. (ed.), (1994), *International Waters of the Middle East*, Oxford: Oxford University Press.

Bobbitt, P., (2002), *The Shield of Achilles: War, Peace and the Course of History*, London: Penguin.

Boutros-Ghali, B., (1996), *Egypt's' Road to Jerusalem*, New York: Random House.

Bulloch, J. and A. Darwish, (1993), *Water Wars: Coming Conflicts in the Middle East*, London.

Carter, J., (1985), *The Blood of Abraham: Insights into the Middle East*, Boston: Houghton-Mifflin.

Cohen, A., (1998), *Israel and the Bomb*, New York: Columbia University Press.

Cohen, M., (1987), *Zion and State: Nation, Class and the Shaping of Modern Israel*, Oxford and New York: Blackwell.

Corbin, J., (1994), *Gaza First: the Secret Norway Channel to Peace between Israel and the PLO*, London: Bloomsbury.

Cordesman, A., (1987), *The Arab–Israeli Military Balance and the Art of Operations: an Analysis of Military Trends and Implications for Future Conflicts*, Lanham: American Enterprise Institute.

———, (1996), *Perilous Prospects: the Peace Process and the Arab–Israeli Military Balance*, Boulder: Westview Press.

———, (2004), *The Military Balance in the Middle East*, Westport and London: Praeger.

Curtiss, R. H., (1997), 'The Cost of Israel to US Taxpayers: The Lies About US Aid to Israel', Washington Report on Middle Eastern Affairs.

Dallek, R., (2003), *John F. Kennedy: An Unfinished Life, 1917–1963*, London: Penguin.

Darboub, L., (1996), 'Palestinian Public Opinion and the Peace Process', *Palestine–Israel Journal*, vol. 3 no. 3–4, pp. 109–117.

Dershowitz, A. M., (2002), *Why Terrorism Works: Understanding the Threat, Responding to the Challenge*, New Haven and London: Yale University Press.

Diskin, A., (1991), *Elections and Voters in Israel*, New York: Praeger.

Dowek, E., (2001), *Israeli–Egyptian Relations 1980–2000*, London and Portland: Frank Cass.

Eban, A., (1983), *The New Diplomacy: International Affairs in the Modern Age*, London: Weidenfeld and Nicolson.

Edelman, M., (1994), *Courts, Politics and Culture in Israel*, Charlottesville: University Press of Virginia.

Eisenstadt, S., (1968), *Israeli Society*, London: Weidenfeld and Nicolson.

BIBLIOGRAPHY

————, (1985), *Israeli Society Transformed*, London: Weidenfeld and Nicolson.

Elazar, D., (1986), *Building a New Society*, Bloomington: Indiana University Press.

Farid, A. M., (1994), *Nasser: The Final Years*, Reading: Ithaca Press.

Feldman, S., (1988), *US Middle East Policy: the Domestic Setting*, Boulder: Westview Press.

Feldman, S. and A. Levite (eds.), (1994), *Arms Control and the New Middle East Security Environment*, JCSS Study Number 23, Boulder: Westview Press.

Feldman, S. and A. Toukan, (1997), *Bridging the Gap: a Future Security Architecture for the Middle East*, Oxford: Rowman and Littlefield.

Fisk, R., (1990), *Pity the Nation: Lebanon at War*, Oxford: Oxford University Press.

Flamhaft, Z., (1996), *Israel on the Road to Peace: Accepting the Unacceptable*, Boulder: Westview Press.

Freedman, L. and E. Karsh, (1993), *The Gulf Conflict 1990–1991*, London and Boston: Faber and Faber.

Freedman, R., (1998), *The Middle East and the Peace Process: the Impact of the Oslo Accords*, Gainesville: University Press of Florida.

Friedland, R. and R. Hecht, (1996), *To Rule Jerusalem*, New York and Cambridge: Cambridge University Press.

Friedman, I., (2000), *Palestine: a Twice Promised Land – The British, the Arabs and Zionism*, New Brunswick and London: Transaction Books.

Fromkin, D., (2000), *A Peace to End All Peace: The Fall of the Ottoman Empire and the Creation of the Modern Middle East*, London: Phoenix Press.

Frum, D., (2003), *The Right Man: An Inside Account of the Surprise Presidency of George W. Bush*, London: Weidenfeld and Nicolson.

Garfinkle, A., (1997), *Politics and Society in Modern Israel: Myths and Realities*, M. E. Sharpe, New York: Armonk.

Gilbert, M., (1996), *Jerusalem in the Twentieth Century*, London: Chatto and Windus.

———, (1998), *Israel: a History*, London: Doubleday.

———, (2003), *The Routledge Atlas of the Arab–Israeli Conflict*, London and New York: Routledge.

Gilmour, D., (1987), *Lebanon: the Fractured Country*, London: Sphere Books.

Giuliani, R. W., (2002), *Leadership*, London: Little Brown.

Golan, G., (1977), *Yom Kippur and After*, Cambridge: Cambridge University Press.

———, (1990), *Soviet Policy in the Middle East: from World War II to Gorbachev*, Cambridge: Cambridge University Press.

Gordon, H., (1999), *Looking Back at the June 1967 War*, Westport and London: Praeger.

Gorst, A. and L. Johnman, (eds.), (1997), *The Suez Crisis*, London: Routledge (collection of documents).

Govrin, Y., (1998), *Israeli–Soviet Relations from Confrontation to Disruption*, London and Portland: Frank Cass.

Gresh, A., (1998), 'Turkish–Israeli–Syrian Relations and their Impact on the Middle East', *Middle East Journal*, vol. 52, no. 2, pp.188–203.

Grossman, D., (0000), *Sleeping on a Wire:*

Conversations with Palestinians in Israel, London: Jonathan Cape.

Gruen, G., (1995), 'Dynamic Progress in Turkish–Israeli Relations', *Israel Affairs*, vol. 1, no. 4, pp. 40–70.

Hahn, P., (1991), *The United States, Great Britain and Egypt 1945–1956: Strategy and Diplomacy in the Early Cold War*, Chapel Hill and London: The University of North Carolina Press.

Halberstam, D., (2003), *War in a Time of Peace: Bush, Clinton and the Generals*, London: Bloomsbury.

Hammel, E., (1992), *Six Days in June: How Israel Won the 1967 Arab–Israeli War*, New York: Charles Scribner's Sons.

Harkabi, Y., (1986), *Israel's Fateful Hour*, Philadelphia: Harper and Row.

Hashem, T. G., (2003), *Palestinian Refugees: Pawns to Political Actors*, New York: Nova Science Publishers.

Hattis-Rolef, S. (ed.), (1993), *Political Dictionary of the State of Israel*, Jerusalem: The Jerusalem Publishing House.

Heikal, M., (1983), *Autumn of Fury: the Assassination of Sadat*, London: Andre Deutsch.

Held, C., (1994), *Middle East Patterns: Places, People and Politics*, Boulder: Westview Press.

Heller, J., (2000), *The Birth of Israel, 1945–1949*, Gainesville: University of Florida Press.

Heller, M., (1983), *A Palestinian State*, Cambridge: Cambridge University Press.

Herzog, C., (1984), *The Arab–Israeli Wars*, New York: Vintage Books.

———, (1998), *The War of Atonement: the Inside Story of the Yom Kippur War 1973*, London:

Greenhill Books.

Hillel, D., (1994), *Rivers of Eden: The Struggle for Water and the Quest for Peace in the Middle East*, New York: Oxford University Press.

Hinnebusch, R., (1998), 'Syria and the Transition to Peace', in Robert Freedman (ed.), *The Middle East and the Peace Process: the Impact of the Oslo Accords*, pp. 134–153.

——, (2003), *The International Politics of the Middle East*, Manchester: Manchester University Press.

Hiro, D., (1996), *Dictionary of the Middle East*, London: Macmillan.

Holbrooke, R., (1998), *To End a War*, New York: Random House.

Hourani, A., (1991), *A History of the Arab Peoples*, London: Faber and Faber.

Hroub, K., (2000), *Hamas: Political Thought and Practice*, Beirut: Institute for Palestine Studies.

Huntington, S. P., (1996), *The Clash of Civilizations and the Remaking of World Order*, New York: Simon and Schuster.

Hurwitz, H., (1994), *Begin: a Portrait*, Washington DC: B'nai B'rith Books.

Inbar, E. and S. Sandler, (eds.), (1995), *Middle East Security: Prospects for an Arms Control Regime*, London and Portland: Frank Cass.

Jones, C., (1996), *Soviet Jewish Aliyah 1989–92: Impact and Implications for Israel and the Middle East*, London and Portland: Frank Cass.

Joyce, M., (1998), *Kuwait 1945–1996: an Anglo–American Perspective*, London and Portland: Frank Cass.

BIBLIOGRAPHY

Kam, E., (2004), 'Exceeding the Boundaries: the Parliamentary Report on Israel's Intelligence System', *Strategic Assessment* 7(2).

Kaplan, R. D., (1993), *The Arabists: the Romance of an American Elite*, New York: Free Press.

Karsh, E. (ed.), (1997), *From Rabin to Netanyahu: Israel's Troubled Agenda*, London and Portland: Frank Cass.

———, (1997), *Fabricating Israeli History*, London and Portland: Frank Cass.

———, (2002), *Essential Histories No. 28, The Arab–Israeli Conflict: the Palestine War 1948*, Oxford: Osprey.

Katz, S., (1996), *Lone Wolf: a Biography of Vladimir Ze'ev Jabotinsky* (2 vols.), New York: Barricade Books.

Kedourie, E., (1970), *The Chatham House Version and Other Middle Eastern Studies*, London: Weidenfeld and Nicolson.

———, (1984), *The Crossman Confessions and Other Essays*, London and New York: Mansell.

———, (1992), *Politics in the Middle East*, Oxford: Oxford University Press.

Kelly, S. and A. Gorst, (eds.), (2000), *Whitehall and the Suez Crisis*, London and Portland: Frank Cass.

Khadduri, M. and E. Ghareeb, (1997), *War in the Gulf, 1990–1991: the Iraq–Kuwait Conflict and its Implications*, Oxford and New York: Oxford University Press.

Kimche, D. and D. Bavly, (1968), *The Sandstorm, the Arab–Israeli War of June 1967: Prelude and Aftermath*, London: Secker and Warburg.

Kimmerling, B. and J. Migdal, (1994), *The Palestinians: the Making of a People*, Cambridge MA: Harvard University Press.

Kinross, Lord, (2003), *The Ottoman Empire*, London: Folio Books.

Kretzmer, D., (1990), *The Legal Status of the Arabs in Israel*, Boulder: Westview Press.

Kumaraswamy, P. (ed.), (2000), *Revisiting the Yom Kippur War*, London and Portland: Frank Cass.

Kurzman, D., (1992), *Genesis 1948: the First Arab–Israeli War*, New York: Da Capo Press.

Kyle, K., (1991), *Suez*, New York: St Martins Press.

Landau, J., (1969), *The Arabs in Israel*, Oxford: Oxford University Press.

Laqueur, W. and B. Rubin, (eds.), (1985), *The Arab–Israeli Reader: a Documentary History of the Middle East Conflict*, New York: Facts on File Publications.

Laqueur, W., (1989), *A History of Zionism*, New York: Schocken Books.

Levran, A., (1997), *Israeli Strategy after Desert Storm: Lessons of the Second Gulf War*, London and Portland: Frank Cass.

Lewis, B., (1996), *The Middle East: 2000 Years of History from the Rise of Christianity to the Present Day*, London: Phoenix.

——, (1998), *The Multiple Identities of the Middle East*, London: Weidenfeld and Nicolson.

——, (2003), *The Crisis of Islam: Holy War and Unholy Terror*, London: Weidenfeld and Nicolson, p. 71.

Liebman, C. and E. Don-Yehiya, (1983), *Civil Religion*

in Israel, Berkeley: University of California Press.

Lochery, N., (1997), *The Israeli Labour Party: in the Shadow of the Likud*, Reading: Ithaca Press.

———, (1999), *The Difficult Road to Peace: Netanyahu, Israel and the Middle East Peace Process*, Reading: Ithaca Press.

Lucas, N., (1974), *The Modern History of Israel*, London: Weidenfeld and Nicolson.

Mahler, G., (1999), *Israel: Government and Politics in a Maturing State*, San Diego and New York: Harcourt Brace Jovanovich.

Makovsky, D., (1996), *Making Peace with the PLO*, Boulder: Westview Press.

———, (2004), 'How to Build a Fence', *Foreign Affairs*, March–April, pp. 50–64.

Malki, R., (1996), 'The Palestinian Opposition and Final-Status Negotiations', *Palestine–Israel Journal*, vol. 3, no. 3–4, pp. 95–99.

Mansfield, P., (1991), *A History of the Middle East*, London and New York: Viking.

Ma'oz, M., (1995), *Syria and Israel: from War to Peacemaking*, Oxford and New York: Oxford University Press.

Masalha, N., (1999), 'A Critique of Benny Morris', in Illan Pappe (ed.), *The Israel–Palestine Question: Rewriting Histories*, London: Routledge, pp. 211–220.

Massalha, O., (1992), *Towards the Long Promised Peace*, London: Saqi Books.

Mazzawi, M., (1997), *Palestine and the Law: Guidelines for the Resolution of the Arab–Israeli Conflict*, Reading: Ithaca Press.

Medding, P., (1972), *Mapai in Israel: Political Organisation and Government in a New Society*, Cambridge: Cambridge University Press.

———, (1990), *The Founding of Israeli Democracy 1948–1967*, Oxford: Oxford University Press.

Milton-Edwards, B., (1996), *Islamic Politics in Palestine*, London: Tauris Academic Press.

———, (2000), *Contemporary Politics in the Middle East*, Cambridge: Polity Press.

Morris, B., (1999), *Righteous Victims: a History of the Zionist–Arab Conflict, 1981–1999*, London: John Murray.

Morris, E., (1999), *Dutch: a Memoir of Ronald Reagan*, London: Harper Collins.

Mutawi, S. A., (1987), *Jordan in the 1967 War*, Cambridge: Cambridge University Press.

Neff, D., (1988), *Warriors at Suez: Eisenhower Takes the US into the Middle East in 1956*, Vermont: Amana Books.

Netanyahu, B., (1995), *Fighting Terrorism: How Democracies Can Defeat Domestic and International Terrorists*, London: Allison and Busby.

Newman, D. (ed.), (1985), *The Impact of Gush Emunim*, London: Croom Helm.

O'Brian, C. C., (1988), *The Siege: the Story of Israel and Zionism*, London: Paladin–Grafton Books.

Oren, M., (1992), *The Origins of the Second Arab–Israeli Conflict*, London and Portland: Frank Cass.

———, (2003), *Six Days of War: June 1967 and the Making of the Modern Middle East*, London: Penguin Books.

BIBLIOGRAPHY

Ovendale, R., (1992), *The Origins of the Arab–Israeli Wars*, London: Longman.

Owen, R., (1984), *State Power and Politics in the Making of the Modern Middle East*, London: Routledge.

Oz, A., (1984), *In the Land of Israel*, London: Flamingo.

Pappe, I. (ed.), (1999), *The Israel/Palestine Question: Rewriting Histories*, London and New York: Routledge.

Peres, S., (1993), *The New Middle East*, New York: Henry Holt.

Peretz, D. and G. Doron, (1997), *The Government and Politics of Israel*, Boulder: Westview Press.

Peri, Y., (2002), 'The Israeli Military and Israel's Palestinian Policy: from Oslo to the Al Aqsa Intifada', *Peacework* 47.

Quandt, W. B., (2001), *Peace Process and the Arab–Israeli Conflict Since 1967*, The Brookings Institution, Berkeley: University of California Press.

Rabinovich, I., (1985), *The War for Lebanon 1970–85*, Ithaca and London: Cornell University Press.

———, (1998), *The Brink of Peace: the Israeli–Syrian Negotiations*, Princeton: Princeton University Press.

Randall, J., (1990), *The Tragedy of Lebanon*, London: Hogarth Press.

Ranstorp, M., (1997), *Hezbollah in Lebanon*, London: Macmillan.

Reich, B. and G. Kieval, (1993), *Israel: Land of Tradition and Conflict*, Boulder: Westview Press.

Reinharz, J. and A. Shapira, (eds.), *Essential Papers on Zionism*, London: Cassell (New York University

Press).

Richards, A. and J. Waterbury, (1990), *A Political Economy of the Middle East: State, Class and Economic Development*, Boulder and Oxford: Westview Press.

Ross, D., (2004), *The Missing Peace: the Inside Story of the Middle East*, New York: Farrar Straus and Giroux.

Rubin, B., J. Ginat and M. Ma'oz, (eds.), (1994), *From War to Peace: Arab–Israeli Relations 1973–1993*, New York: New York University Press.

Rubin, B., (1994), *Revolution until Victory: the Politics and History of the PLO*, Cambridge MA: Harvard University Press.

Rubinstein, A., (1984), *The Zionist Dream Revisited: from Herzl to Gush Emunim and Back*, New York: Schocken Books.

Sachar, H., (1979), *A History of Israel: from the Rise of Zionism to Our Time*, New York: Knopf.

———, (1999), *Israel and Europe: an Appraisal in History*, New York: Knopf.

Said, E., (1994), *The Politics of Dispossession: the Struggle for Palestinian Self-Determination, 1969–1994*, London: Chatto and Windus.

———, (1995), *Peace and Its Discontents: Gaza–Jericho, 1993–1995*, London: Vintage.

———, (1995), *Orientalism: Western Conceptions of the Orient*, London: Penguin.

Sandler, S., (1993), *The State of Israel, the Land of Israel: Statist and Ethnonational Dimensions of Foreign Policy*, Westport: Greenwood Press.

Savir, U., (1999), *The Process: 1,100 Days that*

Changed the Middle East, New York: Vintage.

Sayigh, Y., (1997), *Armed Struggle and the Search for State: the Palestinian National Movement, 1949–1993*, Oxford: Oxford University Press,.

Schiff, Z., and E. Ya'ari, (1984), *Israel's Lebanon War*, London and Sydney: George Allen and Unwin.

———, (1990), *Intifada: the Palestinian Uprising, Israel's Third Front*, New York: Simon and Schuster.

Seale, P., (1988), *Asad: the Struggle for the Middle East*, Berkeley: University of California Press.

Shadid, M., (1997), 'A Housing Strategy for the Palestinian Territories', in A. B. Zahlan (ed.), *The Reconstruction of Palestine: Urban and Rural Development*, London and New York: Kegan Paul International.

Shalev, M., (1992), *Labour and the Political Economy in Israel*, Oxford: Oxford University Press.

Shapira, A., (1992), *Land and Power: the Zionist Resort to Force 1881–1948*, Stanford: Stanford University Press.

Shapiro, Y., (1991), *The Road to Power: Herut Party in Israel*, Albany: State University of New York Press.

Sharkansky, I., (1987), *The Political Economy of Israel*, New Brunswick: Transaction Books.

Sheffer, G. (ed.), (1997), *US–Israeli Relations at the Crossroads*, London and Portland: Frank Cass.

Shepherd, N., (1994), 'Ex-Soviet Jews in Israel: Asset, Burden or Challenge', *Israel Affairs*, vol. 2, no. 1, pp. 245–266.

———, (1999), *Ploughing Sand: British Rule in Palestine, 1917–1948*, London: John Murray.

Sherman, M., (1999), *The Politics of Water in the*

Middle East: An Israeli Perspective on the Hydro-Political Aspects of the Conflict, London: Macmillan Press.

Shimoni, G., (1995), *The Zionist Ideology*, Hanover and London: Brandeis University Press.

Shlaim, A., (1988), *Collusion Across the Jordan: King Abdullah, the Zionist Movement and the Partition of Palestine*, Oxford: Clarendon Press.

———, (2000), *The Iron Wall: Israel and the Arab World*, New York and London: W. W. Norton and Company.

———, (2004), 'The Nation: the Lost Steps', *Political Studies Journal* 47(4).

———, (2001), *The 1986 War: Collusion and Rivalry in the Middle East*, London and Portland: Frank Cass.

Shulewitz, M. H. (ed.), (1999), *The Forgotten Millions: the Modern Jewish Exodus from Arab Lands*, London and New York: Cassell.

Smooha, S., (1978), *Israel: Pluralism and Conflict*, London: Routledge and Kegan Paul.

———, (1993), 'Jewish Ethnicity in Israel', in K. Keith and J. Peters (eds.), *Whither Israel: the Domestic Challenges*, London: I. B. Tauris, pp. 161–176.

Sofer, S., (1998), *Zionism and the Foundations of Israeli Diplomacy*, Cambridge and New York: Cambridge University Press.

Stein, K. W., (1999), *Heroic Diplomacy: Sadat, Kissinger, Carter, Begin and the Quest for Arab–Israeli Peace*, New York and London: Routledge.

Stephanopoulos, G., (1999), *All Too Human: a*

Political Education, London: Hutchinson.

Swirski, B., and M. Safir, (eds.), (1991), *Calling the Equality Bluff: Women in Israel*, New York: Pergamon.

Swirski, S., (1989), *Israel: the Oriental Majority*, London: Zed Books.

Tessler, M., (1994), *A History of the Israeli–Palestinian Conflict*, Bloomington and Indianapolis: Indiana University Press.

Teveth, S., (1974), *Moshe Dayan: the Soldier, the Man, the Legend*, London: Quartet Books.

Thatcher, M., (2002), *Statecraft: Strategies for a Changing World*, London: Harper Collins.

The Middle East and North Africa, Europa Publications, London, published annually.

Vatikiotis, P. J., (1991), *The History of Modern Egypt: from Muhammad Ali to Mubarak*, London: Weidenfeld and Nicolson.

Vital, D., (1975), *The Origins of Zionism*, Oxford: Clarendon Press.

——, (1987), *Zionism: the Crucial Years*, Oxford: Oxford University Press.

——, (1988), *Zionism the Formative Years*, Oxford: Oxford University Press.

Woodward, B., (1991), *The Commanders*, New York: Simon and Schuster.

——, (2003), *Bush at War*, London: Pocket Books.

Wright, J., (1999), *The Political Economy of Middle East Peace: the Impact of Competing Trade Agendas*, London: Routledge.

Yapp, M., (1996), *The Near East since the First World War: a History to 1995*, London and New York:

Longman.

Yishai, Y., (1997), *Between the Flag and the Banner: Women in Israeli Politics*, Albany: State University of New York Press.

Zak, M., (1996), 'Israel and Jordan: Strategically Bound', *Israel Affairs*, vol. 3, no. 1, pp. 39–60.

Ziberfarb, B., (1996), 'The Israeli Economy in the Era of Peace', *Israel Affairs*, vol. 3, no. 1, pp. 1–12.

Index

INDEX

INDEX

INDEX